THE HUMAN CAREER

THE
HUMAN CAREER

A Philosophy of Self-Transcendence

By ROBERT ULICH, *James Bryant Conant*
Professor of Education, Harvard University

HARPER & BROTHERS   PUBLISHERS   NEW YORK

THE HUMAN CAREER

FIRST EDITION

M-D

Library of Congress catalog card number: 54-12159

To my students
from and in many countries

CONTENTS

PREFACE

I.

The vastness of the American continent expresses itself not only through its rivers and mountains, its woods and prairies, but also through the wealth of its cultural strains. America has had its discussions with almost every great Asiatic and European religion and movement of thought, and has added to them its spirit of experimentation and practical responsibility. It is also the country where fundamentalist attitudes have preserved themselves with unusual pertinacity in traditional Protestant and Catholic circles as well as in a constantly bubbling sectarianism. And it may well be that the modern worship of science as the savior of mankind is nothing but religious fundamentalism transferred into a secular language.

In view of that intense interest in matters of the spirit nothing is more erroneous than the tale, constantly repeated even by outstanding European authors, and spreading dangerously all over the world, that the United States of America is the country of unrelenting haste, unleashed technology, and unprincipled greed for money. Some of this is, unfortunately, true. But several of the most severe European critics—who, by the way, have never set foot on the shores of this country—have failed to see that the same dangers have been rampant also on the other side of the Atlantic—even in the most inhuman forms of exploitation of man by man. Certainly, the American, like others, likes to earn money, but he also likes to spend it, often for worthy purposes. Perhaps his spending, rather than his earning, is the reason why other nations consider him the apotheosis of materialism—while accepting his dollar.

II.

But whatever onesided or ignorant critics may say, they should at least acknowledge that, in contrast to other nations, America has, at least so far, tried to recognize its cultural pluralism. It is more than questionable whether other countries would have stood the risks of mass immigration better than the United States, even if they had enjoyed her geographical and economic advantages. People here are generally against forcing their neighbor into their particular kind of faith, provided he acknowledges the rules of fair play. Respect for each other's spiritual birthright is the great achievement of the eighteenth century, expressed with unique strength by the founders of this republic. Without "eternal vigilance" this achievement may be destroyed by the powers of obscurity even behind these shores, for these powers lurk in the depths of every society and quickly raise their heads in times of danger.

But there is an even more subtle danger than the outward attacks on man's freedom which we hope to fend off, something that frightens even the brave. Do tolerance and respect for our fellow man's opinion by necessity end in indecisive relativism, and the attitude of "so what?" even in regard to the most urgent concerns of man?

Let us not forget that every right is accompanied by its duty. The right to have one's opinions respected rests on the duty to dare have opinions. The mind of a coward provides that social vacuum into which the spirit of totalitarianism can enter, in one of its many and omnipresent guises. Decent error, willing to correct itself, is infinitely superior and socially more useful than shoulder-shrugging apathy with its cynical smile.

But if opinions are to be of some worth they must be based on criteria, and these criteria are difficult to obtain and maintain in a society where so many, often the most responsible, no longer are inclined to accept the standards of their fathers' religion or other human claims of divine revelation. Too many creeds throughout the world pretend to have the distinctive privilege of supernatural birth and authority.

The needed criteria have to be gained from a new understanding of the human being, not in the sense of old dogmatic and a-priori speculations about "the nature of man," nor in terms of experimental psychology (however valuable its specific results may be). They have to be gained from projecting ourselves fearlessly into the totality of the human situation, or into man as he exists with all his joys and sufferings, fulfillments and longings, victories and defeats, with all his knowledge and ignorance, and, finally, as a mystery to himself. This mystery we can neither conceal nor escape. It is man's companion; without it he would not be man. It is his depth that becomes all the deeper the more it reveals itself to him. It lies in his power of continual self-transcendence, his restless search for new islands of meaning, his thinking about nature and mind, being and non-being, birth and death.

And while exploring the recesses of our selves we will discover that, although speaking the language of our own time, we still move along the path gone by the great prophets of mankind. There is, if truly interpreted, no great difference between their intuitional wisdom and our modern search. We will be more modest because we will no longer be so certain of having received divine inspiration, but for this same reason we may be more free to profess our ignorance. But we will be especially free in rejecting superficial commonplaces, even if they come from modern "authorities." From the long history of humanity we have learned that man thrives more on honest questions than on mediocre answers.

This book has slowly emerged in connection with courses in which, avoiding philosophical technicalities as much as possible, I have tried to help mature students to think systematically about the problems and obligations of modern man. Since I never felt an essential difference between scholarly pursuits and the more universal concerns of humanity, I cherish the hope that my endeavors may now extend from the halls of Harvard into wider groups of thinking humanity.

I would like to see this book especially in the hands of those interested in the great issue of human education. Not only is a special chapter given to this topic, but the whole discourse is, in one way or another, related to it. During the past decades "philosophy of education" has developed as a separate discipline of thought, and rightly so, for the theoretical and practical responsibilities connected with the continuous transmission and revival of our culture have assumed a range and responsibility wide enough to need the full devotion of the expert. However, he cannot do justice to his subject unless he views it in combination with the universal philosophical quest that is the subject and motivation of this book.

ROBERT ULICH

Cambridge, Massachusetts
September 1, 1954

ACKNOWLEDGMENTS

I am indebted to the Rockefeller Foundation which through a generous grant has helped me to acquaint myself personally with movements of thought in other countries. The Hazen Foundation has kindly permitted me to use parts of my pamphlet "Man and Reality" in one of the chapters.

The help of my wife has accompanied me while I wrote this book. I am grateful to Dr. Hedwig Schleiffer for bibliographical advice. Miss Eleanor Goldman has patiently typed the various versions. Nothing is more helpful to an author than the dialogue with a friend who understands even when sometimes he may disagree. For such help and friendship I am deeply grateful to Dr. Peter Bertocci, Professor of Philosophy at Boston University.

R. U.

THE HUMAN CAREER

"The Tao that can be reasoned is not the eternal Tao. The name that can be named is not the eternal name. The unnameable is of heaven and earth the beginning. The Nameable becomes of the ten thousand things the mother."

"How all-pervading is the great Tao! It can be on the left and it can be on the right. The ten thousand things depend upon it for their life, and it refuses them not. When its merit is accomplished it assumes not the name. Lovingly it nourishes the ten thousand things and plays not the Lord. Ever desireless it can return home to it. It plays not the Lord. It can be classed with the great."

LAO-TZE*

* from *Lao-Tze's Tao-Teh-King*. Translated by Paul Carus, Pen Court Publishing Company, Chicago, 1898. Pages 97 and 53.

CHAPTER 1

Setting the Scene of Modern Civilization

> It is only when measured in terms of dignity and not merely in terms of comfort that a "standard of living" can properly be called "high."
>
> ANANDA K. COOMARASWAMY

I. THE INDIFFERENT

WHEN we look at human beings as they are today and probably have always been, we discover that a large number of them are more or less indifferent to the great intellectual and spiritual issues. They do not "catch fire" when confronted with them. They even avoid such confrontation for they do not want to be "bothered." Perhaps they like to hear and talk about "interesting" ideas, but primarily for entertainment and as a theme of conversation. They are decent people and a necessary thread in the complex fabric of production and consumption, social clubs and political relations. In one or another segment of our life, we all belong to these groups. We cannot know about everything, so what else is there to do but follow? And since there is no particular delight in merely following, we leave the whole business to other people.

Yet they and we are voters, form the bulk of the nation, fight wars, enjoy victories, or at least think that they are better than defeats. Despite all passivity there is much going on. A continual process of communication works through press, radio, television.

1

Propaganda experts are appointed by governments, knowing that the wind that moves the big vessel of public opinion must come from their side, or else it will come from another. Even dictators, however cruel to individuals and groups, respect nothing as much as "the people." Since antiquity they have told the masses that the costly government buildings were for them; they have tried to win them over with public festivals; they have listened to their catchwords. While the absolutist princes of the eighteenth century, catering largely to the nobility and an educated bourgeoisie, built theaters, modern politicians like to be photographed in the company of movie stars and boxers. It makes them "popular" with the populace, and on this popularity they depend.

But it is false to see only the negative in the "masses." They can indeed be misled; individuals, otherwise normal, may surrender their consciences to the evil impulse of the crowd and behave like beasts. Yet even when misdirected from any moral point of view, they can be heroic. They can sacrifice themselves more willingly than their monarchs, presidents, and generals, for the bad as well as the good. They are sensitive to atmosphere.

Who provides the atmosphere? Who creates inclinations and dispositions? Fortunately, not only propagandists and hirelings, but also parents and teachers who try to help a young mind to distinguish between right and wrong, who select out of custom and public opinion that which strengthens the productive and sublimates the destructive qualities in young and old. Seldom does a teacher meet a potential creator in his classroom; most of his pupils will be followers. That which they have learned and perhaps even forgotten may mould the core of their personality. In a good society such social values as decency, honesty, and the spirit of cooperation "go without saying." However, the saying must have arisen in infancy and adolescence, it must continue in the conversations between friend and friend, reader and book, action and reflection. And in all these conversations, even among those who seem indifferent to greatness, there somehow participate, whether dead or living, known or unknown, those who have taken ideas seriously, who bother, who are not satisfied with mere living, but who search for a meaning.

Who are they?

II. THE CONCERNED

From the men who in the course of our Western history have been concerned with the perennial problems of life, there emerge three more or less representative groups. The first of them we call God-centered, the second reason-centered, the third man-centered. We will look at each group with three questions in mind. First, what was its general view of the world and the mood of living that arose from it? Second, how did it apply its world view to the practical tasks of mankind? And third, what influence did the specific world view have on intellectual search and education? In addition we will consider each group not only insofar as it has enriched the cultural heritage of humanity, but also insofar as it has harbored the seeds of disintegration and decay.

But at the beginning we issue a warning. The groups of which we will speak are "types" or "ideal patterns." Though inherent in human reality as formative forces, they rarely appear in absolute purity. To a degree, they are to be found in every single individual, which is the reason for their persistence throughout civilization. They shade into each other, and they are blurred by compromises and obscurities which are part of man's destiny. After all, life is not for logic, but for living.

1. The God-centered or Theonomous Group

Those whom we call *God-centered,* or *theonomous* (receiving their law, or *nomos,* from God), are convinced that their single existences are embedded in a deeper and embracing source of being. In every important decision they rely not merely on their own or their friends' intelligence, but consult divine authority. Though not present physically it may be more real to them than the house in which they live or the neighbor to whom they speak.

Says St. Augustine in the Tenth Book of the *City of God:*

Our heart when it rises to Him is His altar; the priest who intercedes for us is His Only-begotten; we sacrifice to Him bleeding victims when we contend for His truth even unto blood . . . to Him we devote and surrender ourselves and His gifts in us . . . to Him we offer on the altar of our heart the sacrifice of humility and praise, kindled by the fire of burning love. It is that we may see Him, so far as He can be seen; it is that we may cleave to Him, that we are cleansed from all stain of sins and evil passions, and are consecrated in His name. For He is the fountain of our happiness, He the end of all our desires.[1]

And just as man's personality becomes colored by what he does in his immediate environment, so also it receives an enduring mood and mental atmosphere by its discourse with the Eternal. The power that lives in religious contemplation and prayer may even influence a man's physical structure.

Not necessarily does the divine appear to the faithful in the symbol of a personal God, as we are accustomed to imagine in our Western religious tradition. Nor is it necessarily of supernatural quality, for nature itself can be conceived of as the vessel of the spirit and thus receive the character of holiness. Many Indians and Chinese feel themselves and the world nourished and inspired by an inexpressible ground that is immanent in our world. Though the power of this ground radiates into all that is, they hesitate to give it a name. Names, concepts, and myths invented by man can only be distortions. And some Christian mystics are not far from the speculative thought of Asia.

God works without means and images. The more you are free of images the more open you are to His influx, and the more you are lost within yourself and for yourself, the nearer you are to Him. In this regard Dionysius admonished his disciple Timotheus and said: Dear son Timotheus, do not be afraid to rise above yourself, your mental powers, and above all modes of life, so that you may enter into the quiet hidden darkness and into the vision of the unknown

[1] *The City of God by St. Augustine.* Translated by Marcus Dods, D.D., with an Introduction by Thomas Merton (The Modern Library, New York, 1950), p. 306.

God Who is beyond all knowledge of God. But in order to achieve this you must sever your self from all that is: to appear in the things of the senses is against God's nature.

Now you will ask: How without image can God work in the ground and essence of the soul? This question I cannot answer, for the soul can only know in images and must prehend everything in its particular shape. . . . But this is the most wholesome that could happen to the soul: the not-knowing. For it causes it to seek the wonder. The soul senses the divine, but it does not know how and what it is. . . . Only the not-knowing knowing makes the soul stay, yet drives it on to search.[2]

In the great representatives of the God-centered attitude we admire the firmness of the anchorage in which the believers' minds are harbored. It gives them a strength of conviction and a feeling of independence not to be shaken by the hatred of the blind and the threat of the mighty. For God, the center and ruler of the world, will guide His faithful through the valleys of the shadows toward the mountains of salvation. The concept of the polarity of sin and grace, characteristic of developed religion, provides a realistic picture of man's utter limitations, and at the same time allows room for hope and dignity, just as the concept of surrender to God as the only way to real freedom provides an inspiring explanation of mankind's goal and mission, a God-centered philosophy of history, and an ethics of the highest aspiration.

In relation to practical, social, and political tasks a truly theonomous culture will always emphasize man's moral obligations to his fellow men and the principle of religious love (often, unfortunately, with the proviso that these obligations apply only to those of the same faith). During its "prophetic" period religion may work as a revolutionary force against the entrenched powers of personal and collective egotism. But on the whole, transcendentalism will tend to emphasize salvation in another

[2] Author's translation from Meister Eckhart's sermon on "Eternal Rebirth." *Meister Eckhart's Schriften und Predigten.* Edited by Herman Büttner, (Vol. I, p. 81, Jena, 1923).

world and assume a more conservative attitude. For this reason
it has often been criticized by social reformers. When a certain
stability and recognition has been reached, religious institutions,
like all other organizations, reject sudden interference in the
established order. Even Calvin, who—more than Luther—
wanted the Christian to prove himself in political life, rejected
violent changes of government. A bad king is God's punishment.
Suffer him humbly in order to live with the will of the Lord.

God-centered man will consider himself not a "creator" and
"discoverer" of new truths, but an interpreter of the Truth that
is in the world through the presence of the divine. This eternal
Truth is the criterion of all human thought and action. It has
to be upheld against intellectual criticism and arrogance as well
as against the attempts of states and governments to assume
control over the conscience of man.

For these reasons one will hardly convince a fundamentalist
Jew, Protestant, Catholic, or Mennonite of the desirability of a
uniform national school system if the nation consists of followers
of different creeds. Nor will he tolerate, for the sake of unity,
public religious instruction given by special agencies outside the
school. Religion, he will contend, cannot be taught side by side
with and on the same level of importance as other subjects.
Religion is not even the crown, for a crown is something addi-
tional and decorative and, as we know from history, can be put
on or off. Rather religion must be the pervading spirit in all and
everything that is taught.

This may be narrow, but it is consistent. And it is by their
penetration of the whole of human existence that the great world
religions have conquered territories much wider than empires,
and have held them much longer.

But even into movements and institutions where divine spirit
is supposed to dwell, there creep decline and imperfection.

In our civilization the theonomous attitude has been represented mainly by Christianity. It had its two revolutionary
periods in the first centuries and in the age of the Reformation.
The sense of being "chosen," which always emerges when men

believe themselves close to the center of the universe, gave the early Christians and later the Protestants a heroic power of resistance and organization. But it also brought about the ever-lurking dangers of hairsplitting disputes over unanswerable problems, timidity with respect to new ideas, and persecution of heretics. The whole Middle Ages suffered from the forgery of the Donation of Constantine, by which this monarch was supposed to have given the Western part of his empire to the Popes of Rome, who consequently claimed to be the rulers not only over a spiritual, but over an enormous material empire. Political alliances between Church and State made possible a control of souls and bodies resembling the tyranny of modern totalitarianism. For when religion loses its contact with the source of divine challenge and inspiration, then—despite all clamor of cult and worship—it is no longer a well of creativeness, but a prison. Convictions become dead patterns of righteousness, morality a cruel convention, and the divine ground a dry desert. When man professes God but actually identifies his narrow self and his earthly interests with Him he commits the worst of all sacrileges.

In such periods of decay the Christian churches owed their rejuvenescence mainly to those whom they persecuted, the truly religious who led the souls of their fellows beyond the walls of dogma and institutionalism back to the streams of the spirit. The greatest of the medieval mystics, Meister Eckhart, died during his trial before an ecclesiastical court; Pietists and Quakers were hunted by Protestant ministers; and on the Catholic *Index of Forbidden Books* have been put the works of Erasmus of Rotterdam and other wise men venerated by the best of mankind.

2. The Reason-centered or Logonomous Group

In modern men the center of spiritual gravity has shifted from the older form of Christian supernaturalism toward other sources of inspiration. What has happened and when did it happen? To both questions a simple answer is difficult.

Long before the Renaissance, which we generally associate

with the rise of the modern mind, human reason had asserted its right to wrestle with the mysteries of life in a spirit of independence, free from ecclesiastical authority and unquestionable revelation.

When we compare the piety of a man of the ninth century A.D., such as Hrabanus Maurus, with the theology of two representatives of ripening medieval religiosity such as Pierre Abelard (1079–1142) and Thomas Aquinas (*ca.* 1225–1274), we immediately sense the difference between naive acceptance of supernatural authority and an attitude of sophistication.

In his *Education of the Clergy* Hrabanus Maurus says:

Those who read them [the Scriptures] strive for nothing else than to grasp the thought and meaning of those who write them, in order thereby to fathom the will of God, at whose bidding and under whose direction, as we believe, they were written. But those who read superficially allow themselves to be deceived through manifold recurring passages, the sense of which is obscure, and the meaning of which is doubtful; they assign to what is read a meaning that does not belong to it; they seek errors where no errors are to be found; they surround themselves with an obscurity in which they cannot find the right path. I have no doubt that this has been so ordered by God's providence that the pride of men may be restrained through spiritual labor; in order that the knowledge of man may be divorced from pride, to which it easily falls a prey, and then loses its value entirely . . .[3]

There is no sentence in this passage to which Abelard or Thomas Aquinas would officially object. Yet why did Abelard in his *Yea and Nay* compare contradictory statements of the Christian tradition with each other? And why did Aquinas devote his life to bringing about an intellectual marriage between the gospel of Christ and the philosophical writings of the pagan Aristotle?

Exactly that had occurred which Maurus condemned. Both

[3] Translation taken from *Great Pedagogical Essays, Plato to Spencer,* by F. V. N. Painter (New York, American Book Co., 1905). See also R. Ulich, *Three Thousand Years of Educational Wisdom,* p. 175.

Abelard and Aquinas were "rationalists" within the horizons possible to medieval man. They found "errors" and "obscurities" where, according to Hrabanus Maurus, "no errors are to be found." Of course, they did not read "superficially." They tried to prove that the errors existed only in human interpretation. Yet they were constantly concerned with possible errors. Instead of being in the state of simple piety, they were already in the state of dialectic. And as a tool in this dialectic, they needed and joyfully accepted the logic of Aristotle. In this respect Luther, the reformer, was more pious than they. The intrusion of pagan philosophy was for him an offense to the Gospel.

In his *Letters to the Mayors and Aldermen of the German Cities* (1524) Luther complains about the lack of piety of the Christians, both learned and unlearned. Thus God, "in turn, instead of the Holy Scriptures and good books suffered Aristotle and numberless pernicious books to come into use, which only lead us further from the Bible. To these were added the progeny of Satan, the monks and the phantoms of the universities, which we founded at incredible cost, and many doctors, preachers, teachers, priests, and monks, that is to say, great, coarse, fat asses, adorned with red and brown caps, like swine led with a golden chain and decorated with pearls . . ."[4]

Yet, the "ruse of history," to use a famous Hegelian term, seems to have used Luther for a special role in its unfathomable purposes. Through his insistence on every Christian's personal reading of the Bible, his advocacy of a public elementary school system, and his fight against hierarchical authority in the interpretation of the Revelation, he released the pent-up stream of reasoning which even Protestant theology was unable to confine. Thus the final result of Luther's work, as well as that of Calvin and Zwingli, was not a new and simple faith of man in the word and grace of God, but further intellectual self-assertion. It first

[4] Translation taken from F. V. N. Painter, *Luther on Education* (Philadelphia, Concordia Publishing House, 1890). See also Ulich, *Three Thousand Years of Educational Wisdom*, p. 236.

expressed itself in subtle theological argumentations not very different from those of the late Scholastics, until eventually it burst the framework of the strictly Christian tradition and emerged as a youthful confidence in the power of reason itself. Rationalism, or the Age of the Enlightenment, replaced the era of the Reformation and the Counter-reformation. Roughly speaking, it began with Descartes and ended with Hegel, whose system, though already revealing romantic traits, is nevertheless based on the conviction that history can be explained as reason's self-evolution.

Yet this logonomous attitude, after being extinguished at the end of Antiquity because of the decline of Greek-Roman thought and the hostility of Christianity, would have reappeared even without the Reformation and the idealist philosophers. The conquest of the globe and the new scientific discoveries aroused in the advanced men of the seventeenth and eighteenth centuries a degree of intellectual enthusiasm difficult to reconstruct in the jejune attitude of our civilization towards the wonders of scientific research.

There is an enchanting release of optimistic activism in this kind of rationalist piety, as we might paradoxically call it. The world is no longer a magician's platform or the theater of inscrutable and awesome divine dispensation; there are now Method and Order. Of that Order man can be a part if he disciplines his thought and life according to its laws. In every great philosopher's work of the period we have a treatise on "Method." For it is by persevering intellectual discipline, not by belief in the authority of the Bible and of Aristotle, that man receives the revelations of the cosmos. But there is "Method" not only in theory, but also in conduct and action. Moral ideals are not commandments issuing from a divine source, but reflections of laws inherent in the universe.

In other words, the Divine assumed the form of *Weltvernunft,* or World-Reason, or the Neo-Platonic *Logos,* unfolding itself in the constant attempt of history to overcome the conflicts and contrasts of life by ever higher logical syntheses. People now were ashamed of having killed each other because of different interpretations of sin, predestination, and the Eucharist. In recommending thinking rather than blind faith, they also admitted not only the possibility but also the right of error, in other words, tolerance. Yet, though this world view was "secular" from the point of view of a strict theist, it was, in general, not antireligious, for deism also can arouse the sense of religious awe. There were, of course, men such as Voltaire. But Voltaire's famous "écrasez l'infame" was not said against God, or Christ, and perhaps not even against Catholicism, but against the reactionary and cruel clergy whom Voltaire had ample opportunity to observe in his time. Most enlightened men conceived reason as a divine force in which man participated but which nevertheless transcended him. He did not create it, rather it worked in him as the highest self-reflective product of the world's evolution from matter to spirit. Such was, in more or less outspoken form, the conviction also of Americans such as Benjamin Franklin and Thomas Jefferson. Politically it has been incorporated in the American Constitution, and Thomas Paine (1737–1809) has given eloquent expression to this faith in *The Age of Reason*. There appears the challenging and ego-centered statement: "I do not believe in the creed professed by the Jewish church, by the Roman church, by the Greek church, by the Turkish church, by the Protestant church, nor by any church that I know of. My own mind is my own church."

But this "mind" of Paine is not the isolated mind of the skeptic. For Paine precedes the sentences just quoted by saying: "I believe in one God, and no more; and I hope for happiness beyond this life." And in a later chapter he continues:

But some perhaps will say—are we to have no word of God—no revelation? I answer, Yes: there is a Word of God; there is a revelation.

The Word of God is the Creation we Behold. And it is in *this word,* which no human invention can counterfeit or alter, that God speaketh universally to man. . . .

It is only in the *Creation* that all our ideas and conceptions of a *word of God* can unite. The creation speaketh an universal language, independently of human speech or human language, multiplied and various as they be. It is an ever existing original, which every man can read. It cannot be forged; it cannot be counterfeited; it cannot be lost; it cannot be altered; it cannot be suppressed. It does not depend upon the will of man whether it shall be published or not; it publishes itself from one end of the earth to the other. It preaches to all nations and to all worlds; and this *word of God* reveals to man all that is necessary for man to know of God.[5]

Whether consciously or not, a large number of Western men, especially in the United States, are still motivated by the belief that there exists a deep harmony between human thinking and a supreme order, and that it is the function of free experimentation and reason to strengthen that harmony. In spite of their rational and critical idealism they still are Christians, even good ones; but to believe in the letter of the dogma would be for them a sign of backwardness and superstition.

It is the supreme test of any philosophy of life (just as it is the supreme test of a man's or a nation's character) to subject its values and inner strength not only to happiness and success, but also to calamity. The great religions have proved this again and again, but so has great rationalism.

In his *Souvenirs d'Enfance et de Jeunesse,* which are a treasure for the interpretation of the culture of postrevolutionary France, Ernest Renan (1823–1892) describes one of the eighteenth century's rationalists and revolutionaries, called by his neighbors *le bonhomme système.* He lived a lonely and suspected life in the period of the Catholic-monarchical restoration. Renan, author of the "heretical" *Life of Jesus,* who nevertheless speaks with love and respect of the priests by whom he was educated in various Catholic seminaries, says of *le bonhomme système*:[6]

[5] *The Age of Reason.* Many editions. Chapters I and X.
[6] *Oeuvres Complètes de Ernest Renan.* Tome II (Edition Henriette Psichari, Paris, no date, p. 775). Translated by author.

A strange person who remained to us a mystery for a long time, was for some reason one of the causes which, on the whole, made out of me much more a son of the Revolution than a son of the crusaders. . . . He went out every day in order to buy his little food; in the evening, he took a walk to a distant place. His face was serious, but not sad, amiable rather than hateful. Later, when I read the *Life of Spinoza* by Colerus, I felt that as a child I had seen with my own eyes a model similar to the Saint of Amsterdam. People left him unmolested, they even respected him. His resignation, his smile, seemed to be a vision of another world. One did not understand, but sensed in him a superiority to which one bowed.

Le bonhomme système never went to church. He avoided the clergy. His comfort was a library of books of the eighteenth century which for the priests of the town was "une sorte de puits de l'abîme," an abyss of abysses, which after his death they bought for little money in order to burn it.

Naturally I shared that horror. Not before my own philosophical ideas had ripened did I know that in my youth I had had the good fortune to see a real sage. I could easily reconstruct his ideas in remembering words which I had not understood earlier. God was for him the order of nature, the inner reason of the world. He did not suffer if one denied it. He loved humanity as the representative of reason, and hated superstition as its negation. . . . He was right. Far from refusing to accept God, he was ashamed of those who thought they could touch him [*Loin de méconnaître Dieu, il avait honte pour ceux qui s'imaginent le toucher*]. Lost in profound peace and sincere humility, he looked at the errors of mankind more with pity than with hatred. Evidently, he despised his century. The renascence in the new generation of superstition which he had believed to be buried by Voltaire and Rousseau, appeared to him as a sign of complete stupefaction.

As we have already said, certain aspects of this thought and attitude were not new. They existed in full vigor at the height of Antiquity, and they slowly emerged from the scholasticism of the medieval doctors and the Renaissance. But it is the beauty of the late seventeenth and eighteenth centuries that then the enthusiastic belief in reason created a free and courageous man engaged not merely in abstract speculation, but willing to strive for the application of rational method to social and political life. Proofs of this attitude are the American and French revolutions, the establishment of government based on the consensus of the people, and the release of immense energies in industry and technology.

With respect to intellectual search and education, logonomous man shows a marked difference from the God-centered and Revelation-centered type. Rather than humbly remaining within the authority of the Gospel and seeking perfection merely in nearness to the divine center, the rational idealist believes in self-realization through the development of the intellect which connects him with the rational order of the world. In other words, his attempt at self-realization is not selfishness but the attempt to find the self through the discovery of the laws of being. Most of all, through science and education man can grow out of superstition and slavery toward freedom. When governments fail to support this upward struggle of men, the latter are entitled to fight in the name of Reason. Logonomy is aggressive.

Yet is not the French revolution, to which we have referred as an example of aggressiveness, a perfect demonstration of the fact that the polarity of greatness and vice, of strength and decline is in the logonomous world-view as it is in the God-centered one?

Just as the stakes of the Inquisition are the abomination of Christianity, so also are the prisons and guillotines of the French revolution the shame of the rational period. Apparently there is nothing so great in man that he cannot pervert it into its opposite.

When logonomy becomes barren, thinking man feels no longer incorporated in a great and orderly cosmos or logos. Just as in the decay of theonomous man idolizes his self-complacent piety and makes it absolute, so in the decay of rationality the ideals of reason and progress degenerate into an empty catch-word. Individualism, rather than being a grace, becomes a danger, for the individual no longer regards himself as part of a whole, but becomes himself the whole. He no longer speaks of human dignity which he shares with his fellows as both a gift and a responsibility; he thinks only of his ego. "Natural law," the great idea of rationalism, with its roots in religion, becomes a personal law, and the "inalienable rights of man" degenerate from a general obligation into reckless self-assertion. Empirical science becomes the shibboleth and excuse for lack of vision; it mechanizes not only nature, but also man, rather than making him the master of himself and his environment. The logos becomes techno-logy and scholarship slides from the courageous priesthood of truth into the state we generally associate with the university of Alexandria during its decline, but of which, alas, we have so much in our own colleges and universities: big libraries, a large and busy staff, much criticism, collecting, cataloguing, and describing, but no longer profound insight. Finally, justice no longer flows out of a moral conscience that feels itself in unity with the universal principles of creative life; it now becomes a weapon for security among those who wield the power, as in the early period of capitalism. Only a utilitarian humanism and fear of the organization of the masses provide some degree of corrective.

3. The Man-centered or Autonomous Group

Wherein lies the cultural significance of the *man-centered* or *autonomous world-view* in contrast to religious transcendentalism and rational idealism? The answer is not easy. For while theonomy and logonomy, in addition to their prophetic utterances, have produced great philosophic systems—the first, those of St. Augustine, Thomas Aquinas, and Calvin; the second, those of Plato, Aristotle, Spinoza and Hegel—strict autonomy is by nature impressionist and antisystematic. There is the Prometheus myth of the ancient Greeks, symbolizing the rebellion of self-conscious man against the Gods (but the Gods still existed). There are the monumental lines in one of the Odes of Horace:

> Si fractus illabatur orbis,
> Impavidum ferient ruinae.

Amidst the crash of a collapsing world
The stones will hit a man who knows not fear.

(But knowing of the poet's life we may suspect that these lines express more a borrowed than a genuine feeling.)

Paradoxically, a certain autonomy mingles with pantheistically flavored theonomy in medieval and modern Christian mystics, from Meister Eckhart to Angelus Silesius, and from Jakob Boehme to Rainer Maria Rilke. Often it is less the grace of God that descends to them than the intuitive power of the human soul which creates the vision of God. God then loses all substantiality, he becomes "the darkness," "the abyss," more a psychological than a transcendental concept. The same is the case with modern existentialist philosophers.[7]

In a profound poem the great Swiss poet, Konrad Ferdinand Meyer, pictures Michelangelo at the completion of his work in the Sistina. Has there ever been an artist in whom proud humanity wrestled so passionately with the traditional symbols of the divine as Michelangelo? And has there ever been a court and a city where behind the veils of Christianity there raged so unbridled a human autonomy as the papal court of Rome in the days of Michelangelo? Meyer imagines his hero as engaged in a dialogue with his own painting on the ceiling of the Chapel, the painting of the creation of man.

Den ersten Menschen formtest Du aus Ton,
Ich werde schon von härterm Stoffe sein,
Da Meister, brauchst Du Deinen Hammer schon,
Bildhauer Gott, schlag' zu! Ich bin der Stein.

Thou formed from clay the first of mortal men,
Much harder is the matter that I own,
Great Master, here Thy hammer Thou wilt need,
My sculptor God: begin, I am the stone!

(But also here the divine still existed.)

[7] In this context see F. J. von Rintelen. *Philosophie der Endlichkeit als Spiegel der Gegenwart* (Westkulturverlag Anton Hain, Meisenheim—Glan. 1951). See also the quotation from Meister Eckhart on p. 5.

There is Friedrich Nietzsche's vision of the superman. Here in reality, as Nietzsche himself says, God is "dead." But even the beauty and prophetic insights of his masterpiece *Zarathustra* cannot deceive the reader over the fact that in the author's mind greatness, hope, and despair wage a tragic battle with each other. There is no quiet in his atheism. If he does not struggle with God, at least he struggles with God's death. And so does the most recent philosophical representative of the autonomous attitude, the French existentialist Jean Paul Sartre, author of *L'être et le Néant* (*Being and Nothing*).

As a matter of fact, it is difficult to find even in our modern culture (which most writers would describe as man-centered) people with a completely autonomous attitude. Only an almost forgotten German philosopher by the name of Max Stirner (1806–1856) deserves the credit for having driven the autonomous attitude toward its radical extreme. The title of his book, *Der Einzige und sein Eigentum,* is difficult to translate. The meaning is: *The Individual and His Domain.* There is, according to Stirner, nothing provable beyond man's isolated ego; consequently he is justified in using everything, even other egos, for the purpose of his own self-realization. Man *may* do what he *can* do. Transcendental and ethical ideals are illusions stemming from old religious superstitions. If there is any truth it can only be *my* truth, for it is the only truth that my mind is able to conceive.

All philosophies of autonomy subsist on some metaphysical premises, hidden or not—to a degree, even Stirner's does. Political anarchism—Stirner was an anarchist—believes mystically in the goodness of the individual. Materialism believes in the creative order of nature. English utilitarianism and American pragmatism, which both reveal autonomous trends, put the social whole above the isolated individual, or have their trust in the corrective power of well-understood self-interest; a trust which, consciously or unconsciously, rests on an unproved faith in life's innate trend toward progress—in other words, on a kind of watered-down logonomous metaphysics.

In the pragmatism of William James, whom we will mention later, man sometimes appears as the autonomous creator and sometimes as the creature who might do wisely to believe in a God.

John Dewey's theories of "experience" are, from a strictly epistemological point of view, not as far away from Berkeley's idealism as Dewey and his followers are inclined to believe. For if "experience" creates our world, what then is this world but the product of our mind? Even Bertrand Russell, certainly one of the most autonomous and relativist philosophers of our time, who asserts that the unconscious universe "cares neither for our existence nor for our aspirations," wants us "to preserve our respect for truth, for beauty, for the ideal of perfection which life does not permit us to attain . . ."[8]

But how can an individual man have "respect for truth" as such if truth is not believed to possess a uniting power greater than what I, or my neighbor John Smith, or my enemy Adolf Hitler, merely happen to believe? It cannot be a mere accumulation of opinion, a mere "as if." It must be something essential.

If we look for the ways in which the man-centered attitude applies itself to the scene of social responsibility we have to distinguish between individualistic and collective forms of autonomy, though the latter is a contradiction in itself because of the essentially antisocial nature of autonomy. The first, such as Nietzsche's, despises the masses, enslaved by superstition, false loyalties, and voluntary ignorance. According to Nietzsche, it needs the Promethean superman to lead the few outstanding individuals toward new heights of achievement; the "common man" is important only so far as the sheer quantity of his existence may prevent the free self-fulfillment of the great individual; he is a hindrance more than an obligation.

[8] "A Free man's Worship." In *Selected Papers of Bertrand Russell* (New York, 1927), p. 6.

The picture changes completely in the second, the collective, interpretation of autonomy, as today we have it in the Russian revolution.

This revolution, at least in part, has emerged from the philosophy of Karl Marx who rejected both the theonomous basis of religion and the logonomous basis of Hegel's rationalism. Lenin and his friends were dialectical materialists and believed they professed the orthodox interpretation of their master, who, unfortunately, could not defend himself. They drew no vertical line from man to God, or from man to the Logos. They denounced religion as the instrument of feudalism, and logonomous idealism as the ideology of the greedy and imperialist regime of the bourgeois. From a partial point of view, they were not incorrect. But, like Marx, the first communist generation of Russia was also the generation of the visionaries, despite all materialism. They had their great hope and their utopia. It was not Nietzsche's individual superman, but the kingdom of all men, or the classless society. And the metaphysics behind it—falsely interpreted as strict materialism—was the faith in the evolutionary nature of history, as the reflection in the evolutionary nature of life.

But to what degree can the minds of men such as Lenin, Trotsky, and Lunatscharsky be identified with the minds of the Russian worker and peasant? Did perhaps the Party's official philosophy succeed because in the soul of the Russian people it transformed itself into a form of religious transcendentalism, nourished through many centuries of religious devotion? Here again we stand before a phenomenon of bewildering complexity.

The attitude of autonomous man toward intellectual search and education is similar to that of the rationalist to the extent that for both a trained intellect is the main instrument in man's struggle for liberation. But in contrast to other forms of thought, man-centered scholarship and education reject any transcendent interpretation of life as a relic of moribund ideologies. Also, self-realization, as the end of education, is no longer the realization of the self as a part of a cosmic order, but is now identical with increase in power, whether the power be sought by an individual or by a group. "Knowledge is power."

Autonomy has its historical value as the Promethean protest against obsolete institutions and the abuse of the Holy. But wherever it appears, as in modern fascism, it seems to be doomed to a quick decline. The end of Russian communism we cannot yet foresee, but apparently it needs continuous purges. A state of mind whose mission was to rebel against obsolete ideologies loses its right to exist, and totally contradicts its own premises, when it tries to establish itself as an absolute authority. This has always been the danger in revolutions. In trying to become ends in themselves they become cruel forms of reaction.

In the decline of autonomy, just as in its rise, we have two seemingly opposite but fundamentally interdependent situations. In the individualistic form, where everyone is for himself, there appears the threat of anarchy in society, and the sense of anxiety and loneliness in the individual. This happens even in "democracies" when people are no longer united by the spirit of freedom for common achievement, but live in the hollow liberty of mere self-assertion and technological advances. After a while they become uncertain of themselves and in their fear of being devoured by chaos they look for the strong leader to balance the lack of inner discipline by authoritarian methods. Anarchy and totalitarianism are twin brothers.

In the collectivist form of declining autonomy men who have already lost the genuine afflatus and become dogmatic try to convince themselves and others that they still are the vessels of the true revolutionary spirit and become, so to speak, a militant church without ideals—which is the worst of all forces of persecution. They are constantly menaced by their own insecurity; they have no humor; they have no mercy. By impressive pomp they try to conceal the emptiness within.

We do not need describe this kind of life in detail, because we are in the midst of it.

III. SOME CRITICAL QUESTIONS

Yet we should not commit the common error of praising the past (which cannot contradict us) and blaming the present. Was man not always the center of interest to man? Are we today more of the materialist type and more concerned with ourselves than a knight or peasant of the thirteenth century? Probably not. If eating and drinking are accepted as criteria, medieval men—provided they had the means—surpassed us by miles. If medieval statesmen and generals had had the atomic bomb, would they not have used it? Did their interest in heaven prevent them from fighting, looting, and raping? If we read the medieval chronicles and laws, it does not seem so. Their transcendentalism did not always "transcend" their egos; it was, as often today, but another form of self-interest. The devil and his hellish host, distant while men were young and full of passion, usually became frightful reality only when old age knocked at the door. What if people went to church and bought indulgences? Did that really make them better? Since the world for them was full of magic, how else could their will to live express itself but in magical cult? Yet, cult is not essential.

In addition, what do we know about our ancestors' feelings since in the Middle Ages only a small fraction, which with few exceptions had accepted the views of the clergy, could write down their ideas on expensive parchment. Even in the eighteenth century communication by printed word was not extensive. The majority of those whose writings went to the printing press had been trained in Greek, Latin, theology, law, and philosophy. Do these men give us a realistic picture of their little neighbors' attitudes toward life? Perhaps they do not even give us a realistic picture of themselves, wrapped as they were in their specific ideologies about the nature of man.

Nevertheless, there remains the fact that each period is characterized not only by what everybody does and eats, but also by its aspirations. Truly, the material factor in human life is enormously influential and a historian who neglects it deceives himself. But so does the historian who fails to include in the picture of a period its hopes, its dreams, and its rare ideals. The normal and the selected interact. If there is a productive tension between the real and the ideal, the latter will give wings to a culture. It makes a difference to what kind of advisers we listen, and what kind of authors we read; those who hold us down, or those who lift us up. Sooner or later this difference shows not only in the conduct of the individual, but also in his government, his education, his forms of amusement, his competitive behavior, briefly, in the whole wide range of public ethos. The Bible, the only book read in the house of a devout Protestant farmer, was of greater moral significance than a modern library of mystery stories and science fiction. And one sermon of a Bernard of Clairvaux, heard by a medieval man once in his life, may have made a deeper impression than the hundreds of speeches and addresses we hear over the radio.

There is a further question to be asked if we want to avoid false generalizations. Does the behavior of modern man, so extensively criticized by clergymen, educators, and professional reformers, really represent the autonomous attitude? Is it really rebellion against God and the logos, or is it not rather the ambiguous attitude of indifference which has probably existed as long as man had to fight his exhausting struggle for survival with no time for deeper reflection? It is a foolish question whether man in earlier times was essentially better than we. In all likelihood, he was not. Nor is there a simple answer to the question whether man-transcending outlooks, such as theonomy or logonomy, provide a finer sense of moral obligation than a world-immanent self-reliance. All can be productive as long as they rise from deep concern, and all can be sterile when the product of a state of inner decay.

In our old and complex society we have corruption, yet we have also kept alive the great movements of thought and inspiration through which mankind has gone in its long history. We still have saints who die for their religion; we have still explorers who sacrifice themselves for rational truth; and we have still the courage of men willing to die for the sovereign kingdom of man. Are we in a hopeless state of decline, as we may sometimes think in our despairing hours? Who knows? There has never been a period when Armageddon has not been preached. Maybe we are close to it, but the question still is what we do with our chances. And though against their own will, certainly those men most of all invite failure who think that God is only with them and their pasts, and that in other camps there reigns nothing but the devil. Wherever people search seriously, there is hope for truth and for salvation.

IV. THE OUTLOOK

Let us now summarize our opinion about the responsibilities of the three world views with respect to the formation of the twentieth century's culture. Each of them has had its productive and revolutionary, as well as its sterile and reactionary phase.

1. If the *theonomous or god-centered* view still took seriously its doctrine of divine judgment and its pessimistic-optimistic philosophy about the world here and hereafter, it would act as a revolutionary force against the present social and cultural situation. Indeed, we find movements such as religious socialism, and religious neo-conservatism, both coming primarily from Germany and France, which challenge the capitalist-competitive as well as the communist-collectivist societies as materialist deviations from Christian ethics. Even officially the churches have voiced their protest against a world suffering from the diseases of industrial strife on the one hand, and of totalitarian suppression on the other. Since the times of Leo XIII Catholicism has shown its patriarchal solidarity with the modern tendencies toward trade unionism and social welfare (*Novarum Rerum*, 1891). But at the same time Catholicism shows definite signs of hardening of the arteries.

In the great times of the Catholic Church no pope would

have dared to do what Pius IX did in 1870—impose, more or less, on the collegium of cardinals the dogma of papal infallibility in essential matters of faith. The figure of St. Mary has provided for many centuries one of the most beautiful myths of the Christian tradition. But it remained for the present Pope to use the privilege of papal infallibility for declaring *ex cathedra* the dogma of the bodily assumption of St. Mary, against the conscience and advice of many good Catholics. And while Catholicism stiffens, Protestantism ranges from stubborn fundamentalism to an almost complete dilution of Christian faith. It remains to be seen whether Protestantism can accomplish a spiritual as well as organizational self-unification. If so, it will have a new renascence and a new future, while Catholicism, building around itself a spiritual Maginot Line, may strengthen its position for a while, but later discover that it weakens from lack of inner vitality.

2. The *logonomous, or reason-centered* attitude has today lost much of its inspiration. Its optimism, originally based on a deep though perhaps one-sided interpretation of the relation between human and divine reason, became shallow during the prosperity of the nineteenth century and its laissez-faire spirit. It is now challenged to rediscover its original sources and to create a new practical and philosophical idealism. The present "crisis of liberalism," or its serious situation of defense against nondemocratic movements, is but one aspect of the total crisis of the logonomous world-aspect.

3. The *man-centered or autonomous* attitude, as we saw, can be evaluated positively as a protest against authority or authorities which have lost their inner justification. When man has given up faith in all transcendent ideals, when all that he hears sounds to him like skillful propaganda, he may find nothing to fall back upon but his self. The self, however, is little unless it has its anchorage in ideas of more than personal validity. Extreme self-reliance can quickly change into despair and self-isolation.

Or, in order to escape this imprisonment within the lonely

self, man may throw himself into the arms of institutions, especially the State. He may make idols out of politics, organization, and "leaders." In our age of mass organization and technology, we are closer to this error than at any time since the end of the Roman Empire. Even in democracies there is danger to the highly praised values of freedom and individual dignity.

Each of the three world views recommends itself today as a form of "Humanism." Thus we speak of Christian, rationalist or idealist, and naturalist humanism. But if a concept means too many things it loses all value of precise communication. It would be better to preserve the term "Humanism" for the logonomous attitude which began in the Renaissance and found its culmination in the philosophy and poetry of the eighteenth and the beginning of the nineteenth centuries.

Most people would agree that ours is a period during which man breathes an atmosphere of secularism. This view is one-sided. As already said, our complex heritages still live with us in their positive as well as in their negative forms. We are bewildered. But at no time would people have coped successfully with the gigantic tasks that confront us today. Ours is the question whether the various world views here described will still prove capable of productive self-renewal, so that they can lead man out of his present stage of painful transition toward a new rallying of forces. Neither theonomy nor logonomy nor autonomy alone can solve our problems. Those who claim to have the exclusive answer in but one of these world views forget that man is a striving being with many-sided interests. We have to choose between a world-open pluralism which avoids the pitfalls of relativism, and the deceptive security of dogma which easily degenerates into blinding authoritarianism. If we do not want the latter, we have to venture the first.

CHAPTER 2

Man as the Self-Transcending Being

Philosophical Anthropology

> Many the forms of life,
> Fearful and strange to see,
> But man supreme stands out,
> For strangeness and for fear . . .
> And speech, and thought as swift as wind,
> And tempered mood for higher life of states,
> These he has learned, and how to flee
> The stormy sleet of frost unkind . . .
> So, gifted with a wondrous might,
> Above all fancy's dreams, with skill to plan,
> Now unto evil, now to good,
> He wends his way. . . .
>
> SOPHOCLES (*Antigone*)

I. GENERAL CHARACTERISTICS

ARE all the questions and answers by which man relates himself to the universe equally right—or equally wrong? Is there any firm point from which we may start in order to find some solution in the battle of "isms" such as God-centered transcendentalism, logos-centered rationalism, man-centered naturalism, and all the "schools of thought" connected with them?

Let us try to answer these questions with an attempt at a self-interpretation of man, not only because he is himself the source and object of all his interests, but also because the picture which he has of himself colors his practical behavior as well as his theoretical outlook toward the whole world. Without neglecting the findings of the empirical sciences we will mainly consult the wisdom of those who through their insight into human nature have guided their fellow men toward self-understanding.

Is there a common denominator by which to characterize man as a distinct creature in the wealth of creation? He eats, drinks, and sleeps; if normal he avoids pain, seeks satisfaction, and wishes to survive. But these "biogenetic" characteristics are universal not only among normal humans, but also among the dogs with which we play, and the cows which we milk.

Why, in contrast to animals, does man need such a long period of growing up and education? Because he is not specialized, he is not adapted to a specific environment and specific life conditions like a bee or even a higher mammal. His instincts are much less developed than those of the creatures he considers below himself on the ladder of evolution. He is not naturally bound to, and at home in, his world. He stands within and at the same time before it. Whereas under normal conditions nature tells the animal what to do, man has to find out, to select, to decide to a much greater extent. Yet, in spite of his being weaker than animals in many respects, having less strength than a bear, less speed than a deer, his nervous system and his brain interconnect his various sensorimotor functions to such a degree that in the end he is stronger than either of them. Thus, though at a disadvantage in the beginning, he develops in the course of time more skills and specializations than any other living being. The moment a human opens himself to reality, an enormous number of impressions pour into him and make him vibrate with energy. Observe a child during the first years of life and you will marvel at the process of absorption and expansion. It is impossible to distinguish which faculty helps the other, compensates for, and sometimes also fights the other in the process of maturing.

Certainly the upright posture[1] and the opposition of the thumb help in the process of looking freely around and "getting

[1] See the article by Erwin W. Straus, "The Upright Posture." *Psychiatric Quarterly*, October, 1952.

a grip on things." However, the main agent of progress lies in the fusion of man's activities with the faculty to which we have given such names as understanding or intelligence. It is not some faculty that "grows out," or "emerges from" or is "above" the sensorimotor activities of man; rather, it develops *with* them. As an integral part of man's total activity it helps in the building up of his world of apprehension and cognition; together with action itself it is one of the decisive factors in the reduction of danger and tension. Without intelligence our aggressive and defensive, our questioning and responsive dialogues with the near and distant environment could not develop into the form of communication we find in the esthetic symbols of art and the conceptual symbols of language. Through them we escape the necessity which would maintain us on the level of the higher mammals—that of constant repetition of every experience, of returning again and again to the same place, of running around in the small circle of our physical existence.

Through esthetic and conceptual symbols we can explain something without being there, we can make innumerable short-cuts in experience; we can learn from each other and from older generations. By virtue of symbols a talented person can learn within ten years mathematical operations on which the genius of mankind had to work for thousands of years. Not always in equivalent depth and performance, but at least in constructive imagination an artist may traverse within two or three decades the path from cave drawings to Picasso; and the thought of the great religious and philosophical prophets can be conveyed to young people in schools and universities. There is, to be truthful, something deceptive about this vicarious experience. For never can it reproduce the ringing sound of original knowledge; which may be the reason for the tragic fact that people and nations learn so terribly little from the errors and achievements of other men and nations. Yet our whole civilization is built on the possibility of evoking many pasts in our individual present, and of projecting ourselves imaginatively into distant futures.

All this is to say that the human being lives in an order which reaches far beyond his personal existence, which, at least to a degree, overcomes the animal's limitations of time and space, which makes possible productive withdrawal from the immediate and, by dint of such withdrawal, reflection and theory. Thus arises the objective edifice of culture that overarches our individual strivings like an ancient cathedral.

After this allusion to the basic qualities which make the epic of human culture possible, we may now state the following characteristics of the human race.

1. Man—as the most unspecialized creature on earth—lives in the continual state of *self-transcendence*; he never stays quietly within himself but reaches or goes intellectually beyond himself into unknown spheres of reality. The concept of self-transcendence will be central for many of our future considerations.

2. Because of this openness to the world and its impressions, man is *restless*. Observe an animal in the state of falling asleep. Only young children possess this capacity of quick relaxation of every muscle, of sinking down into the ground of self-forgetful nature. Man is full of tension, often even in sleep.

3. Man, who is not naturally and instinctively adapted to a particular way of life, must make his way by *intentional planning*. Without it he could not survive.

4. Man is *political*, the *zoon politikon* of Aristotle. He needs systematic and collective organization in his defense and aggression against a world of threat. He needs the fact and sense of belonging.

5. But man is also *the creature of anxiety and loneliness*. When his planning fails, when there is no reward from his activity, and when he is thrown out of human organization, he quickly loses energy and courage and feels himself utterly isolated.

6. Man is *homo faber*, the systematic *toolmaker*. Only by extending his power beyond his own body can he protect and develop himself and his group.

7. Man is also the *symbol-maker*. By means of esthetic and

conceptual symbols—art and language—he reduces the power which time and space have over the animal, and builds an order and system, a "world," beside and above the natural cosmos.

8. Through living within nature and at the same time in an order of his own, man acquires perspective. This means that he can wait rather than act on the spur of the moment; he can choose and decide from *"a point of view";* he can compare.

9. In consequence of his living in a conceptual as well as in a natural world, or in a second order, as it were, man can *ask questions, think, reflect, and build theories* which help him to assemble his thoughts and impressions in logical sequence.

10. By virtue of his reflective quality man is the witness of, and at least in degree, the director of his own development, *"le témoin de son être."*[2]

11. Only because he is at the same time witness and director, man can have *history*; he is the historical creature *par excellence*.

12. Man is *dependent and free* at the same time. He is dependent to the degree to which he participates in the life-and-death-spending order of nature. He is free to the degree to which he lives in the second order, or the order of mind. But even here he is not "free from . . ." he is only "free for . . ." free to find out to what degree he can make his asking, thinking, acting, and planning compatible with the constructive principles of living, that is, with those principles which teach him how to combine the minimum of harm with the maximum of productiveness. Otherwise he will perish.

13. We have the right to assume that these principles point toward certain laws which would constitute the *third, highest, and universal order,* or the ground and end of all that is.

In consequence of all these qualities of self-transcendence man is the one being capable of *world-wide participation*, or of universality of aspect. He can feel himself as a participant in the three orders, the natural, the intellectual and the order of the

---

[2] Regis Jolivet, *Les Doctrines Existentialists de Kierkegaard à Jean Paul Sartre* (1948, p. 224).

whole, which is too embracing to be denoted by a single human concept. A naturalist might call it the ultimate or cosmic energy, the existentialist philosopher Karl Jaspers calls it the Encompassing (*das Umfassende*), the mystics call it the Ground or the Abyss, and in conventional religious language it is called God. Whatever the thousands of names given to this inscrutable source of all life—the *Summum Verum*, the *Summum Bonum*, and the *Summum Pulchrum*, the Highest Truth, the Highest Good, and the Highest Beauty—it must be something in which the contradictions seen by human eyes and minds dissolve in a universal synthesis. And it is just this for which we have no name.

14. Only through the sense of participation in the three orders of nature, mind, and wholeness can man fully understand his *ethical responsibility,* which extends not only to himself and other human beings, but to life in its totality. This sense of participation interprets to him also the basic meaning of concepts such as freedom, love, and dignity, as well as sin, failure, and aberration. Man's highest aspirations always end in the Unseen yet ever present.

One may object that with these considerations we have gone beyond the realm of science and empiricism into that of metaphysics. Certainly we have. Nevertheless, we have a good conscience. For whoever reads with a philosophically trained mind any psychological book, however emphatically it may claim to be nothing but "scientific," will sooner or later discover the underlying metaphysics, even though it may be hidden to the author himself. The very ideal of scholarly objectivity requires that we try—especially in dealing with the problem of man—to shed light on all factors which are real, though we may not yet be able to subject them to the experimental method of the laboratory. Otherwise even the results of the laboratory will be interpreted falsely.

We will approach our subject of philosophical anthropology in greater detail on two planes, as it were. First, though briefly, because there is no need to repeat psychological textbooks, we will analyze *the main intellectual functions* through which man realizes his being in the world. Second, we will describe the *gradual expansion of his orbits of experience,* or the way in which he becomes an ever self-transcending self.

But before we begin with the analysis of a person's wholeness into parts, let us acknowledge the artificiality of this procedure. If anything is a *Gestalt,* or a configuration, man is. Yet the discursive character of language does not allow us to represent in one comprehensive symbol the simultaneity of various factors, their oneness in variety, their independence and interdependence. We have to describe one quality after the other, though in reality there is no strict chronological sequence. The only instrument man can use to come close to the truth is his conceptual thinking, but it may also lead him away from reality. This is the tragedy in man's intellectual existence. Achievement and failure are combined. However far our intellectual search may drive us, we are confined by this limitation.

Thus, when we speak of "instincts," or "drives," or "emotions," "intelligence," and "reason," we disconnect the connected. From the evolutionist's point of view, all these qualities represent a continuum of the mind which accompanies a group of biochemical events.

II. OUR MENTAL EQUIPMENT

1. *"Instincts" or "Drives"*

As already indicated, if we mean by "instinct" the frozen inherited tropistic response which is conducive to the animal's survival under normal circumstances, but stultifying under changing conditions, then man has no instincts. Sometimes we may envy the amazing social instinct of certain insects, but if we see a whole train of processionary caterpillars coming to a standstill and starving to death because the leader cannot get out of a trap, then we are grateful for being at the other end of the mental evolution and prefer the risk of choice to the determinism of instinct.

If, on the other hand, we mean by "instinct" certain compulsive and unreflective reactions to the stimuli which come from and to our body, such as need for food, air, sleep, and sexual satisfaction—in other words, reactions which are inseparable from normal physical functions—then, of course, man is an instinctive being.[3] Because he is less disciplined, the young child is more instinctive than the mature person, but even the latter is to a high degree. Yet to call someone a "creature of instinct" is a depreciation. We mean that he is not fully on the human level, but a sensuous, underprivileged person.

In other words, man integrates his instincts with his total being to the degree to which, with the development of his intelligence and character, he becomes able to control himself, to reflect and to choose. The more intelligence and freedom of choice he possesses, the less is the tyranny of instinct. Even the most elementary drives, such as hunger and sex, become a part of the total personality during an individual's cultural development. Civilized man, under ordinary conditions, does not devour food but cultivates his taste; he does not violate, but respects a woman's right to choose her partner.

But even the most cultured person is deeply embedded—not only in his physical, but also in his psychic life—in the vegetative struggling and dying of nature. However much man is able to rise toward the lofty, he also sinks toward the deep and dark sphere of life. However great the difference in education, none of us should—or can—remove himself so much from our common biological heritage that he denies himself the proper satisfaction of the drives by which nature announces its will to live. In extreme, this would be suicide.

The biogenetic drives discussed so far have been designated as "innate" or "unlearned." But we are here not interested in the

---

[3] See, e.g., Muzafer Sherif, *The Outline of Social Psychology* (New York, 1948) (Index "Instinct," "Motive," "Need," "Drive").

old and moot question of the "innate" or "acquired" character of our mental functions. Probably they are both, since for every function, however susceptible to gradual growth and discipline, there must have been some germinal or embryonic capacity. In man, just as in nature, there is no *creatio ex nihilo* and no break of the law of causality. Nothing comes from nothing, or everything comes from something. But it is the characteristic feature of man's biogenetic or instinctive drives that they tend to develop through their own immanent power and do not need the kind of systematic learning necessary to man's technical and intellectual achievements.

It is the same with them as with our body, as long as it is healthy. Nature is supposed to take care. Thanklessly we use the gifts of nature, unaware of their intricate functioning. We take it for granted that a boy likes to eat; only when he refuses do his parents become attentive.

Should not the natural "giveness" of such basic life functions as the circulation of our blood, the interaction of our nerves and muscles, and the development of our instincts lead us to think about a general phenomenon in man's relation to the forces of life?

When we speak of "the ego," "the individual," "the person," or "the self" we generally conceive of something independent, something that lives out of its own power. This is arrogance. It is life, or nature, or the creation, or whatever name we may give it, which lives in us and of which we should consider ourselves the reverential keepers, the trustees, the guardians. We are not the individual creators of our selves, rather our selves "partake" in the creative stream of life. If a physician cures a patient, is he not but the adviser who relies on centuries of research into the natural forces of life which he directs rather than creates? One can hear a surgeon say that the operation was successful, but the patient died. What happened? Externally, the body was well repaired, but nature refused to make the heart beat. "Which of you by taking thought can add one cubit unto his stature?" (Matt.

6:27). The consciousness of dependence on forces beyond one's own power is the distinction of reverential or "religious" man in contrast to modern technological man who forgets that even his technical masterpieces do not result from bullying, but from obeying nature. It makes no difference whether this relationship is interpreted naturalistically or transcendentally, whatever these words may mean. Whether "Nature" or "God" gives, *some* power gives, a power greater than man. There can be neither true religion, nor true science, unless it is permeated with the idea of interaction of all individual life with the Life by which it is nourished. Thus, we take up here, though in another context, the concepts of transcendence and participation earlier discussed.

2. Feelings or Emotions

Three characteristics of our drives, namely nearness to physical nature, universal occurrence in normal men, and, in consequence of their elemental quality, an inclination toward irrational behavior, are characteristic also of our feelings and emotions—the two terms being just as interchangeable as the terms "drive" or "instinct." In his emotional life a person betrays often more clearly than anywhere else what he really is. Also, in this sphere he understands his fellow men more easily than in the discussion of intellectual subjects, for men are more equal in their feelings than in their rational achievements. On the other hand, we all know men whom we considered endowed with reason and discipline whom we suddenly "no longer understand." Their passions run away with them.

> The expense of spirit in a waste of shame
> Is lust in action; and till action, lust
> Is perjured, murderous, bloody, full of blame,
> Savage, extreme, rude, cruel, not to trust;
> Enjoyed no sooner but despised straight;
> Past reason hunted, and no sooner had,
> Past reason hated, as a swallowed bait
> On purpose laid to make the taker mad:

Mad in pursuit and in possession so;
Had, having, and in quest to have, extreme;
A bliss in proof, and proved, a very woe;
Before a joy proposed; behind, a dream.
All this the world well knows; yet none knows well
To shun the heaven that leads men to this hell.

SHAKESPEARE: *Sonnet cxxix*

Yet, despite all their power, we are not so deeply nature-bound in our emotions as we are in our instinctual life; we are more free and human, and, which is the same, more individualistic.

Theoretically, one could conceive of a being whose physical needs operated without any emotional overtones; hunger, if not satisfied, appearing merely as emaciation, lack of warmth showing in certain reactions of the skin; sex as a mere result of the blind necessity to procreate. In all likelihood, such a creature could not survive. It would not have at its disposal the motivating as well as the signaling device which we possess in our feelings. Nor would such a creature have the flux and flow of inner experience, the heights of joy, the intimacies of delight, and the abysses of sadness which make human life worth living, because they make it sensitive, exciting, and profound.

After all the contradictions we discover in our affective life, can we wonder that they defy definition?[4]

Five main interpretations have emerged among philosophers and psychologists. This not only because of the complexity of the subject but also because of conscious or unconscious value differences in the scholars' theories of man and life. For it colors my explanation of feeling whether I am—to use an essentially obsolete, but here permissible vocabulary—a materialist, a naturalist, an idealist, or a religious transcendentalist.

With our interpretation of the emotions as a signaling device

[4] See Henry A. Murray, *et al.*, *Explorations in Personality* (Oxford, 1938). Also Clyde Kluckhohn and Henry A. Murray, Editors, *Personality in Nature, Society, and Culture* (New York, 1948).

we acknowledge a kernel of truth in the opinions of a group of thinkers whom we might denote as belonging to the *biological* school.

From Antiquity up to our times feelings have often been explained as symptoms which register states and mutations of our physical nature. W. B. Cannon[5] and R. G. Hoskins,[6] especially, have shown the interaction between the glands and emotional behavior. But as early as in the fourth century B.C. the Greek Aristippus considered the emotion of "pleasure" to be the result of soft movements in our body and displeasure the result of violent movements.[7] In contemporary America the school of behaviorism with its emphasis on conditioned reflexes represents the biological interpretation of feeling.

In contrast to the biological school there exists a second group, the *intellectualists,* for whom feelings are primarily subservient to, or derivatives from, or accompanying phenomena of, the intellect. For this group, as well, the affections need a physical channel, but essentially they are a sort of motions of the mind, or the soul, or results of such motions. In the Enneads[8] the Greek mystical philosopher Plotinus considers feelings of happiness or unhappiness reactions of the soul to its own states of perfection and imperfection. There is also Hegel's beautiful image of *Gefühl* (feeling) as *dumpfes Weben des Geistes*[9] (the wordless weaving of the mind). The intellectualist Herbart,[10] one of the founders of the modern theory of learning, believes that our emotions and desires result from modifications occurring in our conceptual representations. In other words, feeling is a kind of pre-intellectual or post-intellectual state of mental life.

Naturally, Kant is also close to this school of thought. However, he is more comprehensive, or, so to speak, more anthro-

---

[5] *The Wisdom of the Body* (New York, 1932).
[6] *Endocrinology, The Glands and Their Functions* (New York, 1941).
[7] Diogenes Laertius, *Lives,* II, "Aristippus."
[8] On the Essence of the Soul, *Enneads,* IV.
[9] *Encyclopaedie der Philosophischen Wissenschaft,* par. 446.
[10] *Psychologie als Wissenschaft,* par. 106.

pologically minded. In his unrelenting vigilance against false forms of idealism he recognizes the sensuous origin of the emotions and their role as indicators of satisfaction or frustration, abundance or deprivation, fulfillment or danger. Nevertheless, he considers them to be related to cognition. They are, so to speak, mental states arrested on their way from dim presentations to clear concepts, or impressions which document themselves merely as states of pleasure or displeasure. Feelings, consequently, are subjective and have no claim to universal validity.[11] They are, however, so closely related to our conceptual and active world that they can have contemplative, intellectual, and practical overtones.[12]

Then there are, third, the *"enthusiasts,"* or *romantics,* not sentimentalists or idle dreamers who would not be worth mentioning, but men of such profound passion for life and truth that they experience the limitations of reason in comparison with the depth and power of the emotions. So Pascal can say: *"Le coeur a ses raisons que la raison ne connaît pas"*[13] ("the heart has its reasons which reason does not know"). And Goethe has Faust proclaiming: *"Gefühl ist alles, Name ist Schall und Rauch"* ("Feeling is all in all, names are mere sound and smoke").[14]

A fourth group is composed of the *voluntarists,* for whom all living and feeling is primarily an effluence of will, or will an effluence of feeling. A large philosophical and psychological discussion has grown out of the attempt to define the differences and similarities between the two. Whatever the value of such endeavor may be, it has at least proved their close interrelationship. Wilhelm Wundt, who devoted much of his research to the affective life, is convinced that feeling can be considered just as

[11] *Kritik der Urteilskraft,* Einleitung; *Anthropologie in Pragmatischer Hinsicht, passim.*
[12] *Metaphysik der Sitten* I, Einleitung I, pp. 11 ff.
[13] Pensées, Part II, art. XVII. See in this connection Max Scheler, *Der Formalismus in der Ethik und die materiale Wertethik,* pp. 260 ff., who elaborates on Pascal's ideas from the point of view of a modern systematic philosopher.
[14] Faust, I. Part, Scene XVI.

much the beginning of a willing as willing can be considered a composite process of feeling.[15] In the United States William James has brought the emotions and will into close affinity.[16]

In recent times, as a fifth group, there has developed the *psychoanalytical* school of thought with an ever-increasing number of internal differences. It is impossible to subsume under any specific category the work of the man who has contributed more than any other contemporary to the understanding of the emotional process, Sigmund Freud. He makes ample use of the genius' right to prefer the suggestiveness of images and symbols to outworn abstractions; at the same time, he is primarily the physician who diagnoses for the sake of helping and not for the sake of mere analysis. Consequently, even his closest disciples differ in their interpretations of some of his basic concepts. Every new explanation of Freud's thought may lead to another misunderstanding. By outsiders he has often been called a "materialist," "naturalist," and "determinist." Since he was unafraid of directing the light of insight into psychic areas which others would like to leave in darkness because they seem to think that it is easier to find one's way in night than in light, he has had to stand a whole rainfall of epithets, motivated by everything from unconscious bias to willful slander.

Certainly, there are statements in Freud which tend toward so-called "materialism." Perhaps the statement that "the most complex mental operations are possible without the cooperation of consciousness" is offensive to a spiritually minded person.[17] His emphasis on libido has been branded as sexualism. His interpretation of the affective life as directed by the desire to achieve happiness and to avoid pain has been interpreted as supporting a hedonistic ethics. But then Socrates and Thomas Aquinas too

[15] *Grundriss der Psychologie*, Chapter II. par. 12–14 (several editions, Leipzig), and *Grundzüge der Physiol. Psychologie*, Vol. III, Vierter Abschnitt.
[16] See *The Principles of Psychology*, Vol. II, Chapters XXIV-XXVI (New York, 1890).
[17] *The Basic Writings of Sigmund Freud*. Translated and edited by A. A. Brill (New York, 1938, pp. 448, 521, 529).

would be hedonists, for they also knew that man strives for happiness. The question is the meaning of "happiness": lust, luxury, self-indulgence, or voluntary acceptance of one's duty. In addition, one can be realistic about man's exposure to his emotions without recommending them as the guide for human conduct. Freud himself, in his *Formulations Regarding the Two Principles in Mental Functioning*, sets the "reality principle," the capacity of coping maturely with the tasks and conflicts of life, against the "pleasure principle in the merely hedonistic sense of the word."[18]

Yet, if one looks at Freud's work as a whole one cannot fail to discover a certain hedonistic and mechanistic tendency. Like most scientists of his time, he did not discern the deceptive simplicity of nineteenth-century naturalism. His explanation of art and religion by the theory of complexes is a primitive generalization, though it may contain a partial truth. Future research in comparative anthropology and social psychology will probably reveal that some of his basic tenets, especially the Oedipus complex, are not as universal as he assumed. But whatever his faults may be, he has directed our attention toward the rich and complicated interplay of conscious and subconscious forces in maintaining the delicate balance in man's psychic household.

Who has created these forces? What is the ultimate purpose of man, and what is his relation to the universe? Toward these problems Freud maintained, on the whole, the attitude of an honest agnostic. Philosophy, one may suspect, was for him an intellectual luxury. Agnosticism, however, is also a philosophy, shining behind the data thought to be of "strictly empirical" nature.

But would Freud have arrived at his penetrating observations if he and his forerunners had not brushed aside preconceived and traditional speculations about the nature and destiny of man? Even in philosophy this has often been the way toward new perceptions of reality. Renunciation of previous answers is just as

[18] See Freud's *Collected Papers,* Vol. IV, p. 13, and Brill, p. 510.

necessary for the cognitive progress as is the attempt to find new answers. The two complement each other. Thus it has come about that Freud has enriched even those fields of thought which were to him alien, namely philosophy and the theory of art and religion. Finally, now when we have already some historical perspective, is Freud's work really so "revolutionary" as it was considered in the beginning? Many of his ideas about the subconscious were anticipated by earlier thinkers. And is not his triad of the Id, the Ego, and the Super-ego more or less a naturalist interpretation of what other thinkers have called the "dark forces" in the unknown regions of the soul, "self-consciousness" of the person who finds himself confronted with the enormous variety of situations, and the "conscience" which relates the ego to the regulative principles of life? Thus, one may be inclined to ask: "Why all the noise?"

In spite of so many deviations among the interpreters of feeling there is more consensus than seems at first glance. If the various schools of thought did not emphasize their divergent aspects so onesidedly, they would all be right.

First, no one doubts the interaction between our emotional and our physical life, from whatever side the stimulus may come, from within or from without, from the mind or from the body. Nobody doubts that the emotions accompany, enhance, or reflect the functioning of our instinctive drives. On the other hand, no one has expressed any serious doubt that feelings of which we are aware must have something to do with awareness, that is, with consciousness or mind—whatever this may be. Whether one glorifies emotions as the spring of psychic life, or puts them into a position inferior, or even hostile, to the conceptual intellect, there seems to be agreement that they represent a form of energy oscillating between the senses and intelligence. When in the state of passion they may defy or obstruct censorship by our rational qualities; when in the state of balance, they may agree with them. But in either case the emotions tune our psyche, and to a large degree also our body, according to pleasant or unpleasant contacts with the external world. Often the emotional response to a stimulus may stay within or barely rise above the sphere of the unconscious, to disappear like the ripple of a wave without any observable effect on the stream of mental life—a passing sensation for which we may not even have a name. Or the emotional response may create an inner conflict, at first ploughed under and for ever invisible to the untrained perception, but developing under many disguises to destroy the harvest of life.

In the process of evolution, feelings represent a high development of the nervous system and are the harbingers of the intellect. Often they are, as it were, the warning sentinels in man's battle for survival, and often they are the very contrary, the forces of lust and blind action. Often they are almost silent like the last vibrations of a tuning fork, often they produce violent percussions. Has a philologist ever made a study of the vocabulary which great writers—Dante, Shakespeare, Goethe, Dostoevsky, Tolstoy—have used for the thousands of degrees in the scale of emotions? Perhaps in no area of experience is our language more revealing of the wealth of the human soul, but also of its terrific exposure.

3. Intelligence

But where would our feelings lead us without intelligence? Intelligence consists of the individual's capacity to *discern* the various entities within a complex phenomenon, to *raise* a problem, and to *solve* it by logical methods in which a process of trial and error is supposed to lead toward better understanding of the subject considered. Man cannot use his intelligence in isolation from his other energies, but through it he can employ these energies for the achievement of the greatest effect with a minimum amount of external effort.

A certain degree of discerning action can be observed also in animals. It is cleverly used by a cat which chases a bird in our yard; even the ameba approaching its victim has its tactics.

Recent observations of bees reveal an amazing degree of ingenuity in the discovery and location of food and the sense of direction. And though animals follow a pattern, there is in the higher species some flexibility in the pursuit of a purpose. Yet it is still the distinguishing feature of man that in him discernment can separate itself from immediate action and become, as it were, an activity of its own. Thus we can distinguish two stages: first, discerning action, with the discriminating process more or less one with the action itself (a beast of prey sensing and hunting up its victim); and second, deliberate planning with the discriminating process already set apart from the acting, but still with the intention of accomplishing a specific purpose (a person trying to find out on the first of the month how to budget the monthly income). Rarely is anything more important for the rise of civilization than the human capacity to put an interval between stimulus and action. For within this interval grows deliberation, perspective, objectivity—all the higher achievements of the reflective mind.

Nevertheless, we must not assume, with certain religious and idealistic thinkers, that action and intelligence have separate roots. This seems so when we look at the high achievements of theory, such as a mathematical or philosophical system. But, first, thinking—which is the characteristic function of intelligence—is itself action, transposed from the outer toward the inner life. It is strenuous when pursued consistently so that the majority of people shy away from it whenever possible. Second, when we investigate the genesis of the indispensable vehicle of systematic thinking, called *language,* we discover that it emerges from our active contact with the environment. Sound itself, just as thinking, is action, only more overt. It is evoked particularly when we respond to joyous or painful sensuous stimuli. By sound we address objects and events which surprise us or which we recognize. Finally, the language of the child develops largely in play, which is the child's form of self-occupation.

If, in these respects, we agree with the pragmatic theory of language and thinking, we must here, nevertheless, emphasize that theory's shortcomings. In a later chapter we will have to deal with the problems of meaning and truth in conceptual language; problems in no way answered by reference to the undeniable relationship between action and thought.

4. Reason

In attending here to such high achievements of the mind as meaning and sense of truth, we have already passed from the quality of "intelligence" over into the domain of "reason," or the domain which Kant calls *Vernunft* to differentiate from "intelligence," which he calls *Verstand*.

We here define "reason" as a mental quality which is impossible without intelligence, but more comprehensive than, or superior to, the latter in consequence of its depth and universality of interest.

The differentiation between intelligence and reason is, perhaps, arbitrary. Many philosophers and languages do not acknowledge it. However, when speaking of intelligence we usually have in mind the attempt to master an encounter with a puzzling event in our environment. We try to solve an "ad hoc" problem. Reason, on the other hand, is not so much interested in the immediacy of the effect, or in changing a situation as quickly as possible. It may not be at all interested in change. It is the instrument by which we go further than by any other means away from the nature-embedded instinctive life of the animal toward the specifically human quality of contemplative freedom. In instinctive behavior, man is "driven." In our emotional life, especially as interpreted by the idealists, enthusiasts, and voluntarists, we already find a certain capacity of floating freely within limited boundaries of experience. Intelligence, though still "tied" to a problem, already possesses the possibility of choice, planning, and perspective. But only reason makes man "free" in that it gives him the perspective, the distance from the here and now, and the interest in "disinterested" knowledge of the mysteries of his self and the universe. It is reason which in the medium of man creates a spiritual superstructure highly independent of space and time, unthinkable without, yet more embracing than individual minds; a world of values, perhaps also of great errors, but of errors which are still worth thinking about. There are many errors in Plato's *Republic;* yet, we still read it. Reason, in other words, is the consummation of man's self-transcendence.

Or, whereas intelligence appertains to the second, or mental order, of which we spoke in the general introduction to this chapter, reason reaches into the third, the universal or *metaphysical* order.

Within reason we may distinguish three different though closely interconnected functions. We call them *contemplation, intuition,* and *faith.*

A. CONTEMPLATION

In the state of contemplation the human mind is no longer aggressive. It stands before the world without the intention of correcting it, of moving something from one place to another, of asserting itself against external forces. It does not wish to alter; it wishes to understand. Though active, the mind is in a state of "dwelling on," of welcoming openness, of a deep respect for the laws and order it senses in the universe—an attitude most profoundly described two and a half thousand years ago by Lao-Tse in his doctrine of the Tao.[19]

The great Tao is the most perfect—though you cannot see it—and no time can diminish its value.

The sublime Tao permeates the whole world—though it appears to us infinitely high and far—and no time will put a limit to its permeating power.

The sublime Tao is in unity with our reason, yet there are so many who doubt.

[19] The term Tao is untranslatable. Its meaning approaches "the all-penetrating spirit."

The sublime Tao is strong, vigorous and all powerful, yet people do not understand it.

It speaks to us clearly and persuasively, yet we do not hear.

For behold, through being busy you may protect yourself from poverty; through being quiet you may overcome the daily troubles of life. But if you wish to comprehend that which is right, good, beautiful, true, and perfect, and to act accordingly as a symbol of the best in humanity—if you wish to understand all this you have first to do this: to keep your mind pure and clear.[20]

In this attitude the thinkers, prophets, and artists have had their hours of highest productivity. They were not forcing themselves on the world; the world came to them. In losing their selves, they were able to escape the clutches in which the surface of reality holds the thoughts of men. They became *free from multitude*, both the multitude of things and the multitude of men. All high cultures and, as a part of them, all high religions praise contemplation, or, as we might call it, *productive withdrawal* from life's surface, as the art by which man merges his individuality with the spending grounds of creation, and thus becomes himself a spending ground to his fellow men. Through opening himself, he receives; through receiving, he can give. This offering oneself as a vessel, this most sublime form of "partaking," rather than the false originality and sterile zeal of producing something for the marketplace—this is the mark of genius.

B. INTUITION

But the state of contemplation is not merely a state of "being open." It is, at the same time, also the beginning of the road toward intuitive insight. Intuitive insight is not the result of

[20] Translated from the German edition of Lao-Tse's *Tao-Te-King. Der Weg zur Tugend* by Reinhold von Plaenckner (Leipzig, 1870), p. 45. Kapitel. There is, in some respects, a profound similarity between the thought of Lao-Tse, Edmund Husserl's phenomenology, and the existentialist philosophies of Karl Jaspers and Martin Heidegger. See especially the latter's essay "Vom Wesen der Wahrheit" (Frankfurt, 1949), p. 14 (*Das Seinlassen vom Seienden—* "The letting be of that which is"). See also Egon Vietta, *Die Seinsfrage bei Heidegger* (Stuttgart, 1950).

pedestrian logic; it does not follow naturally from an already given fact; it is not a progress along an inevitable sequence of cause and effect. It is, as all higher mental activities, closely related to the gift of fantasy that allows man to conjure up, and project himself into situations which do not exist in actuality. Intuitive insight appears as a flash, as a vision of the deeper unity of so far dispersed entities that gives us the feeling of being no longer before or *with-out*, but *with-in* the object of intention.

There is something that is not *merely* rational, yet not *irrational*. Between the conscious and the unconscious there seems to be an area of twilight, like dawn between night and day. Something "dawns on me," the genius of language expresses it. In this pre-conceptual dawn lies the deepest source of productivity. Without it there would not be the great religious prophecies, the great works of art, nor even the great scholarly discoveries. Among the philosophers Plato represents this kind of thinking. Characteristically enough, knowledge is for him "recollection" rather than invention. It makes no difference what name we give the ties by which the individual mind, as through an umbilical cord, is connected with the creative ground. Goethe, in his Faust, spoke of "The Mothers," the Greeks of "The Daimon," Freud of "The Id," and Jung of "The Great Mother."

Geniuses who have given testimony of their most creative moments often refer to something beyond their own power, to something which needs solitude, which comes after waking from sleep, or announces itself in a kind of dream, or after a period of "incubation."[21] It is as if all willful intentions had to disappear because, like a hard shell, they keep a person within his egocentric limitations and do not allow him to participate in the creativeness of the world.[22]

[21] See W. B. Cannon, *The Way of an Investigator: A Scientist's Experiences in Medical Research* (New York, 1945); and E. M. Forster's Introduction to his *Collected Tales* (New York, 1947).

[22] See in this connection Fritz Kunkel, M.D., *In Search of Maturity: An Inquiry into Psychology, Religion and Self-Education* (New York, 1946), p. 78. "We describe this attitude as creativity, and we assume that egocentricity, in spite of a certain resourcefulness, will always remain barren and uncreative."

Does the disparity between accumulation of learning and the possession of true wisdom in our civilization have its origin in modern man's impotence to create stillness within and around him, in his inability to achieve the state of *Versenkung*,[23] in his preference for the most shallow amusement to an hour of solitude, and in the way in which our college students are trained: being never alone, rushing from class to class, cramming subjects selected for them by "tutors" and "supervisors," hurrying through hundreds of pages of "prescribed readings," and measuring the success of their work in terms of credits and grades resulting from dozens of quizzes and examinations? We have in this country more sport, more mental hygiene, more food, more comfortable dormitories than anywhere else; but at the same time we have a frightening number of nervous breakdowns and of persons who are immature outside their field of expertness.

The contrast between ego-centric and ego-forgetting thinking explains also the difference between idle fantasy or daydreaming, and productive intuition. From an academic point of view, both daydreaming and intuition represent a sort of "unconscious association."[24] But while in the productive intuition a person forgets himself, in daydreaming he floats vaguely on his unorganized desires. Instead of using the imaginative power for opening the door to life, the daydreamer escapes from reality in order to gratify his ego in a fictitious world of his own. Hence daydream-

---

I may add here an observation from my own practice. I have observed several times that promising young scholars who speak fluently and compose excellent letters write a rather awkward style in preparing their doctorate theses. It helps when they learn to forget about the degree, the judges, and other externals of the doctorate procedure. They must become immersed in the object and so "free themselves." The most profound expression of this idea is to be found in the parable by Chuang Tze, "The Wood Carver," reprinted in *Three Thousand Years of Educational Wisdom,* edited by Robert Ulich (Harvard University Press, 1947), p. 28.

[23] The German word *Versenkung,* one of the equivalents for "contemplation," means "sinking into the depth."

[24] In psychological textbooks "intuition" is explained as the working of unconscious associations. But this is no real explanation. No wonder, since even with respect to relatively simple mental operations we are still in the descriptive stage.

ing does not contribute to civilization, whereas trained intuition does.

The term *scientia intuitiva* was used by earlier philosophers, though often with different connotations.[25] But whatever the differences, they all agree that intuitive knowledge is characterized by a feeling of distinctness and comprehension. In recent times Henry Bergson and Edmund Husserl have been especially concerned with the problem of intuition. Whatever the verdict on their philosophies may be, they have the merit of having given new weight and dignity to a concept which in an increasingly empirical age had been relegated to "mysticism" and other "unscientific" brands of thoughts. Actually, the exclusion of fantasy and intuition from the cultural, esthetic, and scientific activities of man would mean his falling back into the worst forms of reaction and sterility. When intuition declines, repetition, interpretation, and re-interpretation take the place of creativeness; the age of commentators begins. Conservatism, not in its positive form, as the tendency to preserve what is good against fads and untested novelty, but in its negative form of lack and fear of vision, always grows where intuition is lacking.

However, under the name of intuitive insight there have gone not only the visions of the great prophets and thinkers, but also the fancies of charlatans and the dreams of tyrants. What is the criterion of excellence? We will speak about this problem more thoroughly in the chapter on thinking. But some facts should be mentioned here.

First, though intuition is not the mere extension, it is by no means the negation of critical intelligence and of the laws of logic. Intelligence elucidates, intuition generates, but its generation goes hand in hand with the continual desire for clarification. The sort of "intuition" which claims to have an alliance with divine providence and withdraws its presumed discoveries from

---

[25] See, e.g., Leibniz, *Meditationes de Cognitione, Veritate et Ideis,* Philosophische Schriften, edited by C. I. Gerhardt, vol. IV (Berlin 1880), pp. 423 and 450.

rational examination, should be called superstition or the arrogance of quasi-intellects. True intuition desires, false intuition hates the critique of empirical science. Rightly, a trained mind is skeptical of actions and opinions that justify themselves with reference to superior personal revelation.

Second, intuition, though appearing like a "gift" and beyond the reach of mere effort, is nevertheless the result of *preparation*, which may be of intellectual character or of other forms of self-discipline, especially those of an ascetic life. The creative scholar's intuition is like the arrow shot off by one who understands how to aim and draw the bow of the mind. It is not wild shooting into the air. The artist's intuition is the result of desire for the realization of form, and of trained empathy with the finest vibrations of the world within and without. For the great prophet intuition is the end of a long way of devotion. *Durum patientia frangit*—it is long patience that breaks the stubbornness of things. Paradoxical though it may seem to speak of "trained" intuition, it is the only form which deserves its name. All other claims are on behalf of quackery. In one of the halls of the Harvard Medical School we find an inscription from Pasteur: *"Dans le champs de l'observation le hasard ne favorise que les esprits preparés"* ("On the field of observation chance favors only the prepared minds"). True intuition is dedication, false intuition is intellectual self-indulgence.

Of course, even the deepest intuition suffers from the frailty of the human mind. The profoundest man's expressive power depends on his language and the culture within which he speaks. The proof of his wisdom is whether successive generations return to it as to an ever-fresh revelation, remould it in their own language, and sense its essential truth despite the differences in interpretation.

Who knows whether we understand the great religious and philosophical prophets of the distant past as they themselves wished to be understood? But we always return to them. Often we have nothing but badly transmitted texts and documents. Yet the spring of wisdom flows despite its loss of transparency.

C. FAITH

Now we invite into the house of reason not only such doubtful fellows as contemplation and intuition, but even reason's historic enemy, faith. Objections to such hospitality may come from two different groups. On the one hand, there is a religious group for whom faith, transcending the boundaries of the human mind, is totally different from reason. To this group faith is not man's merit but springs from the grace of God who opens man's soul to the revelation. Most of the medieval theologians, as well as Luther and Calvin and the disciples of modern neo-orthodoxy, would be of this conviction. On the other hand there are the nonbelievers for whom faith is the hangover from times of superstition and false authority. For the first group faith is hyperrational, for the second it is hypo-rational.

What, then, do people mean when they use the term "faith"? We may distinguish four different statements: (1) "This man has faith in his business." (2) "This man has faith in his friend." (3) "This man has faith in monarchy, or democracy, or communism." (4) "This man has faith in a supreme Being."

Each time the word "faith" is on a different level. In all these there is supposed to exist some kind of evidence, though of a somewhat subjective character, lacking the same degree of accessibility to proof we would demand from a scientific experiment. And the further we go along the sequence from "faith in business" to "faith in a supreme Being" the greater—objectively speaking—becomes the number of transempirical factors and the risk of uncertainty. But, strangely enough, so also does the believer's willingness to set his subjective conviction above the feeling of doubt, until finally the desire for critical proof completely fades before the feeling of "inner" certainty. This, no doubt, is dangerous, but it has always been a part of civilization.

1. "This man has faith in his business" means under normal

and intelligent circumstances that he has weighed the factors of failure and success, the assets and liabilities, and has arrived at an optimistic prognosis.

2. "This man has faith in his friend" means two things: first, evaluation of previous experience as in the first statement of faith, which gives him confidence in his friend's qualities. But second, faith in friendship signifies also a kind of moral quality on the part of the believer. Friendship has for him a great value, to be highly respected as such. He is "capable" of friendship. Not everybody is.

3. "This man has faith in monarchy" can mean two things. First, the institution of monarchy, represented by the monarch, has for the believer definite advantages. He has vested interests or at least believes he has. This is more or less the business situation. But, second, it can also mean that the monarch is for the monarchist a symbol of high transpersonal values. The good officer in an old feudal monarchy was willing "to die for his monarch," though they may never have met. The monarch represented the idea of loyalty, of *gloire* of the nation, and of reward for courage, though personally he may have been a coward and a scoundrel. This kind of faith shades over into the religious. When Fernando Cortes conquered Mexico, he certainly was motivated by many egotistic impulses, but he also believed that he was acting in the name of the sacred trinity of *Nuestra Majestad, Cristo,* and *Nuestra Senora,*[26] of the King of Spain, the King of the Church, and the Holy Virgin.

In addition, in our modern political development terms such as "democracy" for a certain type of American citizen, or "communism" for the Russian comrade, contain strange mixtures of the secular-empirical and the transcendental. Today the creed of a church, which in earlier times was one of the causes of war, has in many minds been replaced by the creed of a political system. We have become more and more secular, which does not

[26] See Jose Vasconcelos, *Breve Historia de Mexico* (sixth edition, 1950), pp. 80 ff.

mean that we have become less and less passionate. Cruelty still accompanies ideological fanaticism, as it did in the sixteenth and seventeenth centuries; only the content has changed.

4. "This man has faith in a supreme Being" is a statement that moves definitely from the empirical into the transcendental. Yet for the pious theist the transcendental, though invisible, is more than the visible; more real, because more abiding and more powerful, than anything on earth. In the typical Christian tradition "The eternal omnipotent, and omniscient God, Lord in Heaven and on Earth" is conceived to be of much higher reality than any earthly monarch could ever be.

In these four forms of faith the central term could well be replaced by "belief." This man believes in his business, in his friend, his monarch, his God. It always means "to accept as true," "to have confidence in," "to trust in the existence of." Something specific is always in point, and though perhaps not existent before our eyes, it is so taken for granted that doubting it would cause disappointment or even offense.

However, faith in *our* sense, as the outer and more far-reaching circle of reason, is of a different nature. It is not the kind of belief that raises its object from the level of possible doubt to the level of merely subjective certainty. It is not the businessman's belief in his business, the friend's friendship, the officer's loyalty to his king, or the orthodox believer's supposed knowledge of his personal God. Rather it is the consciousness of everything seeable being in the embrace of the unseen. It represents the highest degree of man's power of self-transcendence, but it is not to be confused with transcendentalism. It is the hope that each new advance of reason or great action is not a mere trick of brain or will, but a truer vision of a final reality which, though never grasped completely, is nevertheless known to subsist. Faith, in our sense, could also be called the state of partaking in—or living in infinite relatedness with—the whole.

This faith, though unable to express itself except in symbols, is nevertheless the inspiration—though often implicit—that works within all that man does in the state of world-awareness. It is that which provides "meaning," not only in the sense that this or that isolated object in our mind has pragmatic significance, but also in the sense that we can live meaningfully, because there is a deeper order within a meaningful universe.

This faith in partaking delivers us from an artificial, isolated autonomy. It makes it possible for us to hope that our thinking is not accidental, or merely the time- and space-bound operation of individual intelligences, but that it is related to a truth, however far this truth may be beyond our single truths. This faith makes it possible for us to hope that there are criteria for our doing that are not merely intellectual constructs but are rooted in the nature of being; that we are not chaos and surrounded by chaos; that, despite all horror and irrationality, our life has a place within a greater and all-embracing order.

This faith lives—however hidden—in the endeavor of every scholar who does not cynically gainsay the meaning of his work, for this work derives its meaning from an embracing truth. It is every "scientist's religion,"[27] however irreligious or antireligious he may be. This faith lives secretly in all parents who work and hope that "they may live in their children." It lives in the work of the teacher who wants to be more than an instructor. But especially and expressly it is the living element in all great religion. "Now faith is the substance of things hoped for, the evidence of things not seen" (Heb. 11:1). Not only the *content* of faith (which would merely be "believing in"), but *faith as such* changes the personality of the meaningfully living person, colors his experiences, and incorporates all his single purposes into a chain of purpose.

All the great mystics were inspired by such faith. They all knew that it is not the good works we do, nor the accurateness and orthodoxy of a specific cult and belief, but the living in the

[27] See "Science and Religion" by H. B. Philipps, *Technology Review*, April, 1953.

whole or, as they called it, the "grace," that lifts those who are aware out of the multitude of the sleeping unaware.

Yet in most of our Christian mystics, with the possible exception of Meister Eckhart, as in most modern clergymen, insight into the character of faith as the continual awareness of the embracing reality is shadowed by "belief" in a fixed tradition full of antirational elements. One can accept these elements only by divorcing faith, as *"super vires intellectus,"* from necessary rational criteria. Hence the disastrous split between faith and reason that has severed men into the hostile camps of the believers and the unbelievers, or the pious and the enlightened, and still drives deep fissures through our modern civilization.

There is the famous statement of Anselm of Canterbury:

I thank you, Lord, that thou hast created me in thine image, and thinking of your grace I will love you. . . . I cannot try, O Lord, to penetrate Thy heights, for how could I compare with Thee my own reason? Yet, I desire somehow to understand Thy truth in which my heart lovingly believes. For I do not try to understand in order to believe, for I believe that I may understand. For this I believe, that without faith I shall not understand.[28]

And the scholastic philosopher Raimundus Lullus says: "Faith is a state of mind, given by God. Through it the intellect understands beyond its own inherent powers that which it could not apprehend by its own nature."[29]

There is profound wisdom in both statements, however much, at the first glance, they may offend the critical and self-assertive intellect. For all understanding is a gift that we receive from our partaking in the whole, and not from our own powers. Yet the context in which these statements stand, and the way in which they have been interpreted, have opened the door not only to the humble wisdom of the great, but also to obscurantism and superstition.

[28] ("Proslogion,") Cap. 1. *S. Anselmi Opera Omnia* (Edinburgi, 1946), Vol. I, author's translation.

[29] "Philosophiae Principia," Caput III. *Raymundi Lulli Opera* (Argentorati, 1617), author's translation.

Our life is an island, grounded in a depth we do not know, surrounded by unknown waters. We may revere its infinite depth and width in the expressions of creeds and cults; we even should. But never should we forget that we can speak but in symbols. Even if we knew all about the historical origin of life, we would not yet know what it is. Nor would we know whither life goes. When we look into the face of a dead friend, he speaks to us of time, of end, of the infinite, and of our own going toward it. And however much we listen, we do not fully understand. Yet there is a difference between those who turn away in fear and those who listen in faith. These latter know that they are not thrown by some whimsical demon into a life of chaos, but that they are within the embrace of a great spending power in which there are also birth and love, and perhaps also the void or the nothing, as the great opposite of all existence. Rather than turning away, they accept in humility, but also in courage.

Their life is not intelligence alone, as so often is the case with modern man. They know this is not enough. For lack of a comprehensive framework of understanding, such a life of mere intelligence may end in irrationality and despair. Those who have faith know that through their physical and intellectual nature they are connected with the cosmos. They will understand it only within the boundaries of human existence. But this is enough to make existence a rich and valuable possession.

III. CIRCLES OF WIDENING EXPERIENCE

The discussion about intelligence and reason, which are the main instruments of man's self-consciousness and his conscious relation to the world, has shown us that man cannot be understood by himself, but only in his relation to the world that surrounds and interests him. In other words, man can be understood only in his continually self-transcending nature. The longer and wider the bridges he builds between himself and the universe, the greater the volume of his personality. This process is not only quantitative. It builds the road away from the smallness of the undeveloped ego toward the maturity of the self-knowing and and world-embedded self.*

But this road is not only filled with the satisfaction of new vistas, it is also filled with tension, fatigue, and occasional defeat. Is not every passage from a safe port to the unknown a dangerous voyage—one on which the traveler may go astray, or from which he may return tired, and try to hide in the familiar harbor? But then it is no longer the familiar, because the climate of defeat now surrounds it.

How can we explain the frequent failures in the human process of maturation? Many circumstances, some perhaps beyond any person's power, may contribute. During recent decades we have learned much from psychoanalysis, the findings of which here need no further explanation.

In light of the history and behavior of the human race one might ask himself in the language of our forefathers what more "the great deluder Satan" could have invented to help man in rejecting God's mercy and in making life miserable than all the vices of aggression and destruction, of theft and treachery, of murder and of warfare. And perhaps more diabolically than all these overt crimes there work—to a degree in every man—the diabolic forces of unadmitted or unaccepted failure and inferiority with their products of jealousy, envy, delight in degradation and joy in the fellow man's defeat.

Certainly one of the reasons why we have so much unhappiness is that a person ventures, or is pushed, too early from his mental abode into activities which are to him more frightening than inviting. Rarely can a person pass successfully from one level of experience to the next, unless he has acquired some self-

---

* See in this connection: Johann Heinrich Pestalozzi's essay: "Die Abendstunde eines Einsiedlers," translated in part under the title "The Evening Hour of a Hermit" by Robert Ulich (*Three Thousand Years of Educational Wisdom,* edited and commented upon by Robert Ulich, Cambridge, Harvard University Press, 1947, pp. 480 ff.); Kurt Goldstein, *Human Nature in the Light of Psychopathology* (Cambridge, Harvard University Press, 1940); Yvon Belaval, *Les Conduites d'Echec. Essaie Sur l'Anthropologie Contemporaine* (Paris, 1954).

confidence from feeling "at home" and fairly secure on the stage which he is going to leave. Man's self-transcendence becomes chaotic and self-defeating if the ties are broken which from the beginning have helped him in the formation of his self and his sense of belonging.

It is here that we can understand the importance of a family that provides for its younger members a feeling of warmth and confidence, follows them even when they are away, makes them happy in thinking that there is a place whither to return, and accompanies them through their adult life as their most cherished remembrance. If this grounding faith is lacking, every new venture may lead to anxiety and regression rather than to maturity. We all hesitate to jump from one unsafe stone in a river to the next. And if someone forces us we may fall, for we want to prove that our reluctance is justified. Life is full of such stones.

Sound human development, we may say, is unfolding or "organic." It reveals to us the deep unity in all life. No bud bursts into a flower until it has become strong enough to break its covering. Take away too early the sheltering cover and the bud decays. No flower sheds its petals and becomes a fruit until it has developed its reproductive organs. And just as in the life of a plant only the parts with essential functions pass over into the next evolutionary stage, so also in human growth the accidents of childhood and adolescence are shed; but how boring the adult who has lost his childhood and adolescence completely!

Yet the term organic must not be taken too literally in the naturalist's sense, for man is reflective and can decide, so or so. Nor can the confidence of which we speak be acquired in an atmosphere of overprotection. Lack of challenge may make a person fearful of any risk. We then have the adult who behaves like an adolescent, whereas many great and even happy men became steeled on the rugged road of an unhappy youth.[30]

[30] *The Psychoanalytic Study of the Child*, Vol. V., edited by Ruth S. Eisler, Anna Freud, Heinz Hartmann, and Ernst Kris (New York, 1951).

During the past decades we have heard much of education as "adjustment to the changing conditions of society" or whatever the pedagogical jargon may be. But it needs more than adjustment. For how can a person adapt himself constructively to a world of risk unless he is capable of weighing, choosing, rejecting, and acting? Above the category of adjustment we have to set the categories of selection and decision. Only a slave adjusts to every situation; a free man knows when to say yes, or no. Whereas in the realm of matter growth has a goal without a soul, man has not only the grace but also the burden of choice. Therefore, as we said, he is not "organic" in the natural sense. A plant can be in danger, which is physical, but it cannot be in crisis, which is spiritual. One can create symptoms of neurosis in an animal, yet it is not the neurosis of a human being.

Nor can a plant develop the quality which is of importance for a human person, that of *purposefulness*.

Looking back at the composite nature of man with all its centrifugal tendencies we may ask what prevents these tendencies from splitting apart. Often in disturbed personalities one drive may work against another, and emotions cross each other like clouds in a storm until all ends in wreckage. We could also ask what it is that makes possible a faith that our life is not a mere accident, but a meaningful enterprise within the great and universal enterprise of being. The answer lies in the word "purpose." Out of his many interests a healthy individual develops a series of goals to which he can be devoted. They may meander, but eventually they must, like tributaries, unite in a broad and steady river.

Having a purpose helps the ego to overcome its own inner contradiction. It binds the person to an objective world which does not depend on him but on which he depends; which gives him a hold, a sense of contribution and usefulness, and with it a sense of self-respect. The paradoxical fact is that a person gains freedom to the degree to which he is able to sacrifice his smaller to his greater self. Only through lasting loyalty does he become independent, only through transpersonal contacts can he acquire personality.

Through purpose in this sense the individual not only acquires selfhood and finds a place among his fellow men, he also acquires a vantage point within his changing environment. This acquisition of a point where to stand—the capacity to accept that which is conducive, and to reject that which is unconducive to one's development—is not merely a product of intellect, but of a complex mixture of feeling, thinking, and acting. A person driven by his emotions may end in chaos or sentimentality. A person who intellectualizes only will become unable to decide and finally problematic to himself. A person who relies only on action may end his life in a state of exhaustion. Only the person in whom feeling, thinking, and acting have become one can preserve himself among the welter of influences. The sense of purpose will create in him criteria of the important and unimportant, and the increasing clarity of viewpoint can mould the variety of actions into a coherent life scheme. This is learning in its most profound and essential meaning. Hence, it is not only false but dangerous if certain educators, rightly disgusted at the platitudinous utilitarianism of some forms of modern education, throw out the baby with the bath water and in the name of a truly "liberal" education condemn all schooling related to vocation. Is it not through finding a "vocation" that man discovers his purpose? Is it not through his desire to be useful—which can be fulfilled only in some chosen work—that man finds his self-respect?

Here is now also the place to speak of a much discussed psychological phenomenon, namely *"will,"* which we have not yet mentioned. Some modern books on psychology omit "will"; from their point of view rightly, because it does not fit into the deterministic concept of man. For such a philosophy "will" is an embarrassing idea. However, for every other school of thought, "will" is an obstinate subject. Because of its total pervasiveness it is more evasive than any other human quality. It can be explained only as a *Gestimmtheit,* as a tonus, a directing force from within, which colors the total behavior of an individual. This *Ganzheit,* or this wholeness-character, of will explains a fact to which the Swiss psychologist Charles Baudouin has pointed in his revealing book, *Suggestion and Autosuggestion,*[31] that an isolated act of "willing" or "not willing" (I *will* finish this piece of writing; I *will not* smoke) is generally doomed to defeat. Only if the total person is tuned to carrying out the intention will the intention become realized. This can be observed in seemingly trivial occasions. As long as a beginner "wills" to swim, he thrashes about and goes down. Only when he relaxes or has learned to float, or trusts himself and the water, only then can he swim. But how often do we thrash about instead of allowing ourselves to float?

But this is now the basic question. How can one "float" on the stormy waves of life and use the floating to furnish the means for purposeful movement? Only when one allows himself to be carried, when one has a kind of faith which is not an artificial product of "I *will* live, I *will* succeed, I *will* believe," but the result of a deep and sustaining believing or *in-spiratio.* One is not alone; there are forces within and around which will support us, even if it is difficult.

This profound phenomenon, which appears in the little as well as in the great things of life, explains the courage and steadfastness of the believer in contrast to the exposure, fickleness, and insecurity of the unbeliever. By "believer" is not necessarily meant the adherent to any specific religion. If one needs a special and exclusive dogma to hold on to, perhaps even under all kinds of doubts and tribulations, then one is more an unbeliever in our sense than a believer. One is still in the state of thrashing about or of unwillingness to take one's hands off the raft. The really faithful do not care about dogma, about whatever creed or "heresy" they may happen to support. Those converts in whom the conversion was more an act of deliberation than an

[31] Translated from the French by Eden and Cedar Paul (New York, 1921).

outgrowth of the total personal development, are often the zealots; they are tense, intolerant, and mostly intolerable to the really well rooted person. This applies to religious as well as to political converts, and to a type of neo-nationalists one often finds among immigrants. They wish to forget their past, wish to become more American, more English, more French, more German, than anyone else, and are, therefore, constantly insecure and disliked.

But if the power which supports or which allows one to float rather than to scramble is not bound to any particular creed, and may be found even among many who are unbelievers from an orthodox point of view, where does it come from?

The answer leads us back to our discussion of "Faith" as a part of "reason." Faith, as that which supports, though not necessarily springing from any particular kind of *transcendentalism*, springs from the sense of *transcendence*. Every man whose overwork, busyness, egotism, passion, or any isolated ambition has not yet broken his full sense of living, feels in contact with the world as a whole, even if this world is sometimes hostile and threatening. This feeling is also the experience that leads to the deeper form of morality which comes from a loving concern for the great unfolding of life. Prevent this comprehensive experience from supporting an individual and he will not be a generous and free contributor to his society. Cut it off from a nation and you will see a self-glorifying tribe rather than a contributor to humanity. Cut it off from humanity, and there will be nothing but a mass of competing people and peoples. And it will make no difference whether such crippled societies call themselves democracies, monarchies, or communist states. With the source of inspiration gone, they harbor the germs of sickness.

After these general considerations we may now look at the social content and significance of the widening circles of man's experience.

1. Child, Mother, Home

The newborn child is not only physically limited in vision and enclosed in the boundaries of his body, he is also socially and mentally deaf and blind in that—despite his utter impotence—he assumes unconsciously the position of "omnipotence." Because he is not yet a person, no one else is a person, not even the mother. The whole small world around is but a part of his struggling nature as it seeks satisfaction for his constantly rising urges.

The emergence from this absolute ego-centricity and the recognition of the mother as a person who belongs also to herself and to other human beings—the opening of the hitherto closed gates of the ego toward an objective world—is a process full of crises. If not successfully carried through, it provides a continuous threat to the further development of the personality. In all likelihood, this process is only the second critical step out of the self-contained state of nature; the first, and probably most shocking, being the opening of the mother's protecting womb toward an utterly unexpected and aggressive environment.

2. The Community

A false home atmosphere does damage not only to the individual it tries to help, but also to the community around it. When there is hatred at home, the hatred extends into the environment. On the other hand, when charity not only begins at home, but also ends there, the members of the family remain egotistic and refuse to appreciate the wider tasks and problems of human life, social as well as spiritual. Many among us are incapable of judging the responsibilities of the nation or of humanity except by the standards which were right as long as mother still took care of us. Similarly, the religion of such people never grows beyond the infantile stage. The Father of whom Christ speaks remains constantly the *pater familias* who commands, provides, corrects, punishes, and helps his children out of the ditches when they promise "not to do it again." There is a heaven populated by father and mother images and a hell for the recreant, all being an extension of the earthly family into a supposedly "religious" and "transcendental" atmosphere. But in reality this is not religion and transcendence, but pure earthliness and retarded development.

In the history of our culture the feudal society of the Middle Ages represents the most highly developed stage of a family society, with the individual family, the clan, the guild, the nobility, and the dynasty all related to each other like households of greater or lesser importance. The king was supposed to have divine sanction; he was close to the saints. Even up to the eighteenth century, when the modern national state already had political existence, people were expected and willing to shed their blood for their dynasty rather than to help their fellow men.

For how many years of youth does the modern family still serve as the custodian of the child? With the development of our technological civilization the time-span has become shorter and shorter. For smaller children the playmates and the neighbors' homes and gardens are not yet "community," they are extended family. But at the age of six or even earlier there comes the first school day, the first entrance into an objective and impersonal world with crowds of people one does not know and with big buildings belonging to nobody in particular. In many countries the first school day is still celebrated with considerable ceremony. The parents lead the child to the first assembly; there are sermons and prayers, and gifts are given to the neophytes. It is an initiation rite of the sort we find in primitive societies, in religious life, in lodges, and in remnants of feudalism such as guilds, officer corps, and orders.

Such ceremonies are not merely residues of a past magical age or strange disturbances in our busy routine. There are certain "water sheds" in life which should remind man that it is time for inner recollection and composure. The proverb that the way to hell is paved with good intentions contains some wisdom; but a life *without* the solemnity of good intentions may end in platitude.

In the Middle Ages, the larger towns produced the first mature community life. Whereas the villages were still family assemblages over which the feudal lord held sway, there existed in the towns communal self-administration, a proud citizenry, and religious and legal ceremonial for the symbolization of independence. In the seventeenth and eighteenth centuries the New England town became the perfect example of vital community life, with the town meeting, autonomous jurisdiction, and the religious sanction of the congregation. For there is no decisive stage in the social evolution that is not somehow brought into the neighborhood of the holy. Ancestral and house gods are venerated in typical family societies, whereas community saints, processions, and solemn assemblies characterize the conscious community.

For people with a happy and stable youth the community represents even today not only a geographical, but also a social center that could not be exchanged for another. As a sentimental melody the remembrance of it flows throughout a lifetime. One would not like to miss Main Street and the railway station, even if ugly. On Main Street were made the first purchases, from the railway station the first excursions into the world. In the course of time even an unpopular school teacher is remembered with a lyric overtone.

3. The Nation

But just as with the progress of civilization the family or clan no longer suffices, so also the community becomes more and more absorbed by a larger unit. Fifty years ago a peasant woman in the heart of Siberia answered the question as to the name of her village with the words "our village." "Our village" was the center of the world and there was nothing else. Today, as political citizens we are more of the nation than of the village, town, or city. One's language is the nation's language, not the community's; so is one's literature. Whether or not a person wants it, he is collectively united with the victories and defeats, the virtues and sins of his nation. It follows him even when in protest he may migrate to a foreign country. Sound patriotism, in contrast to ugly chauvinism, is the acknowledgment of these bonds in the hearts and heads of the self-conscious citizen.

4. Humanity

The feeling of living within his nation is that stage of interpersonal experience to which average man in modern society has reached. Countries in which this development has been retarded now make up for lost time, often with revolutionary vehemence. Yet we know that just as with the family and community, so also the nation should not be the last stage. Advanced peoples strive out of their political isolation toward humanity. In earlier times the unity of humankind was merely an idea of religious transcendentalism. Only a few utopians dared imagine its reality, and many made the mistake of thinking that one could arrive at internationality only by forgetting nationality—as if a tree which has no roots could grow high and spread its branches.

But today the idea of the unity of national and international citizenship lives in the conscience and consciousness of many, struggling for birth.

Why, then, have we not yet succeeded? Because existing human societies have become bogged down in the middle of the way toward full maturity and humaneness. Certainly they would like to go further. But though having the vision of a league of nations, and having the United Nations with its successes in many fields, they still stumble over themselves. They behave like persons whom we have already described, who wish to pass from one orbit of experience to the next, who are mature enough in their imagination and their intentions, but not yet in their total being, and thus become fearful and hysterical.

In earlier times man's life had too few openings into the width and fullness of the world to allow for the complete development of his talents. Today he stands before horizons beyond his comprehension. Now bigness rather than smallness stifles his growth, just as in the industry of some modern countries it is overexpansion and overproduction which threaten security.

Many lamentations can be heard about this course that history has taken. But who would like to live the life of a medieval peasant with its disease and squalor, or even the life of a European city dweller of the eighteenth century, who was punished when he was not within the walls before the closing of the gates? No, there is much health and even grandeur in this modern growth. But as with all grandeur, there is also danger.

During the past two centuries the fortunate citizen of an advanced country has felt the blessings of progress, of the gradually increased control over the physical and intellectual conditions of civilization. He had freed himself from the grip of cold and hunger. He had struggled out of the threat of the Inquisition and of religious wars. He had untied the fetters of absolutism and won equality and justice before the law. He had acquired sufficient leisure and education to devote part of his life to the cultivation of his mind. No wonder he believed that the courageous use of reason which had helped him so far would lead mankind further and further along the road toward happiness.

How could he know that this released energy would create a magnitude of new problems which, rather than appearing as new challenges to be mastered, would frighten him? Subjected to a mass of contradicting theories he needs today more courage than ever to trust in the final victory of reason. In the face of ruthless war among so-called civilized nations he needs more strength of faith than ever to repel the danger of cynicism. In face of brutality and barbarism all over the world it is hard to believe in the decency of the human race. Thus today people of the greatest intellectual sophistication often turn into irrationality, give up the seemingly useless labor of seeking and groping, and accept magical authorities in order to have "something to believe in." In politics man runs between the extremes of conservatism and collectivism, two seeming contrasts which grow from the same root of uncertainty. Medieval forms of Catholicism and Protestant orthodoxy disdain religious liberalism. Not only the bewildered "masses," but even judges, clergymen, and politicians fall prey to "revivalists," "inquisitors," and "leaders," who to the critical mind betray their sick personalities.

In other words, the belief in organic and historical evolution, which is nothing but the philosophy of progress of the eighteenth and nineteenth centuries, is now in danger. This would do no harm if thus perished the superficial idea of "growth" of man and civilization as an inevitable product of more experimenting and more technology. For this idea is nothing but the primitive and unconscious metaphysics of materialism. But there is at stake the issue of faith in the meaning of life, and the idea of progress in its profound and inspiring form. And this is serious.

We will never succeed in taking the last step from the narrowness of the self into the width of humanity unless we understand the latter not only quantitatively as a grouping of many peoples, but also qualitatively, as a moral concept. By repudiating such values as the dignity and brotherhood of men, the fruit of our common heritage in the same source of life, mankind remains merely a sum total of individuals who can be divided and handled at will. Never will calculating intelligence understand what Francis of Assisi meant by "Brother man." Only when man stands in the world not only with the desire to profit from it as much as possible, but with a sense of commitment to the whole, can he climb up to the level of inner community that renders outer community possible.

Unfortunately, even the existing world religions are themselves not yet mature enough for mankind's last and supreme mission. Since its recognition by the Roman emperors as a public institution, Christianity has possessed little strength to defend itself against the encroachment of national power. In their dogmas the various sects of Christianity have never freed themselves from separatist tendencies. Despite all assurances to the contrary, in practice most of them have done their work within the limits of a strange polarity. On the one hand they have built up man's idea of human brotherhood; on the other hand, through the narrowness of their creeds, they have also fostered division.

Christianity in this respect has perhaps the least enviable record of all great religions. Yet man will succeed in combining respect for himself and his nationality with homage to mankind only when the religious interpretation of life—as the most far-reaching of all human visions—provides him with a sense that the divine unity of mankind should support rather than prevent the plurality of ways by which we may strive toward a better society.

IV. CONCLUSION

We have now described our theory of man. Such a theory, as has been shown, must encompass more than the science of psychology, however much it may profit from it. For a comprehensive theory of human existence will reveal that man's physical and mental life reaches into a nourishing and embracing power that he senses and that works in him, though it is beyond his intellectual grasp. In other words, whereas psychology is man-immanent, a theory of man in his wholeness is man-transcendent.

Analysis of man's intellectual equipment has proved that he represents a product of the creation which, though deeply grounded in its physical base, has risen above the vegetative level to the heights of reflection and self-reflection. The world in which man stands is at the same time the world which he comprehends by virtue of intellect and of reason. The degree of this comprehension constitutes at the same time the degree of his freedom. He is the being that is not only *had* by the world, but that *has* a world.

We have also arrived at this conclusion by the experimental approach. The widening orbits of man's experience lead him to the insight that his environments are of both a physical and a spiritual quality. In order to achieve the fullest degree of maturity, he should pass beyond ever-enlarging social organizations toward a qualitative concept of humanity—humanity as being not the totality of human beings, but the brotherhood of men conscious of their common ground in the creation. Also, here "world" in its fullness of concept arches in its grandeur above the small "worlds" around us.

The continual interaction of the physical, the mental, and the spiritual features of man is his blessing, but it is also his risk. No animal can lose itself in such a depth of loneliness, crime, bewilderment, and despair as man. Only out of the many purposes which may occur in his life, and through an organic development of his various capacities, can he develop a meaningful and single purpose. And only when this development is inspired by his awareness of lasting commitment to the world to which he belongs, can he achieve the highest level of devotion, and at the same time the highest level of existential self-realization.

Man is the creature which is not only formed, but which also forms himself. He is the being full of contrasts. He cannot grow and create without the experience of tension and conflict, yet he must be able to bind the opposites into some whole. If he does not succeed in this never-ending attempt, he breaks under the burden. He knows of himself and his being in the world, and the more deeply he goes into himself, the more embracing becomes his knowledge of the cosmos in which he participates. No other living organism owns his consciousness, yet this very gift provides that he does not know where he is. Born into the world, he has to accept exposure and servitude; having the power of reflection and decision, he also can be, to a degree, free and of his own. He loses himself unless he allows his emotions and his reason to lead him toward orbits of being far beyond his immediate surroundings, but his transcendent mind is also his peril. For the more it pushes him toward infinite horizons, the more it makes him realize his finiteness. The universe is constantly with man, but it never fully reveals itself to him. Only when with the expansion of his reason his power of faith grows, can he rest from time to time in himself and the world and receive the inspiration which he needs in his struggle for a final meaning of human existence and history.

CHAPTER 3

The Nature and Future of the Individual

Things are in the saddle
And ride mankind.
EMERSON

IN OUR analysis of the mental equipment of the individual and of his widening circles of experience we have followed a procedure which is justified in that all scholarly understanding of the phenomena of life, be it a metal, a plant, or a human being, requires the power of generalization. The mineralogist, the biologist, and the humanist simply extend the great quality of language, the symbolic representation of things by means of abstraction, into the field of systematic endeavor. Yet there remains the unique beauty of the precious stone in a ring, the rose on a desk, and despite all philosophical and psychological works about human behavior there remains the completely distinctive quality of a beloved person.

This is the difference between the scholar and the artist. The scholar wishes us to understand the unique through the universal, the artist wishes us to understand the universal through the unique. As the artist can make the unique symbolic of the possible truth in every man, so the scholar would like to relate his generalizations to life's individual events. Otherwise the artist creates bad art, and the scholar bad science.

71

In order to avoid the latter danger we must add to the preceding chapter on the general characteristics of human individuals, as a plural, a discussion of the problem of the human individual—the self, the I—as a singular.

I. MODES OF LIVING

Are there not in every person rhythms or fluctuations of intensity which have not merely to do with age, health, fatigue, courage, or depression, but represent basic modes of living? Each individual is distinguished from the other by his greater or lesser susceptibility to a certain psychic climate. Or different moods may prevail at various periods of each life, often to a degree that borders on or reaches the psychopathic.

We may, for example, differentiate between three basic levels of awareness: "vegetating," "living wide awake" and "living in the state of routine," though there are always transitions between the three—twilight stages, as it were.

By *"vegetating"* we understand the state of unity with nature in which we are not the "persona" or the "mask" through which life expresses itself by choosing us as one of the countless channels for its ever-spending power. When we vegetate we are similar to the plants in our garden, or the cat which sleeps on our window sill. The instinctive part in us is greater than the differentiating.

But the striving of man for self-realization does not permit much slumber. His feelings are alive; they desire an outlet, are longing for clarity, and push toward action. Thus there is constant increase in awareness up to the most intense levels of attention, feeling, and rationality. Vegetating is necessary for the health of the human household, but it is not the specific mark of humanity.

In *living wide awake,* closely related to the state of reflection, man finds himself not only in and before himself, but also in and before the world. Nowhere does man's "individuality" or "personality" appear so clearly and disinguish itself so evidently as in this attitude with all its grades of sagacity and intensity of interest. He builds, changes, creates, and destroys an objective world of ideas and institutions. He begins to ask what he is, where he belongs, whence he comes, whither he goes. He becomes a philosopher and the more he asks, the more he finds himself in an endless universe of transcendent relations, elevating and bewildering at the same time.

This life of continuous wakefulness and openness to problems great and small is strenuous. Therefore nature helps man to go back to a state that is near to vegetating but is at the same time different. We call it *"routine"* or *"automatic"* living. After the stage of learning is completed, we drive a car without being conscious of the manipulations with which we had to struggle at the beginning. This automatism occurs in the mental as well as in the physical sphere. The mathematical operation, the process of writing and reading, all great problems for the young child, become habits which we use almost without thought for further purposes.

In the same way "we get used to" the activities in our social and mental environment. This is partly wholesome, for it follows the life-preserving law of parsimony, but it can also be disastrous for the free development of the individual and a whole society. For "we get used to" or "adjust ourselves" to many practices and ideas conducive neither to the integrity of our own personality, nor to the productiveness of society. The customary takes hold of us by its sheer weight and repetitiveness, irrespective of its intrinsic value. Multitude overpowers creative solitude. Inadvertently, we are in the state of "indifference" which we described in the first chapter.

Why does the vividly self-conscious adolescent so often live in bitter conflict with society? Because it demands from him not only respect for the positive sides of convention and for standards which he ought to follow, but also submission to rules which are against his conscience and deeper sense of personal identity. He despises the hypocritical older generation on which he is dependent and which controls him against his will; he is sorry to see his parents compromising, though they told him not to lie, always to be fair, to be honest with oneself. Growing into adult society and acceptance by it, he feels, is not only a process of maturing, but also a process of degradation and resignation. Against this he rebels, and there is no one to help him. But finally, like most of us, he becomes "conditioned" in order to survive, and joins the ranks of the social automatons.

We live, then, in a situation of ambiguous value; good insofar as it saves us from the strain of attention to things and processes which are merely instrumental, but dangerous insofar as it may breed the delusive comfort of withdrawal from individual responsibility, and loss of one's self through surrender to habit.

This mode of living has neither the beauty of nature, nor the grandeur of spirit. It is neither childhood nor manhood; because of its fear of dangerous greatness, it may well end in cultural senescence. If it is still capable of strong feeling, this feeling is of collective excitement but not of individual and genuine courage. It produces neither the humility of the Psalmist: "What is man that Thou art mindful of him?" nor the exalted hope of St. Matthew: "Ye are the light of the world."

II. THE MYSTERIOUS I

In the preceding chapter we made the tacit assumption that in all the various mental operations and expansions of experience through which man goes there is a mysteriously stable factor, the self, or the I. But what is the "I," or the "self," within which and through which all this happens? What is behind such phrases as "Know thyself," or: "I no longer understand myself"?

Apparently, in the individual, the I, or the self, there is immanent perspective; it is, as we have said, self-reflective. This expression, however, merely denotes a mysterious phenomenon; it does not explain it.

One of the outstanding philosopher-psychologists of our time, the late William Stern, describes the human individual, or the I, in the following way.

[An individual] is something singular, unique, at no place and time existing in the same form. We discover it in the working of certain general laws and the embodiment of certain types, but it is never completely characterized by any reference to laws and types; there always remains a plus through which it is distinguished from other individuals which underly the same laws and belong to the same types. And this last kernel of existence [*Wesenskern*] which causes the individual to be a this or that, different from all other existences, is, from a scientific point of view, inexpressible, unclassifiable, and incommensurable. In this sense the individual represents a concept moving on a boundary toward which research may strive but which it will never reach; it is, so one could say, the asymptote of thought and science.[1]

Yet, though the riddle remains—it is essentially the riddle of life's creativeness expressing itself in endless variations and stages of self-evolution—we may come closer to the understanding of the problem of individuality if, instead of the primarily descriptive, we try the philosophical-interpretative way, going one step further in the transcendent process of man's self-interpretation. To use a modern term, we may use the "existentialist" approach.

III. THE TRANSCENDENT INTERPRETATION OF MAN

In the state of wide awake living, man partakes consciously in the world. In paraphrasing the essence of Hegel's metaphysics, which in this respect is but a part of mankind's religious tradition, we could also say that man in the state of wakefulness is the vessel which life uses for sailing toward infinite horizons of self-realization. Such ideas seem to be "mystical," "unreal," and "fantastic." Yet are they more mysterious than the materialist's

---

[1] *Über Psychologie der Individuellen Differenzen* (Leipzig, 1900), p. 15, Translated by author. Compare also Gordon Allport, *Personality: A Psychological Interpretation* (New York, 1937).

assumption that isolated nervous systems and brains create minds which communicate with each other and produce progressively more universal interpretations of reality?

As a matter of fact, in every skeptic's writings we find such universal notions as "life," "nature," or "cosmos." Either these notions are meaningless phrases from his own point of view, or they point towards a creative and uniting power. Though hidden behind the screen of doubt, there appears the vision of a universe the parts of which are interdependent and of which man himself is a part. This vision has all the characteristics of faith as defined in our second chapter; it is of the nature of the religious and the ground for inviting man out of autonomous skepticism into the camp of those who speak of a universal order.

Needless to say, religion in this sense is not the same as belief in the dogmas argued out at the Council of Nicaea and other ecclesiastical conventions. As we will show later, the essence of religion, as opposed to the shell, lies in its capacity of opening the mind to the influx of those reverential thoughts through which man realizes his dependence on the abiding laws of life, the interaction of the finite and the infinite, of the single and the cosmic, and finally the mysterious consonance of individual search and total meaning. *In hac hora est eternitas* ("In this hour dwells eternity")—these words which the medieval monks wrote on their sundials express better than theological treatises the fact that even the briefest moment in our life is not ours as a possession with which we can do what we wish. Whatever we do during every hour, we do it not only to this hour or to ourselves, but to the whole. Only in this mood of mind can we understand the old religious wisdom which seems ridiculous from a modern individualistic point of view, yet is nevertheless true and most empirical—that each of us is responsible for all mankind, both in space and time, and all mankind is responsible for each of its members.

When we accept this concept, our ideas about individual and society receive new content. According to modern positivism, the individual is a unit connected horizontally with other units, and society is an aggregate of such units. According to transcendent understanding, every individual lives within a continuum which relates him not only horizontally to his material and human environment, but also vertically to the universal order. In this way, his thinking can meet the world; he can deeply sympathize with his fellow men, and thus "community" and "human dignity" can exist over and above mere community of interest.

Modern man's political situation would be different if he would restore in himself this conviction rather than merely talking about it in more or less conventional religious terms. One scene may be suggestive to the reader's imagination. In the Germany of Hitler, a few people met every week to read Goethe, or Shakespeare, or the New Testament, in order to lift themselves above their misery and isolation. They later wrote to their friends abroad that only this had saved them from despair. They did not talk about politics; for who knew where the spy might be; they all were suspect. Goethe is no longer alive, nor Shakespeare, nor the Apostles. They live only in the sound of their words. But, suppose someone listened who did not know German; he would have heard but would not have understood. Would the Apostles understand Luther's translation, or Shakespeare the translation of the brothers Schlegel through which he then spoke to the members of an enemy nation? Yet Shakespeare, and the Apostles, were *in* the translations. So there must be something universal within and behind human languages, a self-revealing spirit in the variety of tongues. Even more, was it Goethe, or Shakespeare, or the Apostles, who "created" their works merely out of their own individual existences? Do they not represent the genius in mankind because they lived deeper in reality, and reality lived deeper in them than in other human beings?

Who brought this community of men and women together? Hitler? The great books? The person who invited them? Their intellects? Their language? Certainly, all these factors played a part. But they are not the whole. Is not the truest, though seemingly the least direct, answer that these men and women were brought together by the inner light which shines in the souls of all humans who heed its flame?

IV. THE LONELINESS OF THE INDIVIDUAL

The more man develops beyond the instinctive and emotional response to the challenge of life into the greater freedom of rational reaction, and the more he dares to choose, to decide, and to rely on himself and his environment, the more—paradoxically enough—he has not only the elevated feeling of conscious participation in the spiritual order of the world, but also the sense of his isolation from the beautiful and quieting matrix of nature. It is exactly the most developed type for whom the relaxed motions of an animal, or the sleep of a child, can be an object of envious contemplation.

Together with pride in the fact of human individuality, there also goes a sense of the tragic through the history of mankind. The Old Testament begins with the symbolic expression of this mood.

But of the fruit of the tree which is in the midst of the garden, God hath said, Ye shall not eat of it, neither shall ye touch it, lest ye die. And the serpent said unto the woman, Ye shall not surely die: For God doth know that in the day ye eat thereof, then your eyes shall be opened; and ye shall be as gods, knowing good and evil. And when the woman saw that the tree was good for food, and that it was pleasant to the eyes, and a tree to be desired to make one wise, she took of the fruit thereof, and did eat; and gave also unto her husband with her; and he did eat. And the eyes of them both were opened, and they knew that they were naked; and they sewed fig leaves together, and made themselves aprons.

Why is the tree of consciousness exactly "in the midst" of the Garden? Because it is through the reflective I that men feel themselves "in the midst" of life like gods "knowing good and evil." But at the same moment they also discover what the first men discovered, that they are "naked"; that they have been thrown out of the embracing simplicity of nature. While they become thinking, they also become separated and fearful, unable to live without hiding. When parents observe the development of a child, do they not have a joyful feeling of participating in the mysterious growth of a human being's consciousness? But the more the child grows, the more his parents will observe that he begins to hide, that there will arise in him the first sense of loneliness, the first desire to lie, and the first and inevitable sense of failure and frustration.

In the story of Paradise—in which most of us no longer can believe literally—the profound Jewish mind projected into symbolic narrative the whole meaning of man's existence, his nearness to, but also his distance from the source of life; his wisdom, but also his error; his achievements, but also his guilt; in terms of the Christian myths, his loftiness, but also his "fall."

V. SALVATION THROUGH DEVOTION

But just as all the great religions, and all the really great philosophies, speak of man's loneliness, so they also speak of the possibility of his re-unification with the creation.

They emphasize the mystery of "dying and becoming," or they speak of devotion, or of love, all essentially one and the same way of forgetting one's ego and finding one's deeper self through communion.

1. The Greek Concept

In Plato's *Symposium,* Agathon has the following words in praise of the God of Love:

Therefore, Phaedrus, I say of Love that he is the fairest and best in himself, and the cause of what is fairest and best in all other things. And I have a mind to say of him in verse that he is the god who

"Gives peace on earth and calms the deep
Who stills the waves and bids the sufferer sleep."

He makes men to be of one mind at a banquet such as this, fulfilling them with affection and emptying them of disaffection. In sacrifices, banquets, dances, he is our lord—supplying kindness and banishing unkindness, giving friendship and forgiving enmity, the joy of the good, the wonder of the wise, the amazement of the gods; desired by those who have no part in him, and precious to those who have the better part in him; parent of delicacy, luxury, desire, fondness, softness, grace; careful of the good, uncareful of the evil. In every work, word, wish, fear—pilot, helper, defender, savior; glory of gods and men, leader best and brightest: in whose footsteps let every man follow, changing a hymn and joining in that fair strain with which love charms the souls, gods, and men. Such is the discourse, Phaedrus, half playful, yet having a certain measure of seriousness, which according to my ability, I dedicate to the God.[2]

But even attachment may sometimes throw the person back into himself. Our work may become meaningless and unrewarding; children may die or leave; a man may run into conflict with his community and his nation; love may become blind passion, a source of jealousy, perhaps the bitterest disappointment.

Therefore, since the dawn of the great ancient civilizations, the I has been searching for sources of devotion and attachment beyond the vicissitudes of nature and human affairs. Detachment has been praised beyond attachment by certain forms of Brahmanism, Buddhism, Taoism, of the Stoa and of Christianity.

Modern psychiatry is inclined—and rightly so—to include certain forms of this withdrawal among the psychopathic forms of human behavior. The history of asceticism no longer appears to us as always productive sublimation.

But there are forms of the ego's detachment from the vicissitudes of desire which belong to the highest achievements of the human mind.

When, in the Platonic *Symposium,* Agathon has ended his encomium to Eros, in which, no doubt, there still lives a certain sensuous and hedonistic element, Socrates relates to his friends

[2] *The Works of Plato,* translated by B. Jowett (New York, no date, Vol. III), pp. 324 ff.

the instruction on the mysteries of love he received from the seeress Diotima of Mantineia. With this revelation he has given us at the same time the Song of Songs of the ideal teacher. The mystery of man's salvation from the narrowness of the self is not "love of the one, which he will despise and deem a small thing," but that he "will become a lover of all beautiful forms."

This will lead him on to consider that the beauty of the mind is more honorable than the beauty of the outward form. So that if a virtuous soul have but a little comeliness, he will be content to love and tend him, and will search out and bring to the birth thoughts which may improve the young, until his beloved is compelled to contemplate and see the beauty of institutions and laws and understand that all is of one kindred, and that personal beauty is only a trifle; and after laws and institutions he will lead him on to the sciences that he may see their beauty being not like a servant in love with the beauty of one man or institution, himself a slave mean and calculating, but looking at the abundance of beauty and drawing towards the sea of beauty, and creating and beholding many fair and noble thoughts and notions in boundless love of wisdom; until at length he grows and waxes strong, and at last the vision is revealed to him of a single science, which is the science of beauty everywhere.

2. The Christian Concept

There is hardly a passage in literature that reveals so clearly the greatness of Greek thought as the Diotima passage in the *Symposium*. And the same passage makes understandable the fact that with the decay of the aristocratic pattern of ancient society, Platonic philosophy gave way to Christianity. For by its very nature the Eros, through which Socrates wishes to dissolve the ego in the vision of Beauty Absolute, can be but the privilege of a few. It contains the idea of universality in that it perceives beauty, or form, "everywhere," but only the chosen ones can attain this ideal. The Socratic Eros cannot serve as the spring of salvation and inspiration from which the humble can drink.

This source was provided by the Christian idea of love in the sense of *"agape."* It springs from the conviction that there is kinship among *all* men on earth through their continual birth and rebirth in God.

Ye have heard that it hath been said, Thou shalt love thy neighbour, and hate thine enemy:

But I say unto you, Love your enemies, bless them that curse you, do good to them that hate you, and pray for them which despitefully use you, and persecute you:

That ye may be the children of your Father which is in heaven: for he maketh his sun to rise on the evil and on the good, and sendeth rain on the just and on the unjust.

For if you love them which love you, what reward have ye? do not even the publicans the same?

Be ye therefore perfect, even as your Father which is in heaven is perfect. (MATT. 5:43—48)

But it is not only its specific version of love by which Christianity conquered the ancient world and created a new concept of the individual, it is also the idea of *victory over death*, or the idea of immortality. In the eighth chapter of Romans, St. Paul writes:

For we know that the whole creation groaneth and travaileth in pain together until now.

And not only they, but ourselves also, which have the first fruits of the Spirit, even we ourselves groan within ourselves, waiting for the adoption, to wit, the redemption of our body.

And in the fifteenth chapter of Corinthians St. Paul answers his brethren:

For since by man came death, by man came also the resurrection of the dead.

For as in Adam all die, even so in Christ shall all be made alive. . . .

Behold, I shew you a mystery: We shall not all sleep, but we shall all be changed.

In a moment, in the twinkling of an eye, at the last trump: for the

trumpet shall sound, and the dead shall be raised incorruptible and we shall be changed. . . .
O death, where is thy sting? O grave, where is thy victory?

Three motives which are more or less one and inherent in the experiences of all mankind became apparent in the two biblical quotations: first, the "groaning of the creation"; second, the connection between life and death; and third, the longing of the I for preservation through "adoption." The groaning of the creation is the cry for salvation. But there is no salvation, for the end of life is death. As all life lives on death, so death lives on life. Death is the most absolute and irrevocable fact before and within all life, the most majestic and at the same time the most unknown.

Anthropologists tell us that, in spite of all variations in man's history, they can point at no culture without death rites. The Greek philosophies, partly believing and partly not believing in immortality, tried to capture the infinite in the finite and overcome the curse of death by experiencing the absolute or "beauty everywhere" in the perfect form of individual life.

This, however, leaves the problem of personal immortality unsolved. In contrast, the Christian believer expects salvation from death by an act of divine grace. Only through God's decision to end his wrath over the first man's sin by the sacrifice and resurrection of His Son "shall we be saved from wrath," and "receive the atonement" (ROM. 5, 9, 11).

"Now if Christ be preached that he rose from the dead, how say some among you that there is no resurrection of the dead?"

In all higher religions, individualism and transcendentalism go hand in hand. The passionate interest in a life hereafter is nothing but the self-assertion of man against his supreme enemy, the end.

A similar dialectic between spiritual self-assertion and transcendentalism is found also among the great idealistic philosophers and poets of the Romantic period. In them the consummation of modern individualism develops the finest shades of theoretical speculation and poetic self-expression. But at the same time they are struggling for the mystical dissolution of the individual I in an Absolute Mind, freed from the delusions of earthly form and matter. Certainly Schopenhauer was one of the most rabid and egotistic individualists who ever lived. Yet, his philosophy of will ends in the Indian Nirvana of self-renunciation.

VI. THE CHANGE OF FAITH AND THE SURVIVAL OF INDIVIDUALISM

The religious and idealistic philosophies are now on the defensive against the various forms of critical positivism, though perhaps not so much as they were fifty years ago. But even among the so-called Christians, Protestant or Catholic, how many still believe in the literal truth of the Bible, or in the hell, the purgatory, and the heaven of Dante? For how many are even the basic spiritual tenets of Christianity a power of living truth?

What effect will this change have on the modern individual and his civilization? Though for centuries Christ's gospel has been misused as an instrument of division instead of unity, of bondage instead of liberty, it has also been the warming fire in the life of man. This fire smouldered even in the movements which helped to destroy the older Christian tradition. Renaissance humanism, the Enlightenment, idealism, romanticism, democracy, humanitarianism, and socialism developed in discussion with Christian transcendentalism. For Hegel the source of individuality does not lie in Greek, but in Christian thought. Even Marx's protest against human exploitation stems from the Old and New Testaments and from German idealism. For in the protest against exploitation lives the acknowledgment of the dignity of the human soul.

This is not to say that all important factors in modern society owe their origin to Christianity. Many have their roots elsewhere, and many have grown out of protest, if not against the Christian religion, at least against the Christian churches. For example, it is impossible to state definitely whether the eighteenth century, from which we have the modern concept of free and co-responsible citizenry, should be described as the age of final application of Christian principles to the social problem, or as the age of liberation from political and ecclesiastical absolutism. Seen from a deeper point of view, one explanation does not exclude the other, for absolutism has nothing to do with Christianity, but liberty has.

Whatever the answer, the great deeds of the eighteenth century were done by men deeply convinced of the rational and self-transcendent power of the human being, by men of a logonomous mentality completely different from the modern autonomous politician, educator, and social scientist who intend to "engineer" human society.

If this picture is true, then the future of genuine individualism is critical. Our political institutions tend toward collectivism. So does our economic life with its big trusts on the one side, and its big labor unions on the other. The automobile and the airplane give people a feeling of pride, but rather than coming from inner strength, this feeling springs from the desire for power and prestige. The quiet order of family life, concentration, and contemplation become rare achievements. Traveling today is certainly quicker. But, we may ask, how much has a man seen and learned of the world who has flown around it "in a few days"?

A Russian proverb says: "If a wise man travels, he gets wiser; if a fool travels, he becomes still more of a fool." Despite all efficiency, our modern machines of transportation do not make man more knowing, but often plunge him into the mediocrity of the multitude, whether he be a senator, a business executive, or a college president. There are no places in the world less revealing than an airport.

Even in democracies the comfortable idea of the citizen's control over the government does not eliminate the danger of loss of freedom. For there are all kinds of solons—those who work for all, and those who work only for themselves. The modern citizen surrenders to centralizing bureaucracies responsibilities which he had hitherto considered his own or those of his community. This is inevitable, for who can pay today for our public school system, our hospitals, and our welfare, and who can individually regulate the national and international complexities of modern production and distribution?

But the concession that such collectivist trends are inevitable, and in certain respects even desirable, does not eliminate the fact that man can meet them in the spirit of Mussolini, Hitler, and Stalin, or in the English people's spirit which grew out of the combination of Protestantism and Rationalism.

Now, if there exist on the one hand a fading away of bold transcendent motivations, and on the other hand a growth of technology and associationism, how then can we hope for the survival of individualism, true democracy, and respect for dignity. Will we slowly subside into a managerial feudalism?

Certainly, it will make no difference whether, out of hypocritical respect for a great tradition, the name of democracy be retained. Everybody claims today to defend "the people's democracy."

Of the two trends toward collectivization the economic-technological will persist. Production of food and tools, concentration of capitalist power in the form of trusts or state bureaucracies and of working power in the form of unions, political centralization of public education and information—all this will make it increasingly difficult for the individual to find himself and to be himself. In these areas the "I" will be buried more and more by the weight of the "they."

So there remains only the question whether *inner* motivations and convictions can be built up which are conducive to the growth of mature and free personalities and able to counteract the intellectual peril of collectivization. These motivations must give the individual a feeling of belonging to a spiritual sphere of life from which he receives the strength to maintain his self amidst the pressure of his surroundings.

Thus not merely for the sake of the individual, but for the survival of freedom and justice—without which there is no true self-realization—must we learn one great and difficult art. Instead of sacrificing our whole personality to the mechanizing environment, we must learn to use this new environment in superior fashion. We must understand how to free human energy, no longer absorbed by physical struggle for food and shelter, for the development of new and great inspirations. These aspirations should not remain merely on the plane of nice sentiments and abstractions. They should give us the courage to reconsider our forms of political organization. One may constantly talk about the democratic way of life, and nevertheless be mortally afraid of any novelty in thought and action. Never did the Romans indulge in so much idle oratory about their republic as when they were losing it. Are we perhaps on the path toward a similar situation?

If we simply "give in" without asserting in ourselves the imaginative-constructive power of man against the weight of external circumstances, then we will coalesce into an amorphous jelly. Hardly then will we understand why or how there ever arose free civilizations. But if we are mindful of the transcendent strength that the human race has been able to demonstrate in the struggle with threatening environments, we will have before us a period of unparalleled possibilities. Being free from the daily threat of a cruel and untamed nature, and at the same time being free from old myths and superstitions, we will be free for the first and real beginning of true religion and true human culture. Is this utopia? Perhaps. But without a utopia, has there ever been hope and achievement?

VII. SUMMARY

We have come a long way in our attempt to understand individuality, and we may well look back at our journey.

The nature of the human "I" is inscrutable. However, just as a biologist can describe the human individual's physical behavior, so we can give a picture of its main modes of living, the vegetative, the wakeful, and the automatic. In the vegetative mode man is, as it were, not yet completely man; in the automatic, he is mechanized. Only in the state of wakefulness do the specific human qualities appear; he realizes that he lives not only on the plane of horizontal contact between himself and his environment, but that in all important relations he reaches into a deeper source of vitality. Just as in every hour of time there is a part of eternity, so in every deep state of man's reflection on himself as a being who feels, thinks, loves, and errs there becomes clear to him his partnership in a spiritual universe. Only to the degree to which there exists this self-transcendent partnership is there also self-understanding; for how can the man comprehend his self who sees it only in artificial isolation?

Yet as Judeo-Christian mythology indicates, however much the awareness of self-transcendence may give man the sense of communion and belonging, it also gives him the painful feeling of isolation. He never and nowhere belongs completely. Always he is both within and without. Hence, the history of self-reflective man is full of a deep longing for communion or reunification which, according to the particular culture, expresses itself in various images—the Platonic myth of the origin of the human soul in the *Phaedrus* or of the essence of Eros in the *Symposium*, or the Christian concepts of love and immortality.

The most sublime and at the same time most real elements of our Christian-individualistic and democratic culture spring from these symbols of transcendence. What, then, is going to happen when—as is the case at present—the power of these symbols weakens? How can an individualistic culture with its specific appreciations of responsibility, justice, and dignity maintain itself amid the threats inherent in collectivist-totalitarian tendencies?

This is the cardinal question of our time. Either the heritage of centuries is going to perish—as it has already in parts of the earth which we considered to belong to the Christian sphere of culture—or we re-vitalize old and find new motivations which remind man of the fullness of his psychophysical existence and which, by their very nature and intention, belong in the category of the religious. In the following chapters we will give more substance to these ideas. But the old and the new can be harmonized only if the old is freed from dogmatic accretions which, though meaningful in earlier times, now insult our intellectual conscience; and if, on the other hand, the new does not live in a mood of infantile protest against any idea which leads man beyond the boundaries of the scientific laboratory. For science, let us not forget, is a most useful and ingenious yet limited device in the whole panorama of human history.

To arrive at a new and world-open self-understanding of man is the intention of the modern movement of "existentialism." There are many versions in this form of thought. And frequently, as happens to all labels, the term "existentialism" conceals more than it reveals. Its founder, Søren Kierkegaard (1813–1855), as well as our contemporaries, Gabriel Marcel and Paul Tillich, connect the problem of human existence primarily with the religious quest; Karl Jaspers conceives of the human individual as living in the freedom of realizing the possibilities inherent in his ever-transcendent existence;[3] Martin Heidegger conceives of man as "the guardian of being" who should nevertheless know that he can never be its master;[4] finally, Paul Sartre assigns to the human mind the task of courageous deciding, though in full awareness of the constant threat of the nothing.[5]

Despite all differences these various thinkers would agree with William Stern's emphasis on the uniqueness of each indi-

[3] *Der Philosophische Glaube* (München, 1948), pp. 41 ff. English translation by Ralph Banheim with the title *The Perennial Scope of Philosophy* (New York, 1949).

[4] *Platon's Lehre von der Wahrheit*. Mit einem Briefe über den Humanismus (Bern, 1947), p. 90.

[5] *L'Être et le Néant* (Paris, 1945), passim.

vidual, on his freedom to be this or that, different from other existences, and on the trans-scientific mystery by which he is surrounded. And since they set this undefinable individual in the center of their philosophical systems, they all are skeptical about the validity of the rational philosophies that appeared between Descartes and the German idealists. Such systems, they feel, do not do justice to the more than rational depth and richness which "human" implies. But often we fail to see that we could not criticize ideas profoundly unless they had been expressed systematically. That means that among our greatest spirits must be those who have the courage to weld the wisdom of generations into a unified whole and thus to build cities of the mind within which men can dwell, which they can defend against attack, but whose doors they can hold ever open to new influences.

CHAPTER 4

Thinking as Theoretical Self-Transcendence

How Can We Have a Common World?

Man is but a reed, the weakest in nature, but he is a thinking reed.

BLAISE PASCAL

WHENEVER man has spoken of himself as different from the other creatures of nature he has described himself as the being who thinks. In his capacity of *homo sapiens* he has seen his special dignity, and, since the beginning of his philosophical endeavor, he has tried to give himself an account of the reliability and validity of his reflective endeavors.

During this self-critical process the early Indian and Greek philosophers soon discovered that man's perception is to a large degree deception. The image we have of reality depends on preconceived assumptions which cause us to look at it in one mode or another. These assumptions stem from earlier experiences, from the way in which we have been told that the world is, or should be, and from guesswork which we constantly perform in our daily confrontations with old and new environments. Since ancient times men have wondered at the perfidy and double dealing which sometimes goes on in the interplay between our senses, our mind, and the concrete world. Recent experiments prove strikingly the assumptive character of our images of reality.[1]

[1] See Merle Lawrence, *Studies in Human Behavior* (Princeton, 1949).

But if all this delusion is something to wonder at, still more should we wonder at the fact that, in spite of it, we do have something of a common world. Why is all not chaos? Why can we live with some assurance in this most uncertain of all environments, provided we can rely as well on our beloved fellow men as on the things around us?

There is one obvious answer. The essential identity of the instruments with which nature provides the members of every species for their survival guarantees a certain identity of reaction to the environment. Healthy humans have the five senses, each of which, despite all differences in acumen and quality, works in each of us in the same fashion. We begin our earthly career about the same way, develop in the course of time the same drives and feelings, and common factors of health and sickness play their roles in human survival and death. This community makes possible among us a form of preconceptual sharing, much wider and more important than we generally assume with our onesided idea that communication has to be by word of mouth. Animals, which have no verbal-logical language, but only signs, have amazingly efficient means of contact and information. Also many of our deepest experiences take root in the preverbal period. The primordial depth of creation constantly emerges in elementary feelings and affections, centered around the most elementary facts and experiences of life. These emotions possess a degree of persuasion in comparison to which words are but fleeting sounds.

Because the source of these experiences is preconceptual and subconscious, it is impossible to give a full account of it. Even the greatest of our psychological interpreters have told us little about the work of Eros in human life, and of the aura that sometimes tells us at the first glance that one person may become our friend, while the other may not.

Yet, however penetrating and directive the power of our emotive experiences, they do not give us a "world" in the sense in which man understands this term: as the widest of all *Gestalten,* or as cosmos, with all parts interconnected into an inherent order. For the construction of such a world, man needs rational concepts, or thinking.

Thinking is the activity through which man combines, compares, and analyzes his impressions and ideas with the aim of arriving at meaningful conclusions. These conclusions, so man hopes, should have enough logical cogency and empirical persuasiveness to compel his fellow men to accept their content with some degree of confidence. In other words, through thinking, man tries not only to give form to his own chaotic experiences and thus to maintain himself in a world of uncertainty, but also to increase his own confidence through the similar confidence of other people. There is a Latin adage to the effect that man does not enjoy his own knowing unless he knows that others know about it.

Like any other human activity, thinking cannot be understood merely by itself and with reference to itself. Though the most distinctive function of man, it is nevertheless, or perhaps for the same reason, the function most deeply embedded in all his other energies. It is, as it were, only the top of a pyramid built mainly from nonintellectual material. For this reason it may have the widest outlook, and also some directive quality—provided the pyramid has not been put upside down with the emotions on the top, which sometimes happens. But even under favorable circumstances, the theorizing faculty of man can do no more than his dependence on the whole constellation of physical and emotional forces allows. A certain subjectivity remains even in a person's most abstract and objective thinking. This fact, of course, is not an anti-intellectual excuse for the neglect of truthfulness and objectivity. No ideal can be completely actualized. But this does not mean that man should have no ideals.

I. THE THREE LEVELS OF MAN'S RELATION TO REALITY

When we try to analyze thinking in its most comprehensive sense we discover that it functions, so to speak, on three levels.

There is first the level of "natural reaction," second the level of "system," and third the level of "meaning." From each of these levels man sees a different aspect of reality.

In speaking of these three levels as first, second, and third, a certain development from a lower to a higher state, an evolution, even a certain evaluation, are indicated. This allusion to a hierarchy of values, however, must not be understood as separation. Even on such high planes of human activity as abstract thought, religion, and education, all three stages of development will be found. For in whatever man does the totality of his existence is with him. The terms "level" or "state" or "stage" should be understood only as metaphors. Nor is there any strict sequence; the level of natural or impulsive reaction does not always precede the second, nor the second the third. Plato realizes that his "wise men" or "guardians of the state," who by "the power of dialectic" are "able to disregard the eyes and other senses and go on being in company with truth,"[2] will live most of their daily lives on the first and second levels and be subject to all their errors. Nor does there exist any "primitive" civilization in which we would not find a certain tendency toward organization, search, and experimentation, and especially a strong desire to give meaning—however magic or mythological—to human existence.

1. The Level of Natural Reaction

On the first level, the response to environment is motivated by a healthy and undisputed use of thinking for the sake of self-preservation in a world of change and danger. In this state, our picture of reality, of the world in which we live, is simple. The real is that which man can sense, that which he can hit, or which hits back if he fails to respect it: a wall, a tree, the hoof of a horse, a business enterprise, or a political power. The philosopher, speaking in more sophisticated language, will say that for man in the state of natural thinking, reality is that which is refractory

[2] Plato, *Republic,* Book VII, 16.

or incorrigible. It is independent of and outside of us; as the word implies, it is that which is *in re* and not merely *in intellectu*. It is that which exerts its will upon us and resists. According to modern pragmatic philosophy it is the content of our consciousness and the stimulus to action; it is that to which our emotional and active life responds.[3]

A child who begins to feel himself a person and consequently experiences his first confrontation with environment, "thinks" on the level of natural reaction. Without being able to examine systematically what he does, he interrelates and orders impressions forced upon him. Such thinking is not yet the result of a deep intellectual urge (one may ask whether it is with many adults), nor does it extend beyond immediate response to an inescapable problem.[4] Any complex operation, such as a syllogism, is too difficult; two items are linked together only according to the fundamental intuitions of space and time and the categories of identity, similarity or difference, and mutual exclusion. This is done without finer logical distinction. For example, the category of causality is too advanced to be clearly conceived; *post hoc* is mistaken for *propter hoc,* and analogies serve as explanations and justifications. For medieval man the analogies between sun and pope, and moon and emperor, were sufficient cause for establishing the claim of ecclesiastical superiority. As already indicated, these simple forms of thinking—which, however, form the basis for all later intellectual effort—are presumably a projection of our own actions and experiences into the behavior of the outer world. The world, or reality, is supposed to behave as *we* do. That which hurts us *is* bad, that which seems to us dissimilar, *is* different, and so on.

On this level of mentality the higher forms of thinking, as found in organization and science, or in philosophy and religion, express themselves only in the germinal forms of groping, hap-

[3] William James, *The Principles of Psychology,* Vol. II, Chapter XXI, "The Perception of Reality" (New York, 1893).

[4] See Jean Piaget, *Judgment and Reasoning in the Child* (London and New York, 1928), Chapter I, "Grammar and Logic."

hazard experimenting, or as magic and myth. Thought still moves in a kind of twilight; it is difficult to differentiate it from feeling and willing. These first attempts to master life or to penetrate its hidden grounds, however, are of great importance for the individual, the group, and the whole history of mankind. If directed toward an emerging goal, they often betray an amazing degree of observation, as in the hunting of primitive tribes, or attain profundity of insight, as in ancient myths or the sudden questions of children.

"Enlightened" misunderstanding, or wanton destruction and ridicule of these early stages of man's development, have brought disastrous results. In history these have often produced a sad misinterpretation of earlier stages of human development. In actual meeting between more advanced and more primitive civilizations they have blocked the paths on which men in different cultures may learn from, or help each other. Often the so-called "civilized" man is not even more mature than the "primitive"; he is only technically more advanced.

In contacts between young and adult, the show of superiority on the part of the older has often disturbed the mental and emotional development of the child whose little flower-garden of fancy may by crude corrections be destroyed and never grow again. Children whose natural desire for myth and fantasy has been suppressed have little chance to succeed later in fields of thought which need a cultivated intuition. They may become successful "experts," but with respect to esthetic and metaphysical imagination they may remain on a lower level than a tribesman who decorates his tent, though they may surprise their friends with sentimentalities and prejudices. Persons in whom essential parts of a full psychic life lie barren are always in danger of lapsing from smartness into romanticism and superstition. Hence an education that addresses primarily the "brain," will always be incomplete and even dangerous. It may achieve little even in the domain of the intellect, for in the curiosity and forming power of the creative mind works a large dose of reverie.

2. The Level of System

The longer and more intensely man becomes occupied with the world around him, however, the more he becomes dissatisfied with a merely natural and impulsive response to it.

Behind the "hard" reality before his eyes, he envisages other, or deeper, or more essential layers of being. For with developing experience the concrete surface of appearance—seemingly the only thing to rely upon—proves to be of transitory and deceptive character. Thus the second level, the level of system, comes to the fore. Man begins to plan and search systematically for insight into the more permanent and unifying qualities behind the changing facets apprehended by our senses.

It is this second reality for which the farmer is looking when, with the help of a chemist, he tries to find out why one of his fields yields a better crop than the others. It is the one which the scientist hopes to detect when he forces a number of supposed "reals" or "variables" into a controlled set of experiments. Reality, at this stage, is no longer a heap of things and events which have to be accepted at face value; it receives a certain coherence, is considered to work according to certain rules and laws, and can be mastered by man to the degree to which he understands how to discover and apply these laws. Thus Francis Bacon could say in his *Novum Organon*:

> Man, as the minister and interpreter of nature, does and understands as much as his observations on the order of nature, either with regard to things or the mind, permit him, and neither knows, nor is capable of more. . . .
>
> Knowledge and human power are synonymous, since the ignorance of the cause frustrates the effect. For nature is only subdued by submission, and that which in contemplative philosophy corresponds with the cause, in practical science becomes the rule.

On the level of system man's logical power engages in complex operations; he argues, discusses and contradicts. He uses experiment and causal thinking not only *ad hoc*, but for the discovery of rules and laws that provide better understanding and mastering of the environment. He becomes a believer in method. The wreath of legends clustering around the learned Pope Sylvester II (Gerbert), and some centuries later around the German figure of Faust; the fight of theologians against Galileo and the theory of evolution; and in our own times the controversy over psychoanalysis on grounds which were not merely philosophical and scientific (and consequently legitimate) but largely emotional and conventional—all these incidents testify that the transition from the first to the second level of thinking, from simple response to system, is generally accompanied by serious conflicts. Though the curious among men like to apply their intellect to complicated operations—there have always been problem-solvers—the average man protests vigorously against the exposure of his cherished beliefs to the light of analysis.

Of course, there have always been rationalizations of such timidity: the gods might object to the invasion by man of their secrets, or society or the individual might be upset. This latter fear, often springing from a selfish desire to maintain comfortable privileges over the ignorant "masses," is historically justified, for knowledge is by nature not only contemplative, but also restless and revolutionary. It is the systematization of knowledge, the search for cause and effect, and the application of insights thus won to nature and society which have resulted in the greatest change in human history, the transition from a primarily magical to a scientific and technical civilization.

Modern man, in his managerial and scientific optimism, has, on the other hand, overestimated the effectiveness of cultures moving primarily on the level of systematic organization, observation and description. He has failed to realize what happens when a civilization lives in dissociation from simple natural reaction and deeper metaphysical interpretation. He mistakes a part of his existence for the whole and suppresses other and just as essential constituents of culture. The average citizen of the West, still proud of his airplanes and highroads, begins now to realize the havoc that the disrespect for simple, intangible, and seemingly useless values has wrought upon humanity. A new boredom and barbarism have arisen. But, "what can we do about it?" The printed words many read, the movies they see, the radio performances they listen to, and the so-called works of art they buy are often far below the taste not only of our educated forebears, but also below the standards demonstrated by the orally transmitted epics, the festivals, the folksongs, and the utensils of illiterate man in ancient India, China, Greece, Rome, and medieval Europe. Says the late Indian scholar Ananda Coomaraswamy about our modern education:[5]

In every sense of the word, modern education, whether in its own context or proudly exported by the English-speaking peoples, is isolationist; the degeneration of language, the slipshod ignorance of scientists whenever they attempt to deal with problems of philosophy or theology, the facile positivism of the great majority of teachers, all these things cut off the student from the possibility of any real understanding even of his own past.

3. The Level of Meaning

On the third level of thought man wishes to discover the abiding ground behind his self and the world. Though being moulded by numberless influences, he wants to be more than a mere meeting place of energies. He desires to give expressive shape to the stream of experiences in which otherwise he would drown. He acquires the perspective to recognize visible and tangible things for what they are—phenomenal and transient—but at the same time he tries to explain them as parts of a larger, permanent, and inclusive universe.

In contrast to the supporters of modern scientism, Bacon, though the first great philosopher of empiricism, recognized transcendent mystery behind the realm of the observable. He speaks of "the subtilty of nature" which "is far beyond that of

[5] "For What Heritage and to Whom are the English Speaking People Responsible?" Kenyon College Conference (1946), pp. 48 ff.

sense or of the understanding," and of the "ideas of the divine mind" which are essentially different from "the idols of the human mind." He also acknowledges that the approach toward the final level of meaning and integration can be accomplished not through thinking in the ordinary, or even scientific sense of the word, but through "mystical" experience. Bacon has seen the truth that the Indians called Brahma; the Chinese, Tao; and Plato, "the colorless, formless, and intangible truly existing essence," or which the medieval theologians intended to identify when they spoke of the *ens realissimum,* or "the most real being." They all, as well as the modern metaphysicians, wish to express one and the same idea, namely that of the cohesion of all the various parts of life in a meaningful universe. Through a strange paradox, for all these thinkers that which is generally called the "ideal" becomes more real than the "real."

In this contemplative and intuitive mood man is no longer satisfied with meeting the tasks emerging and vanishing *during* human life; he attempts to find the mission and essence *of* human life. That means he becomes self-reflective, philosophical, and religious. He realizes a third, or universal, order behind the physical and mental order of things.

Let us now apply this contemplative attitude and search for a meaning to the mystery of thinking in and of itself. In other words, let us look at thinking not from the point of view of its daily use, or its scientific and organizational value, but in regard to its deeper philosophical implications. We thus enter into the field of epistemology, or the theory of knowledge.

II. THE MEANING OF THINKING

1. Thinking as Self-Transcendence

Thinking can be conceived as an essentially spontaneous process occurring in the human being as part of the design of the cosmic order. It is an imperfect process—perfect thinking is either the ultimate expression of the evolution of the mind,[6] or

[6] See Hegel, *Phaenomenologie des Geistes.* VIII. Das absolute Wissen (Ed. Georg Lasson), 2 Auflage (Leipzig, 1921).

the abiding quality of God.[7] Such is the position of the various schools of philosophical and religious idealism. According to this concept the individual mind, bound to a specific body, is but one of the many vehicles by which the Universal Mind carries out its continuous process of self-realization.

Thinking also can be conceived of as a volitional process occurring psychophysically in an individual whenever his attention is directed toward a certain thought goal or thought object which first appears in the senses and then becomes an object for intellectual comprehension.* According to modern experimental theories of learning the formation of concepts and the whole process of cognition can be built on basic psychological phenomena such as sense perception, association, integration, motivation, reward, and tension reduction.

Even if, for the time being, we accept the second and more "empirical" position as the one which may appear more plausible to the majority of modern men, thinking cannot be explained merely with reference to individual man himself. For the person who thinks relates himself to the other objects in the world; he extends, as it were, his mental antennae outside himself into a universe which is not his own, though he is a part of it. Without this process of "going beyond oneself," or "self-transcendence" the individual would be mentally closed in his own shell.

How, under the assumption that there exists a relationship between subjective mind and objective reality, the two join in a world of thought, is beyond human grasp. For only a part of the total process of thinking is explained by referring to the senses, the nervous system, and certain brain functions. Nor is the mystery resolved if we accept, over and above the epistemological theory of the dichotomy of the mind and its objects, the ontological hypothesis that the world, including the mind, is ultimately an indivisible, dynamic, and constantly evolving expression of

---

[7] See Thomas Aquinas, *Summa contra Gentiles,* Chapter XLV, "That God's Act of Intelligence is His Essence," translated by the English Dominican Fathers, First Book, p. 101 (London, 1924).

* This is the point of view of all so-called empirical philosophers from Locke and Hume up to modern naturalism.

energy in which all parts somehow interact with each other. What kind of energy is it? Thus from any possible point of view we are dealing with problems for which our mind and language have no adequate symbols. The transcending process, however, is going on in every meaningful experience, even of the most mundane sort. Always the mind bursts the walls of isolation within which the individual would otherwise suffocate.

2. Thinking as Order

The process of self-transcendence is not of an irregular character, a play of fancy, or a sort of daydreaming. Rather it is an amazing process of selecting and ordering the continual influx of impressions.

The way in which the mind performs this task of changing a potential chaos of isolated prehensions into a comprehended and somewhat orderly world has been the object of scrutiny since the beginning of systematic philosophical thought, with Immanual Kant's *Critique of Pure Reason* (1781) as the most gigantic effort at a solution of the problem.

We have learned two things of fundamental importance from Kant and his French and English predecessors. First, the relation between what we call mind and what we call reality is highly dynamic. The mind constantly forms and transforms the sense impressions conveyed by the outer world, and the ever-changing outer world constantly transforms the content of the mind. Second, man cannot make any definite rational statement about the inner essence and nature of life, since he has no guarantee that his necessarily man-bound reason is capable of transcending itself to such a degree that it can adequately understand reality in itself, or *das Ding an sich,* or ultimate Being.

However, there is something permanent in this process of ordering. It operates according to a certain inner logic which, though perhaps subject to change during the total evolution of man (which Kant did not believe), demonstrates certain qualities of identity, unity, and coherence. Otherwise man could not repeat his own thinking; there would be no human history and no human person.[8]

This intellectual cosmos or conceptual world of man is possible because, according to Kant,[9] there operate within our mind two fundamental "intuitions" (*reine Anschauungen*), space and time. Whatever we perceive, it is somewhere and somewhen. In addition, it has a certain quantity and quality, it is related to other phenomena in that it may be their cause or effect. In addition, the relationship has a certain modality, a quality of possibility or impossibility, necessity or contingency.

The further development of the theory of knowledge has revealed several doubtful points in Kant's work. But whatever we may think about the details of Kant's theory of knowledge, there remains the depth of his insight into the creative, transforming and at the same time ordering and stabilizing quality of the human mind.

In order to make these abstract ideas more concrete, let us ask what happened when Copernicus performed the supreme act of self-transcendence and re-ordering of our reality by approaching the problem of the universe in a new and scientific way.

Instead of adhering to an interpretation of reality suggested both by the sacred Aristotelian tradition and by sense impression —for the latter confirms the hypothesis that we humans walk around on a motionless and somewhat rugged disk in the center of the universe—Copernicus believed in the supremacy of certain organizing, logical principles. When he discovered that by a new method—already envisaged by some ancient philosophers—

[8] As one of hundreds of possible references: Locke, *An Essay Concerning Human Understanding,* Chapter 27, of Identity and Diversity; Section 9, Personal Identity. "Which (the person), I think, is a thinking intelligent being, that has reason and reflection, and can consider itself as itself, the same thinking thing in different times and places" (Philadelphia, T. Ellwood Zell, no date, p. 210).

[9] I. Kant's *Critique of Pure Reason;* translation by F. M. Müller; Part II (London, 1881). "Transcendental aesthetic," pp. 17 ff., and "Transcendental analytic," pp. 56 ff.

he was able to close certain gaps which the mathematics of his predecessors from Ptolemy to Regiomontanus had been unable to explain, he decided that the inherent authority of logic was of greater value than all traditional authority.[10] However, despite the revolution he created through his thinking, Copernicus did not discover a *new* logic, or revolutionize the process of thinking as such. Nobody ever did. Like Euclid and Ptolemy before him, and Leibniz and Newton after him, he applied principles of thinking which possess a perpetual inner coherence more imaginatively, skillfully, and courageously than lesser minds, and thus moved the frontier of human thought closer to reality.

Hence, when we speak of thinking as ordering we must not conceive of it onesidedly as a process by which the sovereign individual minds of men give structure to a medley of facts, or change a world of chaos into a logos. Whether, with the idealist Kant, we consider the categories of the intellect to be a priori or transcendental qualities, or, with the pragmatists, "controlling concepts of inquiry,"[11] in either case it is inconceivable that every human mind creates these ordering instruments merely out of itself. The capacity of forming or of making a *Gestalt* out of the flux of prehensions, is not derived from an individual experiencing itself, but is inherent *in* experiencing, or makes it possible.

If human reflection, or thinking, or however we may call it, were not operating according to principles common to all thinking minds and, in a mysterious way, to the world, it would not order, but end in arbitrary and meaningless dialectics, in nonsense, and nobody would be able to correct it. Even concepts such as "tentative," or "experimental," would be illusory, for "trying out" is worthwhile only in a system that responds to the effort; total chaos would not respond, therefore we hate it.

---

[10] Nicolai Copernici, *De Revolutionibus Orbium Coelestium* (Basileae, 1566), "Ad Sanctissimum Dominum Paulum III Praefatio."

[11] John Dewey, *Art as Experience*, p. 317; see also his *Logic*, passim.

3. The Interpersonal Character of Thought

Without our mind's capacity of developing logical principles—which, nevertheless, none of us "invents" individually—we would live in complete isolation, unable to cooperate, unable to agree even when looking toward the same goal. As a matter of fact, we could not have the same goal. Thus it would be impossible for man to rise from a state of blind arbitrariness and vague groping into a state of disciplined and communicable thinking.

We take the act of thought, as a trans-private act, for granted because it happens millions of times every minute. Yet it is one of the greatest wonders of life that an idea occurring to one individual can be communicated to another by word of mouth or by script. Scholars and research workers cooperate with each other over space and time. The Socratic dialogues still speak to us as does the music of Palestrina, and the abstract formula expressing the result of an experiment made somewhere in the United States can be re-awakened into life and meaning by a chemist in India. Only through the meeting of minds which despite enormous dimensions of space and time can still awaken common consent or dissent has human history and civilization become possible.

But if we ask why knowledge and the meaning of experience are communicable and reproducible, we can answer only by referring to the fact, already mentioned, that nobody creates the principles of thinking individually. Thinking is a universal process that somehow is related to an "ontic" quality of being which enables life to present itself to us as a coherent and unified whole, whatever our metaphysical belief may be with respect to its ultimate goal and meaning. In other words, we discover on the level of thinking, as we discovered in our analysis of man's existence, that man can understand himself only as a sharing communicant in a cosmic process of being and becoming.

4. The Mutuality between Thought and Reality

The fact that thought is interpersonal—that is, communicable and reproducible—is not explained completely by the concept of an inherent order.

Whether we conceive of the relationship between thought and reality monistically, subjecting either matter to spirit or spirit to matter, or dualistically, assuming a certain polarity between the two, in either case we cannot deny that good thinking is "relevant" to its object. These terms are not intended to support the time-honored concept of truth as *adaequatio* between an idea and its object. However, we hope that correct thought expresses a certain convergence towards the part of reality with which it is concerned. It is as if thinking were not satisfied until its own inner order and the order of the world around somehow harmonize with each other.

Therefore, as the Greeks knew,[12] all thinking not only tends toward the general and essential, but also creates for us a meaningful life. Again, we are faced here with the contrast between the religious-idealistic and the empirical-sceptical schools of thought. The strict idealist would explain the unity between an idea and its object as the result of the essentially ideal-logical quality of the universe as a whole. In contrast, the empirical-sceptical philosopher would say that the mind's tendency to imagine itself as a part of a logically ordered universe is a kind of projection—the result of wishful thinking. The individual mind, the radical empiricist would say, prefers the feeling of belonging to the feeling of isolation; the first provides security, the second breeds anxiety. Such feelings, however, are without empirical validity.

Whatever the differences in explanation may be, only when the conviction of unity between an idea and its object is present do we acquire some degree of confidence about our own or someone else's intellectual operations.

[12] Aristotle, *De Anima;* II, 5, 417b, pp. 22 ff.

In other words, when Copernicus performed his mathematical calculations and won confidence in the process, he not only believed in its internal order and consistency, but he also believed that the symbols on his paper were symbols of reality. And although Pope Paul III accepted the dedication of Copernicus' work, because it was then considered a hypothesis without great consequences, later the hierarchy became aroused when Galileo proved experimentally—by evidence taken from reality—that the Copernican theory was more than just speculation. For us who are accustomed to the work of the scientist it needs some imagination to realize the impact made on the men of the seventeenth and eighteenth centuries by the discovery of the congruence of mathematics and the wide and unseen orbits of the universe. The philosophical and political enthusiasm of that period was largely due to the feeling of emergence from a world of magic into a world of order and definable laws. To be sure, the enthusiasm led to disappointment. Rationalist firebrands changed rational inquiry into rationalist absolutism and tried to reshape human society according to their theories. The result was that the French revolution, born out of the Enlightenment, soon collapsed from a movement for human freedom into tyranny. Nevertheless, it remains true that the origin of modern thought is not to be sought so much in Renaissance humanism, or in the Reformation, as in the discovery of the convergence of methodical-systematic thinking and the apparent behavior of reality.

Of course, mutuality between an intellectual operation and its object takes place only if the premises are correct—if the thought-starting intuition of the individual mind is approximately adequate to the reality within and behind the object which it wants to apprehend. Here is the weakness of all merely deductive speculation in comparison with the empirical sciences.

Speculation may be false in its premises, or without any ground in fact. Yet the logic of the speculative process itself may be so persuasive that we overlook its fallacious or doubtful foundations, thus being led away from reality rather than into it. A master of dialectic may render us incapable of immediate effective contradiction without really convincing us. Later we may discover that we fell prey to his logic because we had no time to examine his premises. The French call this "l'esprit de l'escalier," the insight at which we arrive when, unfortunately, we have already retreated from the debate. In contrast to abstract speculation, experimentation becomes the more self-corrective the more systematically it is applied.

5. Thinking as Means of Survival

All the characteristics of thinking we have mentioned so far— its self-transcending quality, its inherent order, its interpersonal quality which allows intellectual cooperation and communication, its kinship with the laws of reality—all these factors allow us to introduce a fifth notion in our analysis, that of survival. This term has to be understood not in a merely Darwinian, or biological, but in a much more total sense, comprehending not only of the physical, but also of the intellectual and spiritual side of human existence. Simply speaking, the more man thinks, the more he discovers. The more he discovers, the greater is his chance of avoiding danger and living wisely. One could also say that thinking is an "existential" process,[13] or a process in which the total existence of man is at stake.

In performing this process successfully, he fulfills the destiny of the human self. Instead of vegetating, he is mentally and morally awake; instead of moving on the surface, he dares face

[13] In Germany, the relationship between thinking and survival has been emphasized by Nietzsche, according to whom thinking has its roots in the will to power; also by Francé, who explains thinking as *Biotechnik* (*Die Welt als Erleben*, 1923), and by such idealistically oriented activists as Rudolph Eucken, according to whom thinking is an action in the service of life and culture, or an activity by which life tends to perfect itself. In France, Henry Bergson, with his theory of the *élan vital,* has been the main representative of a similar school of thought. See *L'Évolution Créatrice* (ed. 12, Paris, 1913), p. 151. Needless to say, American Pragmatism, as elaborated especially by William James and John Dewey, can easily be related to this trend of thought. In all likelihood, the direct or indirect influence of Darwin works in all these philosophical systems.

the depths of being; instead of living in the company of lies, he tries to live with truth. If he fails in this endeavor, he alienates himself from the structure of life and helps in the self-destruction of mankind. For, as the Old Testament says, God visits the sins of the fathers upon the children. This is true not because revengeful and furious gods must satisfy their wrath—that is an anthropomorphic and offensive conception of the Divine—but because the world's order, in the long run, is always stronger than willfulness.

Man can use his freedom and intelligence negatively and may even "profit" personally thereby. But in the course of time the distorted conditions of life will try to restore themselves. This is why "sin and untruth do not pay." Reality has its majesty and dignity. It respects man if he respects it, but it refuses to be an object of arbitrariness. Hence thinking, as man's most effective means for understanding the real, is also one of the principal means of his survival. Dictatorships, which by necessity must forbid man to think and express his ideas freely, may not necessarily perish at the hands of external enemies, but in the course of time they must perish from within. And so will even democracies if they are afraid of dissenters who earnestly help in the common search for truth.

6. *Thinking and Religion*

Only after the previous discussion on the relation of human thinking to the mystery of reality, can we comprehend the meaning of a contemplative life, as advocated by the great religions and philosophies. If Aristotle says in the *Nicomachean Ethics* that the contemplative form is the highest,[14] he is far from encouraging an idle and self-centered existence. Rather he

---

[14] Aristotle, *Nichomachean Ethics*, Book X, 7: "But if happiness consists in activity in accordance with virtue, it is reasonable that it should be activity in accordance with the highest virtue; and this will be the virtue of the best part in us. Whether then this be the intellect, or whatever else it be that is thought to lead and rule us by nature, and to have cognizance of what is noble and divine . . . it is the activity of this part in us in accordance with the virtue proper to it that will constitute perfect happiness; and it has been stated already that this activity is the activity of contemplation."

recommends the kind of contemplative practice that harmonizes the soul of man with the deeper rhythm of life, or, to use a term of the French philosopher, René Guénon, harmonizes *l'ordre human* and *l'ordre cosmique*.[15] Only those who sense this harmony can act well and be free. Due to the emphasis of our technological civilization on quick results, or "efficiency," many modern men have lost the contemplative and with it the religious quality. They are afraid that these stand in opposition to the "scientific" attitude. But the tools which man uses to gain his profoundest insights into the world are, though not anti-intellectual, nevertheless not *merely* "intellectual" or "scientific." They belong to "reason" in the *wide* sense of the word which we earlier explained. They involve not only contemplation and intuition, but also "faith" in the sense of an order to which we can have some positive relation. Thus the innermost contact between man and reality is somehow in the nature of *religion*. It never emerges in us so clearly as in hours of creative love, or when we look into the stillness of death, or when we see a strong man overcoming his hatred against his enemy. And always when the depth of life reveals itself, we also discover our own depth; the two merge into one. This is the genuine "mystical" experience. It must be classed as a form of thought, but it is more than that. Men can be productive in many ways, but whenever they really create, they always do so in contact with something greater than themselves. Man alone never creates.

7. Summary

Since it was necessary to divide the discussion of the complicated problem of thinking into various sections we may, in summary, approach it once more in a different manner.

All our knowing about outer reality is the result of a mutual response between the individual mind and the world. What we know about our environment, our fellow men, and the universe comes partly from them and partly from us. The dynamic reality

[15] Le Règne de la Quantité et les Signes des Temps (Paris, 1945) p. 58.

that lives within us enters into an alliance with the world around us, which is possible because there is some kind of progressive and purposeful convergence (*Thinking as Self-Transcendence*). In part, we conclude by analogy. We infer from that which we feel in us to that which we perceive outside. We *are*, hence there is being generally; we feel the form and extension of our body, therefore we have a sense of form and space; we feel the effect of an action in which we are either the active or the passive part, therefore we have causality. States of feeling stay or change in us, therefore we know about likeness and difference. Certain cause–effect and identity–difference relations occur with a certain regularity; therefore we develop a sense of coherence and of time.

The story, however, is not so simple. First of all, it must not be interpreted as advocacy of a merely biological or associationist theory of knowledge. The fact that thinking and our body are interrelated says something about the unity of the world, but little about the origin and quality of thinking. For in order to feel my body and myself as a structure endowed with space, time, likeness, and difference I must have a mind capable of developing these sensations to the level of awareness. In a newly born child these mental capacities exist only germinally. Thus we are always thrown back on the problem of the relation between cosmic and individual evolution and the emergence of the reflective mind within this evolutionary process.

In addition, the mental processes just mentioned are, after all, operations, that is, they presuppose a certain mental activity. The simplest perception, whether it result from an interior or exterior stimulus, is never complete passivity. Perception, as already indicated, is an operational or functional process of an organizational character (*Thinking as Order*). Even the most empiricist theory of cognition requires the assumption of an inexplicable and "given" mental dynamic which does not necessarily *pre-cede* experience, but works in the most basic mental operation as well as in the progress from particular to general and from simple analogy to complex abstraction and conclusion. Each of us has different experiences and lives in a different world but we are nevertheless united by the experience of communication and community. Thus there must exist some common dynamic which permits us to order the world not only for each of us individually, but collectively for the race as a whole (*The Interpersonal Character of Thought*).

In impulsive and resolute living we believe that the organizational activity of our minds produce an accurate picture of reality—whatever it may be. We hope that the alliance between our thought and the part of the universe we wish to comprehend is a sort of gentlemen's agreement in which neither part lays value on cheating the other (*The Kinship between Thought and Reality*). But no one reveals his innermost secrets to just anybody, and frequently not even to himself. There still remains the question as to whether and to what degree our conceptual thinking opens to us the "essence" of being. In other words, when the common man speaks about nature and life, the scientist about "laws," and the theologian about the Divine (which would be the law of all laws), do they speak merely of their own mental creations, or do they say something about reality?

From the critical point of view—which later we will try to elaborate—this question will never be answered. Man's thinking, even if driven to its last unimaginable refinement, will always remain *human* thinking, or anthropomorphic. And we have no scientific guarantee as to whether the existence of man is so deeply embedded in the essence of being that this essence can ever be fully reflected in human ideas, however subtly and logically we may try to proceed. Not only do we know nothing whatever about the essence of reality, but we cannot even be sure of this ignorance. This idea was advanced by the Roman sceptic Sextus Empiricus. Perhaps that which we denote by the symbol "reality" or "the world," or "life" has not even an "essence." This concept may be human invention about which the universe does not bother. All we can say is that there exists an objective structure.

Yet we should not drive the pessimistic attitude too far. From our own as well as from historic experience we know that thinking helps us toward orientation in the world. For whenever man is prevented from using his rational power, he is at the same time prevented from living creatively and he thus eventually destroys himself (*Thinking as Means of Survival*).

If we realize this fact, and if at the same time we realize that the dynamic and inherent cognitive capacity is *not created by us,* is it too bold—is it not almost urged upon us—to believe that there must be something which does create it? Something that, as we already indicated, gives us the capacity of thinking for the purpose of helping. Something in which we cooperate, not because of our own merit, but by a mysterious act of nature, or evolution, or the spirit, that brings the existence of man close to the creative center of life. This is perhaps the deepest experience behind the religious concept of revelation (*Thinking as Religion*).

There are many interpretations of the wonder of world and thought. Whether these interpretations are "supernatural" or "naturalistic"—to use the two most current, but most unfortunate and confusing terms—somehow thinking man must acknowledge that he is not his own creation, but a participant in a greater whole. He may stand before it with a conviction of the nature of the ultimate unity, or as an agnostic. But unless he chooses to live in indifference, he cannot help but live in an attitude of reverence.

III. THE CRITERIA OF THINKING

But now a question should be answered which is as old as speculative thinking: where are the criteria to tell us whether an idea is true or not true—as far as fallible man is permitted to speak of truth? This is not the place to review the multitude of answers which have been given; they can be found in any scholarly history of philosophy.

Our evolving criteria must of necessity follow from our previous analysis of thinking, otherwise either the first or the second—or both—are wrong.

If we take up the idea of *thinking as self-transcendence,* then it follows that all true reasoning must be open and ever widening, must be the product of continuous striving and longing for deeper insight. The process of self-transcendence is by nature antagonistic to closed systems of thought and society. It joins in the dynamic and evolutionary character of the world. From the idea of *thinking as an ordering process* it follows that good thinking has the tendency toward the creation of coherent structure. If we admire a good theoretical argument or the handling of a mathematical problem, we esteem not only the solution, but also the form. There appears an element of *beauty* which is the reflection of order. Insofar as thinking is *interpersonal,* it must aim at the idea of universality, for only under the auspices of this great ideal can it achieve the highest degree of consensus. If we follow the concept of *kinship between reason and reality* to its logical consequences, then human reason cannot be an isolated, individualistic, and autonomous process, but must spring from man's living within the spending power of the world. The more he overcomes his partiality by forgetting his self in this power, the closer he comes to what we might call the truth. Not knowing what truth really is, we nevertheless feel that we are close to it when, for example, we can repeat an experiment under different circumstances, when we can anticipate the motions of the heavenly bodies, in other words, when our search receives a positive response from reality. From this premise follows the justification of the concept of *thinking as a means of survival,* for right reasoning helps man to understand better the productive qualities of the creation and to live accordingly. But after all that has been said, this idea of survival carries with it not only the pragmatic component of success in the competitive battle of life, it also involves the reverential or *religious* idea of an inner accord between us and the universe. Despite all dissonance, there is also consonance. Here enters into the analysis of thinking a factor already indicated, but to be elaborated later, namely the deep interrelationship between the true and the good. Thinking has not only intellectual and esthetic, but also *ethical* qualities.

The criteria of good thinking can also be expressed in the following way. Truth becomes realized to the degree to which the dynamics of inquiry open ever wider vistas into the appearances which reality has made accessible to the human mind. Is a chain of thought self-opening or self-closing? Has it form or does it contradict itself? Does it aim toward universality or is it merely subjective? Is it suggestive of "world" rather than of an isolated ego? Does it help in the psychophysical survival of mankind or is it based on shortsighted egocentric interest? Does it evoke in us the feeling of striving within, and belonging to, the wonder of being, or is it just one or another sign of arrogant intellectual self-assertion? These are the questions one can ask, and these questions are at the same time the criteria of our thought. There is no more. But it is enough to give us faith in the productivity of our relation to the world and in the meaning of human existence.

There remains, of course, the question as to what extent the various functions and criteria of true thinking are permanent, or have developed in the course of human history. There is certainly identity in the structure of thought which, despite all differences of opinion, has created also some identity in content. So far as we can look back no change has occurred in man's basic intellectual operations as such. Otherwise we could not understand the logic in the early documents of mankind. Furthermore, despite all accumulation and refinement of knowledge, is the content of our thinking superior to that of Lao-tse, or of Plato? Certainly not.

On the other hand, what are twenty-three centuries in comparison with the thirty million years of man's existence? The Greeks had a different concept of time to ours. The Egyptians and our ancestors in the Middle Ages had another concept of space and perspective.[16] So there may be change, even in certain fundamentals. And in between the static and the changing there always is the factor of error involved in all human existence. We are just at the beginning of the first understanding of these great problems of the evolution of the human mind and have to confess ignorance.

But for the much or the little he knows man has reason to be grateful.

[16] See Jean Gebser, *Ursprung und Gegenwart;* Vol. I, Die Fundamente der Aperspektivischen Welt (Stuttgart, 1949).

CHAPTER 5

Metaphysics as Speculative Self-Transcendence

Aspects of Reality

> Without Contraries is no progression. Attraction and
> Repulsion, Reason and Energy, Love and Hate, are
> necessary to human existence. . . .
> Excess of sorrow laughs. Excess of joy weeps.
>   WILLIAM BLAKE

I. THE GROPING

WE ARE now at the stage of our inquiry where we must ask: in
what matrix, or ground, or framework is all this struggling,
thinking, and erring of the individual and his societies embedded?
Or, to phrase the question more technically: what is the nature
of reality? Is the universe which man constantly feels as a surrounding and spending force, logically definable?

The task of dealing with this problem has been given to the
philosophical discipline of ontology (the theory of being) as a
part of metaphysics. Subtle differences have been emphasized
between the two disciplines, the first supposed to be concerned
with the essential nature of being, the second with the ultimate
nature of human knowledge, especially in its relation to "truth."
Historically, however, the term metaphysics is the more inclusive
of the two.

Since from our point of view, the world is a unity in which
"stuff" and "mind," the "material" and the "nonmaterial," the

"natural" and the "spiritual" cannot be clearly separated in the sense of being "here" and "beyond," we do not like the term "meta-physics" which indicates a separation between the "physical" and something supposed to be beyond or outside the "physical." Still more doubtful are we of the term "onto-logy" because, according to our critical theory of knowledge, man may have a vision of truth and being that guides and inspires him, but the essence of being as such is beyond his intellectual grasp. In other words, an ontology in the strict sense is too great an enterprise for human reason. With the utmost effort it cannot jump beyond its own limitations. Even the works of the two most profound modern ontologists, Alfred North Whitehead and Nicolai Hartmann, prove that neither the recent development of science, nor the recent development of the theory of knowledge has changed this situation. Though it is an empirical fact that man participates in the continual self-revelation of the ground of life, it still remains more a matter of faith and courage than of science whether we believe we know its essence. Even the divine revelations which various religions claim to have received concern themselves not with all, but only with parts of reality.

When, therefore, we use the terms "metaphysics," or "ontology," we do it in modesty. Actually, we will deal with "aspects" of reality, or with reality as it "appears" to us, from our philosophical point of view without any claim to reveal the ultimate nature of things.

1. The Metaphysical Temptation

How can we explain the confidence of certain metaphysicians in their knowledge of ultimate substance?

First, there is in every great thinker, as in every great artist, a strange feeling that his work does not spring out of his isolated self, but that "it" thinks and works in him. What this "it" is would be difficult for him to define. He might call it spirit, creation, or self-revealing reality. In our words, he feels as though he were an instrument through which the world manifests its reflective power. This feeling may well lead to overestimation of one's mortal self; the participant presumably has not full knowledge of that in which he participates.

Second, not only the undescribable "it," but the spirit of a whole period tries to express itself in a great work of thought. Plato and Aristotle spoke for Greece, the Prophets for Israel, Descartes and Hegel for the beginning and the end of Europe's Enlightenment. Like all great contributors to mankind's progress, they expressed in their individual language the collective intellectual achievement of their time. Here also lies a source of deceptive self-trust.

Third, a further factor of confidence is the thinker's belief in "method." Since Aristotle and even earlier, each of the great philosophers has tried to avoid arbitrariness by assuring himself of reliable method as a framework for the truth in his endeavor. But even the best method used by a human mind does not guarantee complete validity of a statement or complete objectivity with respect to the premises from which it starts.

These three factors, however necessary for great achievement, often combine to give the philosopher too strong a conviction of contact with eternal truth. This conviction, however, is not only the metaphysician's and theologian's fault. Scientists are also to be blamed. The more emphatic the author, the more self-discipline he needs in order to realize that his work also will need criticism, and that the only thought which has hope of lasting is the one which can be constantly re-interpreted and even corrected without losing its challenging power. All other theories, though of interest to the historian, are like ruins left by extinct nations.

Or if, by force of vested interests, certain theoretical, religious, or political systems are kept alive artificially, they work as confusing elements in civilization. Their external power protects them, yet their obsolescence fetters man's curiosity and advancing knowledge. They claim to represent "the faith of the fathers," but their inner authority is gone. In philosophy as well as in politics and religion there is only one choice: either the continual attempt at critical and comprehensive reason with all its voluntary exposure to revision, or slow decadence. It is sad to think that often this decadence is not so much due to the weakness of the system itself as to the timidity of the disciples. For great ideas *rien n'est plus gênant que les disciples*.[1]

2. Metaphysics and Religion

Systematic speculation has always been for the few. Indirectly, it may influence later generations, but most people are untouched by it. Plato and Aristotle have moulded the culture of the Middle Ages, Hegel and Marx that of our times. Yet even the greatest philosopher's influence lags far behind that of the religious prophet. The latter addresses the emotions, the former the intellect.

However, metaphysics and religion are akin. Thinkers whose curiosity reaches from the safer fields of thought toward the mysteries of reality are near to religion, though they may be skeptical about it. If only from the "professional" point of view, a philosopher needs some knowledge of theology, and a theologian some knowledge of philosophy, though without such knowledge one can be deeply religious. Yet there remains an essential difference. Religion is a permeating feeling, a mode of inner certainty of which the humble and the weak may possess more than the erudite. There is the sense of grace and of contact with the Divine; there are ritual, worship, and prayer. In contrast, the philosopher's relation to God, if it exists consciously, is not the way from God down to man, or the way of revelation; rather it is the hard way from man up to God, full of doubt, search, and labor.

3. Metaphysics and Art

There seems to be little similarity between the abstractions of a metaphysician and the concrete creations of an artist. Yet as

[1] Henry Massis, *Maurras et Notre Temps* (Paris, 1951), p. 59.

long as art is great, it strives for the same depth as philosophical speculation, only in a different way, with a different discipline, and with other symbols. Great poetry is rich with philosophical, and especially with metaphysical thought and so are many paintings and sculptures. In every great artist's soul is the struggle for the meaning of human existence. When art becomes its own end and loses the power of transcendence, when it becomes art for art's sake, it becomes sensuous, refined technique, a mere desire for "absolute" form. Even the esthetic longing remains then unfulfilled. For there is no great form that is not a window to wider vistas of life, just as there is no great culture without universal vision. When the esthetic criterion overshadows all other criteria, men become hedonistic, shallow in thought, and lose ethical directive.[2]

On the other hand, there is something of the poet in many metaphysicians. Not only have some of them written poetry and revealed poetic talent in their style, but metaphysics itself is the most "poetic" of all philosophical endeavors. Though it demands logical and technical training like any scholarly discipline, it reaches into spheres where the merely analytical talent would fail; though dealing with abstractions, it fills them with meaning symbolic of form, order, and cosmos. There is a peculiar beauty in great systems of speculation whatever we may think about their content; ideas there interact, and bear and support each other like pillars and arches in a cathedral.

4. Metaphysics and Science

At the turn of the nineteenth century men hoped that science would take the place of all the earlier attempts to understand the nature of being. This confidence sprang from the reliability of the quantitative method and its stupendous results in the

---

[2] See in this connection the books by Pitirim A. Sorokin, especially his *Social and Cultural Dynamics* (4 vols., New York, 1937–1941). For further elaboration of the affinity between art and metaphysics see Robert Ulich, *Conditions of Civilized Living* (New York, 1946, Chapter V, "Art"). See also Chapter IX of this book.

realms of matter. But the deepest questions of man are beyond measurement and scientific laws. The scholar who believes that through science alone he can answer all the problems of man has either a limited view of the problems of humanity, or he transgresses surreptitiously the method and domain of his discipline and becomes a philosopher, usually a bad one. Laymen who have lost confidence in the clergy often look for spiritual guidance and for proofs of God and immortality in so-called "scientific" books. Such books may even be welcomed by clergymen who are no longer sure of themselves and their persuasive power, but they rightly arouse the suspicion of the man of research and the critical philosopher.

The relation between science and speculative thought is, however, not merely negative. In all his speculations the philosopher must respect the scientific method and its discoveries. He may think beyond, but not against them. The self-sufficiency of metaphysicians like Spinoza and Hegel, who thought that without the laboratory they could decide on matters of nature belongs to the past.[3] This clearance of territory and refinement of scholarly conscience are due to the scientist's censorious eyes. Let us hope the give and take is mutual—each party learning from the other.

5. The Survival of Metaphysics

There is something amazing about the survival of metaphysical endeavor. Though under constant attack from the religious who are often oversuspicious of the rational, of the artists who think it is too abstract, of the scientist and the positivist philosopher who find it not sufficiently empirical and analytic, it continues to survive. Apparently no person of intelligence is exclusively religious, artistic, or scientific; he looks also for some comprehensive *explanation* of his life's cosmic background. Every one of us is, to a degree, a metaphysician. As a matter of fact, being so is the sign of a full and mature life; not being so is the sign of dullness.

[3] As an interesting example, see Spinoza's correspondence with Oldenburg. *Spinoza Opera,* ed. Carl Gebhardt (Heidelberg, Vol. IV, 1927), passim.

It is unlikely that a hundred years hence more than a few university classes in the history of science will use the original works of our present scientists. But unless our civilization goes bankrupt, people will still acquaint themselves with the great speculative systems, just as they will read the great religious documents. Apparently, there is in them a challenging search for reality which remains significant despite error and incompleteness. So let us now engage in this search.

II. THE WORLD AS POLARITY

The world appears to us as composed of contrasts which are complementary. For this reason Plato says that all true thinking must be "dialectic,"[4] aware of the fact that in every truth two seemingly opposite factors enter into unity. Since Plato every great philosopher recognized this principle in one way or another until Hegel built his whole system on the concept of the world as a process of dialectical synthesis. His onesidedness has aroused opposition, and rightly so. Yet, whenever we speak of "world" in a meaningful sense we allude, consciously or not, to a system of apparent polarities. Whether these polarities are merely methods by which the human mind tries to grasp the complexity of being, or whether they are inherent in being itself, we cannot be sure.

First Polarity: Transcendence and Being

The terms "transcendent" and "transcendence" are used here in a sense different from the similar English word "transcendental" or "transcendentalism." By the latter people generally mean "the supernatural," whereas by the term "transcendent" we wish to denote a fundamental ontological fact. So far as we can observe, nothing in the world is merely for and within itself. It reaches beyond itself and lives from and within a wider system of forces; and nothing remains at the state where it is at a particular moment. The universe is a cooperative enterprise of

---

[4] *Republic,* 511 B, 543 B; *Phaedrus,* 265 f, 276 E.

continuously self-transcending units of energy; each of them, besides constantly changing within itself, depends for its continued existence upon the possibility of working with, living on, and taking part in a wider context of forces and relationships. What we call "evolution" (intuitively envisaged by philosophers many centuries before Darwin) is but one of the many signs of the self-transcending power of the world. And when we spoke of man as a self-transcending being, or of thinking as a process of transcendence, we meant the continuation of the fundamental world process of transcendence to the level where it has acquired the capacity of self-reflection, or self-consciousness. On this level begins history, culture, "world," in the sense of a system that looks at itself.

On this level begin also the great questions: Why does all this energy not lose itself in shapelessness? Whence does it come: Why does it allow "being" and "staying" despite all "becoming"? There must be an element of order behind all these forces: the *ontos on,* or "the being of being" of Plato,[5] "the way" of Lao-tse, or the "God" of Philo and the Christian philosophers.[6] And the same sense of wonder we have for being, we should also have for becoming. For both emerge from the same inexplicable ground, one being unthinkable without the other. Yet there seems to be at several times and in several persons a different accent of interest. Whereas the conservative marvels at being, for it represents the abiding, the progressive marvels at becoming, for it represents the element of change. The contemplative Plotinus venerated the eternal "One and All," and so did the ancient theologians. Both Hegel, insofar as he is a dynamic dialectician, and the modern scientist look at the universe as an evolving power. Neither group has been able to remove the veil which hides the ground where both being and becoming interact. If we could, we would be in the center of the creation.

---

[5] *Phaedrus,* 247 E.
[6] See H. A. Wolfson, *Philo,* Vol. I (Cambridge, Mass., 1948), pp. 210 ff.

Second Polarity: Causality and Purpose, or Determinism and Freedom

Since Newton formulated the law of gravitation and its various corollaries, we have believed the material universe to be subjected to and permeated by the law of cause and effect. The material universe apparently does not know of itself. It is man who tries to find out what may move it—gravitation and electromagnetism or the latter alone—and whether it has to be understood as a unified whole or not. Even man does not know the ultimate purpose of his existence, but at least he is aware of something like planning and purpose. And this is exactly what the scientist denies the material world. He has no room for sudden changes from within, nor for miraculous intrusions from outside. If there is a creator who has had in his mind an ultimate purpose and goal for the visible cosmos, he certainly no longer interferes with the laws he has set up for the regulation of its matter. This matter is in the determinist state, even though the atoms seem to behave according to their own fashion.

Yet how could the scientist investigate nature if he did not possess a quality he cannot find in his object, a quality of purpose, reflection, thinking, planning, or whatever is connected with "mind"?

What are the possible explanations for this greatest act in creation, the emergence of life's self-consciousness through the mind of man?

Four possible hypotheses offer themselves.

a. Reflection, or mind, can be interpreted dualistically as the result of a spiritual force which is totally different from matter, a divine creative principle, part of God or emanating from God, the abiding element in the flux of things, appearing in man as his immortal soul. This theory, in various forms, has been accepted by the higher religions and, to a degree, the idealistic philosophies.

b. In contrast to this dualistic-spiritualistic theory is the materialistic-monistic hypothesis, according to which reflection, or mind, is but a result of natural selection among highly advanced organisms. There is no reason to assume anything but a biological cause.

Between these two contradictory theses stand two of a more compromising nature.

c. Reflection, or mind, emerges at a certain stage of the natural evolution, showing its first signs in the behavior of animals and coming to full flower in man, but being itself of an intellectual quality which cannot be explained by any reference to physical processes alone.

d. Reflection, or mind, emerges at a certain stage of the natural evolution, but nature, or life, is falsely conceived if interpreted as of merely "material" and "deterministic" nature. Instead, nature, or life, must be understood in a cosmic sense, as an immensely complex unity. The concepts of "mind" and "matter" are but two terms by which the human intellect (inadequate to the task of comprehending the whole in its essence) expresses the modes in which the world appears to human understanding.

There are unsolved and perhaps forever insoluble problems in each of the four theories. The dualistic hypothesis can only by most artificial means explain the interrelation between mind and matter. The materialist-monistic cannot tell us how matter produces reflection. The third hypothesis, mixing dualism and naturalist evolutionism, raises the problems inherent in both without answering them, but it holds the door open for the evolutionary doctrine while, at the same time, saving the genuineness of mind. The fourth hypothesis, which we might call the cosmic, shifts the whole bundle of problems back into the concept of "animated nature." Nature, for this theory, is but a term for the inexplicable psychophysical unity of life.

In view of our theory of man as a participant in the whole of the creation we believe that the fourth, or cosmic view is the most plausible. In its physical origin and operation the human mind depends on the conditions and laws of the material universe. A man without brain cannot think, but the brain alone does not explain the thinking and its products. When life, at a particular stage of its evolution, developed in man the power of reflection, it was nevertheless life, and it was man; in other words, it was in nature that it occurred. But having reached this level of evolution, nature is no longer exclusively "matter" which merely follows scientific laws (which today, anyhow, have to be understood as statistical generalizations rather than as pronouncements of inherent necessity).

There is no need for "super-naturalism," but there is need for a cosmic view of nature in which the scientist's approach, correct in regard to his special purposes, no longer excludes the humanist's aspect of mind.

To a degree, the whole question is, as so often, one of names. If someone insists that nature is only in the scientist's laboratory and vocabulary, and that everything which, at least so far, eludes his method, is "beyond" nature, or "supra-natural," he cannot be forbidden to do so. But this tacit permission does not imply that with the use of the term "supra-naturalism" he acquires the right to offer as "revelations" all kinds of explanations which contradict well-established evidence.

The main point is to understand that with the evolutionary development of mind a chain of events is started within the universe which unreflective nature itself does not initiate. What we call "freedom"—this most noble characteristic of reflection— is neither outside nor against nature, but it brings to fruition potentialities within nature beyond the power of matter in its unconscious state. The farmer who changes the crop in his field, the engineer who builds a machine, the statesman who organizes physical and human resources, are none of them free to change or escape the laws of material causality. But each of them has the chance to assemble new aggregates of causality. In them nature becomes culture, willing is disciplined, and the struggle for survival goes on within a framework of civilization. The highest level of these achievements is the capacity of reflecting systematically upon one's own reflections and actions—the development of intellectual and moral self-criticism. Thus, as Kant has shown in his *Critique of Pure Reason*,[7] man develops not only the sense of the theoretical, but also of the moral "ought." Both are possible only because of the distance that the reflective mind creates between that which *is,* and that which *could* or *should* be. Here lie the dignity and responsibility of man. To repeat: the moment he plants his activity in the realms of reality, he meets the causal organization of nature. He himself is within it. But he can think and choose this action or another and build a realm of mind into and over the realm of matter. Here is his sphere of reflective freedom. Man lives in both.

Yet let us admit that even with our concept of an evolutionary world we have not solved the problem of the possibility of freedom within an overarching order. How can something act freely within a closely knit system? This is the question which Kierkegaard, in his insistence on the supreme value of individuality, raises against Hegel's dialectic structure, and the question has tortured not only Kierkegaard, but the theologians and metaphysicians of all times. If the unity and final harmony of the world is one of causality then we arrive at a mechanical interpretation of the divine. God created the world as the supreme scientist. But then he was forced to let his clockwork run according to its own inner dynamic. But is this the God of religion?

Even if God can intervene, he is nevertheless described as the "Omnipotent," the "Pre-scient" and "Omni-scient," the "Provident," the unlimited and timeless "One." If these are God's attributes, why should He, at a later stage, find Himself forced to intervene? And how can man act against Him unless He has wanted him to do so from the beginning? Ultimately, the latter question leads to the concept of predestination, of the pre-elect

[7] Translated by Max Müller (London, 1881). "The Antinomy of Pure Reason," Section VIII, p. 440.

and pre-condemned, a concept which, paradoxically enough, re-sembles in many respects the mechanical-causal concept of the scientist. After a long theological history the idea of predestina-tion was elevated to the rank of central dogma by Calvin.

Predestination we call the eternal decree of God, by which He has determined in Himself what He would have to become of every individual of mankind. For they are not all created within a similar destiny; but eternal life is fore-ordained for some, and eternal damna-tion for others. Every man, therefore, being created for one or the other of these ends, we say, he is predestinated either to life or to death.[8]

There is an iron consistency in Calvin's theology. But where, under his doctrine, remains the small niche that we all would like to see preserved for human freedom and decision?

Third Polarity: Wholeness and Singleness, Time and Space

This world is innumerable things: stones, plants, animals, human beings and their instruments. Each is for itself and lives by destroying the other.

This world is also joy and suffering, hope and disappointment, kindness and cruelty, devotion and egotism, sharing and loneli-ness—it is all and even more than we find described in Ecclesiastes and the Song of Songs, in the tragedies and the lyrics of our great poets, in the painting of our painters, and in the melodies of peoples. And who has not sometimes had the feeling of being thrown into a world where living is not worthwhile?

Yet nothing is for itself. When we perceive the table before us we perceive it as being in a room, the room as being in a house, the house as in a city, and so on. Behind the needle we pick up is the universe. In the words we exchange with our children is the interest of mankind.

Except when we are in a state of despair, we realize that in and behind all the chaotic situations we may encounter there is

[8] *Institutes of the Christian Religion*, translated by John Allen (sixth American Edition, no date) Book III, Chapter XXI, V.

the continuous. Otherwise there would be no world. There would not be the recognizable "I" within the temporality of the body. There would be no scientific experiment which could predict or which could be repeated—for both predictability and repetition require a nature that has some aspects of the orderly and static. Within chaos one cannot meaningfully experiment, or try out, or develop a hypothesis. Within the sequence of our ideas and the expansion of our concepts there must be the possibility of method and system, otherwise they would be nonsense. Also, within the constant change of the shape of things there must be space and structure, for things must be able to rest, to "dwell" and to "settle."

But the continuous has the corollary of time. Whereas space reminds us of solidity, time reminds us of fluidity. It runs, moves, escapes. There is the specific moment, an ever-changing boundary we call the present. In the present lives the past, and with it all the millions of past events which are totally beyond our reach and which have left no observable trace. "Where has time gone?" we ask. Only in extreme intensity of experience, or in the state of *ekstasis* such as the unity of love or creative intuition, may we sometimes have the feeling of time "standing still."

But in the present we have also the "not yet," or the "future." "World" is not merely the present and the past; we think of it not merely as appearing and disappearing, but also as emerging. And with the emerging we somehow connect the quality of endlessness. Physicists tell us of our earth's possible heat death, but even when this earth will have disappeared, when there will no longer be the "space" of the earth, there still will be the expanding world and its future; there will still be time. Then our perished earth would be a part of the world's past, but still a part of its being. But how is this possible? Can something "be," that "was"? Can we say that there "is" nothing, when "is" denotes to us existence, and "nothing" non-existence?

Despite the apparent difference, time and space cannot be separated. The daily vocabulary of the Indo-germanic languages shows the inner unity. A river runs and flows, but so does time. A man escapes from prison, but time also escapes. The word "temporal" (*tempus:* time) in our dictionaries is synonymous with the special concept of "transitory," which comes from *transire* (to go across).

Modern physics has proved that which language has intuitively known: Space and time are no longer conceived as existing separately by themselves and apart from events.

Fourth Polarity: Energy and Form

Not only the basic intuitions but also the other intellectual operations by which thought structures the world appear to us as self-complementing contrasts.

Since the time of the Greeks, who together with the great Asiatic civilizations raised man to the state of world-consciousness, we have preferred to see life under the aspect of energy and form. The spending power of "energy" needs "form" in order to create a cosmos, and not a chaos. Every effectual energy enters into form. For Aristotle forms were the prime movers in the continual creation and recreation of the world.[9] As the goal-procuring agents or *entelechies*, forms help the energies of life to achieve their proper self-realization. And since Aristotle lived in an age when theoretical abstractions and mythology had not lost their original kinship, forms became for him something not unlike the eternal Ideas of Plato, with the difference, however, that they did not hover above, but were immanent in the world. Whereas the individual bearers of forms, such as humans, animals and trees, perish, the forms themselves are the eternal guarantors of a purposeful and orderly universe.

Once the road from particular forms of appearance to ontological principles of formation was entered, it was natural that "the soul," giving life and purpose to man, also became a form. And since the human mind likes to see diversities related to a final

[9] Metaphysics VII, 7, "I mean by form the very nature of everything and the first essence." See also VII, 8 and II, 1.

unity, there had to be a highest and purest form, a principle of principles, mover and goal combined in one, free from all vicissitudes of materiality. This, of course, was God.

More than a millennium after the flowering of Greek thought the Scholastic theologians, in their attempt to build up a Christian philosophy, naturally grasped eagerly the Aristotelian concept of soul-form and its relation to the divine creator.

The older concept of substantial forms has now changed to the scientific concept of general laws. There is for us no longer a special will and tendency in every phenomenon of life which drives it into this or that form and behavior, and a hierarchy of inherent aims ending in God as the supreme goal.[10] Despite alterations in detail, ours is the Newtonian world. Yet the basic questions which Aristotle, his teacher Plato, and the Scholastics asked about the relation between energy and form are still with us. They have entered into Christian theology with its belief in the immortal soul. But even when in everyday life we use words such as growth and decay, birth and death, or formation and deformation, of what else do we speak but energy and form and their opposites?

Fifth Polarity: Good and Evil

There is the great problem left: Why does energy turn into evil just as intensely as into good?

Most philosophers would contend that this is not an ontological problem, but one of human evaluation. Heraclitus, at the start of a long pantheistic trend in mankind's thought, is convinced that "God is all beautiful, good and just, only men call one thing unjust, the other just."[11] Consequently, good and evil are not problems of ontology.

Hobbes, among many, says: "That which is desired by man's appetite is that which he calls good," whereas evil is that which,

[10] See J. Bronowski, *The Common Sense of Science* (Harvard University Press, 1953).

[11] *Die Fragmente der Vorsokratiker,* edited by Hermann Diehls, Heracleitos, Fragm. 102.

according to man's judgment, "is the cause of aversion and hatred."[12] According to Spinoza, life as such is neither good nor evil. "We call evil that which causes sadness because it diminishes or coerces our acting power."[13]

For Origines and the Scholastics, evil is that which has fallen out of being, which is non-being, or privation.[14] Closely related to this form of argument are also the theodicies of St. Augustine and Leibniz: God is universal harmony; all that exists must contribute to the beauty of the divine world plan.[15] Evil, consequently, is a sort of defect in man's understanding, and has no reality.

Let us first agree that in *unconscious* nature, in a plant or stone, there is no good or evil; presumably there is only causality. But is *conscious* nature not also an ontological fact? The moment the first signs of reflection arise, and with it will and struggle, there also arises the conflict between fulfillment and failure. If an animal could speak, it would call good that which helps in its survival, evil that which does damage to it. This is the reaction also of most human beings. They call joy and satisfaction good, and suffering evil, for they do not like to be sick, to be frustrated, to lose their dear ones through death. If one wants to say so, this is a matter of human language and "evaluation." But it is not merely that. It is stern and cruel fact deeply embedded in reality. When we are hurt, there always is a concrete cause for it in the world as such. A stone that kills is not conscious of it, but it may nevertheless take a child away from his mother. No philosopher can dispute away the prime tragic conflict that life lives on life. Nor can he argue away the fact that the world pays for its evolution towards reflection by creating the constant clash of freedom and causality. This is a primordial or ontological fact.

---

[12] *Leviathan*, I, 6.

[13] *De Deo*, II, 4.

[14] Origines, *In Johannem* II, 7; Albertus Magnus, *Summa Theologiae*, Tract. VI, Quaestio 27; *Thomas Aquinas*, Summa Theologiae I, 49, 1; 48, 5.

[15] St. Augustine, *De Civitate Dei*, XI, 18.

Conscious life—to repeat—is not less "true" than unconscious life.*

In high stages of human development a new attitude toward good and evil emerges. Evil is not merely that which hurts me personally, but that which prevents life from growing. It is Ahriman in the Persian, and the devil in the Christian mythology. Good is not merely that which is useful for private survival, but that which is supposed to be creative in a universal sense. It is Ormazd, God, the angels and the saints. Naturally, ideas change about what is dangerous or wholesome. Yet, despite all change, all high cultures have been aware that in the spheres of good and evil man deals not only with his own wishes, but with forces at the heart of reality. But if someone insists that all that we have said here about good and evil does not belong to ontology, he may just change the names. He may substitute the term "constructive" for "good," and the term "destructive" for "evil." He may also contend that this fifth of our polarities is merely a subdivision of the fourth polarity on energy and form. For the two presuppose also their opposites, for which we can use the terms weakness and chaos. The essence remains the same, though terms such as construction and destruction, or form and chaos, may sound less subjective and consequently more deeply anchored in the world of fact than the emotionally loaded concepts of good and evil.

The more man matures, the more he acquires a pervading reverence for the totality of creation. There is no frivolous attempt to belittle the blessings of joy and the miseries of suffering, but though the latter are not welcome, they are accepted. In the Judaeo-Christian tradition we have the great symbols of Job and of Christ's cross. Man includes in his existence the painful dialectic of the world to which he belongs. Though suffering from the conflicts of life, he knows that the tragic is part of humanity, and that the greatest chance for happiness lies in living boldly with one's destiny, even when it is hard.

---

* With the acceptance of these ideas there arises also the ontological problem of truth and untruth. This has been discussed in Chapter IV on Thinking.

We naturally try to protect ourselves and those we love from defeats. But we also learn that without such experience no human person can become really adult. Thus, we must wish for our children what we do not like to wish. What more can be said about the world's polarity?

III. THE UNITY IN POLARITY

If the creation appears to us as a sum total of complementary polarities, how, we may ask, do these polarities flow together and form a universe, a cosmos, or however we may call this most gigantic of all *Gestalten* which we call the world?

In his discussion on Cosmological Ideas[16] Kant makes the statement that "in the empirical regressus of ideas no experience can be found of an absolute limit." Consequently—Kant believes —all our ideas about the world's finiteness or infinity, the real and the void, the beginning and the end of being are speculations without empirical correlates.

Yet about one essential factor of the world, its unity, Kant gives an answer. He says that "nature," or the "quantity of the world"[17] is held together by the law of causality. "The correctness of the principle of the unbroken connection of all events in the world of sense, according to unchangeable natural laws, is firmly established by the transcendental Analytik [a part of Kant's Critique] and admits of no limitation." Though perhaps with subtle variations, our modern scientists would agree with this Newtonian-Kantian interpretation of the world's unity.

But whence, Kant asks, comes the law of causality? It regulates the phenomena, but it cannot have been invented by them. A crystal, a plant, our own body are completely unconscious of the laws that work in them. Kant's answer is that "the absolute totality of the series of conditions in the world of sense"[18] is a product of our own reason. And since, despite all its wondrous qualities, our reason remains a humanly limited instrument of

16 *Loc. cit.*, p. 14.
17 *Loc. cit.*, p. 450.
18 *Loc. cit.*, p. 446.

cognition—it cannot even explain itself sufficiently—the essence of reality may forever be hidden to our eyes. Therefore we too started this chapter with the contention that an ontology in the sense of a complete theory of being will forever remain a goal to be striven for but never reached. And, as we said in the beginning, some skeptic may suspect that our polarities are not inherent in reality, but inherent only in our mind.

However, this concession does not force us to repudiate any possibility of valid conclusions concerning the relation of human reason to reality. Our concepts of the psychophysical totality of the universe and of man's participation in its ever self-transcending evolution, these and similar concepts, though partly rising from faith, possess a high degree of probability. Against the skeptic we may contend that the dialectical polarities by which we humans try to build up an image of the world's structure are signposts which point toward reality. Certainly, they do not lead us away from it. Although they are within the world of man, connected with his physical and mental structure, they have nevertheless not been erected by each man as an isolated individual—they would then be utterly unreliable—but are instruments of the power of self-reflection which itself has grown out of the creative process of the world, and is part of it. They point toward an *Order,* implicitly or explicitly recognized by every thinker for whom ideas are more than a play with words, by every artist who tries to symbolize in his work the great harmonies between sound, rhythm, form, and color, and by every experimenter who hopes that others may check his experiment and thus help to reveal the inner system in the world of things.

To use, for the sake of brevity, the medieval technical vocabulary: the philosophy presented here is not in agreement with the "nominalists" for whom human concepts are mere inventions of man, nor with the "realists" for whom the mind is the total representation of the Real because the Real itself is Mind. Or to express the same idea in the modern vocabulary, we do not belong to the skeptical schools of positivism, for which human ideas are like the figures on a chessboard moving around in describable fashion, but without anyone knowing about the place of the chessboard in the world. Nor do we belong to the idealist school which tries to solve the mind-object problem by making the mind the exclusive creator of the world.

To repeat our own position: in the world's evolutionary process the lower organisms are not capable of conscious self-transcendence. Being unconscious themselves, their universe is also unconscious. Plants, in reacting to the stimuli of light and heat, sense the creative power of the cosmos, though with the lowest degree of awareness. The higher the organism, the richer the internal experience and the greater the interchange between it and the outer world. In addition, the more highly developed organism retains in itself the basic features of the lower stages of nature. In this wonderful process of unfolding, man is, for the present, the final flowering. In him so many elements of life have assembled in so admirable an assembly that he can have a sympathetic relation to a large part of the world. The whole is not assembled in him and he commits errors. But in part at least it is reflected in his existence.

These considerations give us the right to think more optimistically about the possibility of a philosophical ontology than we have so far. We still maintain that an ontology in the sense of a complete science of the ultimate structure of the world is impossible. But at the same time we believe that a *critical* ontology and the conclusions related to it are a legitimate part of philosophy.[19] The polarities and syntheses here discussed may be not merely *human* aspects of the great wall behind which there hides reality, but modes of its self-expression. At least, they may have symbolic truth as the reflection of that Great Life the beginning and end of which we do not know, but of which we are cooperative members.

[19] See in this connection: John Wild, editor, *The Return to Reason. Essays in Realistic Philosophy* (Chicago, 1953).

IV. THE METAPHYSICS OF LEARNING AND COMMUNICATION

This comprehension of the human person and his position in the universe helps us better to understand the depth of the specific human characteristic called learning. Psychologists have given us valuable information about the observable functioning of learning. But by its very nature the science of psychology cannot answer the ultimate philosophical question: How is it possible that we can learn, teach, and communicate with each other in the spirit of understanding? Our answer is that learning represents the highest and freest form of the participation of the self, in a world whose endless growth weaves its various elements into a unified whole. Learning is possible only because there is a mutually sympathetic universe with a harmonious interrelationship between the I and the objects intended in the learning process; or because there is system, not chaos. Learning would not be possible in a situation where mind and objects, either one having its order in itself, would stand parallel to each other instead of converging. Such a world would not be a uni-versum (several turned into one) but a dichotomy. Were not the philosophers who believed in such a bilateral constellation forced to resort to such artificial theories as "psychophysical parallelism"?

In the authors of the Upanishads and the Presocratic philosophers, such as Pythagoras, we find the idea that knowledge comes from the relation of like to like. In modern philosophy we meet the idea that knowledge is an infinite process with the goal of placing the variables of experience through constant elements within "a functional coherence of data."[20] This idea of the functional coherence of data which runs through the whole history of philosophy as the prerequisite of systematic pursuit of truth receives its confirmation through our philosophy of the

[20] See Ernst Cassirer, *Philosophie der Symbolischen Formen* (Berlin, 1923–1929) Vol. II, p. 95.

self-transcendent and reflective I as a conscious participant in a sympathetic world.

V. SOME ULTIMATE QUESTIONS

As long as men have speculated they have been faced with the last and deepest of all possible polarities, the polarity of *truth versus illusion.* We find it in Plato, and in the great religions, especially in the Indian doctrine of Maya.[21] Is this world of phenomena, in which every thing passes away and changes into something else, illusion and a web of fancy? If it is, is it *only* illusion, or is the illusion tied to an ultimate truth, to reality in its essence? If there is some truth in the fancy, how deeply does the first permeate the second? How distinguish one from the other?

It may be fortunate that most men live in the naive acceptance of their environment as possessed of the character of reality. Even the Indian sage while reciting to his disciples the *Vedanta Sutra* accepted his disciples as sitting before him. Yet, on many of the deepest thinkers, whether philosophers or scientists, the problem of illusion and reality, of *Schein und Sein,* of mere appearance or of truth, has impressed itself with irresistible vigor.

But even if we believe that our senses and our reason reflect some actuality, is there a still greater world behind the humanly conceivable cosmos or universe, or behind the unity of our vision of reality? In other words, are we not in danger of mistaking the logos in which our mind moves—because terms such as cosmos or universe are logical terms—for the totality of being? Being may be greater, and even totally different from *our* universe. The world of law and order, as the astronomer sees it, may be but a part of something infinitely vast in which there is not only law and order, but also lawlessness, disorder, and chaos. Perhaps forces of this unfathomable radiate from time to time into our little cosmos. Which thinking man has not sometimes been in the grip of the fearful idea that there is not only being, but also

[21] S. Radakrishnan, *Philosophy of the Upanishads* (London, 1924).

the void, something completely different even from death, which is merely mutation, something we might call the utter Beyond?

These questions are more or less identical with speculations coming to us from the times of the Presocratic and Indian philosophers: why is there consciousness and not merely unconsciousness, or why *are* man and mind? Why did the evolution of life break the boundaries of the inorganic? Why is there something rather than the nothing?

With such questions we transcend the possibilities of human thought. There is no other way for mortal man but to search boldly for all that is and may ever be within the limits of the explorable, for only in this way may he reduce the territory of darkness. The inexplorable and unachievable of today may be tomorrow's scene of victory. But there will ever be cause for man to bow his head in humility. For the great Unknowable will always stand before him in silent majesty, exciting his endless curiosity, yet unconquerable.

CHAPTER 6

Ethics as Practical Self-Transcendence

> The greatest enterprises perish in their defeat, and even more surely in their victory. The devotion that inspired them remains an immortal example . . . for it was the foolishness of martyrdom without which man has never founded anything great and useful in the world. Cities, empires, republics rest on sacrifice.
>
> ANATOLE FRANCE on Joan of Arc

WITHIN the immense productivity and waste of life man can embrace the constructive and destructive, the meaningful and the futile, the good and the evil.

Even the pious may "struggle with his God," as the old saints used to say when they felt themselves thrown into the conflict between faith and doubt, between light and darkness. And the greater a man's responsibility, the more will he understand the tragic ordeal of King Arjuna who ordered his troops to battle, yet hated "triumph and domination, wealth and ease, thus sadly won."[1]

In spite of its long history, neither in action nor in thought has humanity been able to master the problem of good and evil. This is partly due to man's nature, but also to fallacious concepts of the ethical demand.

[1] From the *Song Celestial* (Bhagavad Gita), translated by Sir Edwin Arnold (Philadelphia, 1934).

141

I. THE FALLACIES

1. The Fallacy of Absolute Freedom

As we saw, there is in human existence an inexplicable quality which we may call "freedom," or the power of self-transcendence. It never releases man from the limitations of humanity, but it drives him at the same time to look at them with a sense of impatience. Unless man possessed this freedom, it would be meaningless to apply to him the concepts of conscience, sin, guilt, and responsibility—categories which are not willful abstractions, but the motivating forces of human civilization.

Yet honest men have called the idea of ethical responsibility an illusion. They have been overwhelmed by the sight of human bondage; they have been impressed by the scientific law of causality and its seeming contradiction to the concept of freedom; often also they have reacted to the unreal picture of the human person which teachers, preachers, and parents had conjured up before them. As children they had been brought up with falsely understood and rigid religious ideals which could only end in a sense of failure. Later they listened to so-called idealists about a world of "spirit" in comparison to which the world of "matter" was mere illusion. But, fortunately or unfortunately, the world of flesh and matter has proved to be enormously stubborn.

Both the mechanist's denial and the enthusiast's exaggeration of freedom are wrong. Man is neither a machine subject to nothing but mechanical law, nor is he a god endowed with absolute freedom. From his spirituality spring his dignity but also his mistakes, from his corporeality his beauty, but also his vulnerability. Only if he accepts the resulting tension can he live a life with high aspirations and the admission of sin and guilt, without at the same time running into neurotic despair. Ethical behavior is the recognition of freedom and non-freedom at the same time.

2. The Fallacy of Generalization

The second cause of confusion lies in the tendency to identify the good with one single concept of virtue: the Aristotelian *eudaimonia,* the old Roman *prudentia* and the Ciceronian *humanitas,* the Christian *agape* (love or charity), the *felicitas* of Thomas Aquinas, the happiness of the Enlightenment, the utility of Bentham and John Stuart Mill, the "gentleman" concept of the English, the progress ideal of the evolutionist, the well-being of modern pragmatists, the democratic way of life of the American, or the reverence for life of Goethe and Albert Schweitzer. Each of these concepts points at greatness, but in logical isolation it is either too narrow or too general. Values are not "variables" which can be kept apart from each other, but work inseparably within the total flow of human life.

No single virtue can be the total cause or end of the good; rather it must be only one of its many facets. As Christ symbolically gave evidence when he chased the moneychangers out of the temple, there may be situations in which love would not be a virtue, but a vice. Or it may be too late for prudence; nothing else might help but to grit one's teeth and go through. Joseph Conrad describes such an hour of stress in his story *The Typhoon.* The captain was the victor over the hurricane because of stubbornness, not prudence.

Another question: of what does "felicity" or "happiness," or "well being" consist? St. Thomas would say, of devotion to God; the rationalist philosophers would say, of a life devoted to reason; the pragmatist would say, of a life of successful experimentation. Or, what has to be understood by utility, and to whom should it apply? To me? To my neighbors? To my nation? To all mankind? The American democrat would give an answer different from that of a member of a feudal society. And how far should reverence for life extend? Does it mean pacifism, vegetarianism, or some kind of compromise between regard for all things existing and self-preservation?

Also, it is difficult to establish a hierarchy of virtues. The good life is not a pyramid of pleasant things, but a mode of living. For the Platonist the highest values were wisdom, fortitude, prudence, and justice. But these are abstractions difficult to concrete. Even the Bible's and St. Ambrose's beautiful triad of faith, hope, and charity is useful only if, together with it, the whole framework of Christian thought and human life is accepted. When the French revolutionaries judged every political event and idea according to the triad of equality, liberty, and fraternity to be achieved immediately and absolutely, they created tyranny, as does everything that arrogates to itself absolute supremacy. It is indicative of the logical weakness of these isolations, hierarchies, and generalizations that every age produces a new one.

This, however, does not imply that such ethical concepts are useless. They have inspired men with high ideals, have served to clarify the great in distinction from the mediocre, and, like all good categories of thought, have provided a communicable vocabulary and the possibility of meaningful articulation and contradiction. The difficulty arises when these ethical concepts lead men to think that they have exhausted the depth of the ethical problem, or when an individual is judged according to his conformity to an isolated standard.

3. The Fallacy of Conformity

Just as great as the danger arising from onesided abstractions is a mistaken concept of conformity. Also here, the positive and the negative sides are closely interconnected.

We have two general terms for all that has to do with the nature of virtue: "ethics" and "morals." Like identical concepts in other languages (e.g., the German *Sitte*) these two words have a homely origin.

"Ethics" stems from the Greek *ethos,* which originally had a concrete meaning such as "dwelling," or "habitat," or that which is customary at a specific place. The person who disturbed the peace of the community, or milked the neighbor's cow, or used secret charms against his fellows was an outlaw. Thus the term, *ethos,* soon acquired the connotation of approved behavior and was used in an abstract meaning, as theory of conduct.

"Morals" stems from the Latin *mos* or *mores* which connotes custom, social habit, or social agreement. In his philosophical work *De Fato*[2] Cicero uses *mores* in place of the Greek *ethos.* Here too the term implies something like concrete behavior in a social setting, character, moral duty, and the science of conduct. There is, however, a difference. For the more esthetically minded Greek the human ideal of perfection was the *aner kalos kai agathos,* the man of beauty and virtue, while for the more legalistic Roman it was the *vir constans et fortis,* the steadfast and brave man.

The variety of meanings implied in the terms "ethics" and "morals" have had a confusing effect. As has been shown, generically they relate to the art of living in peace with neighbors; in other words, to custom or conformity. Now custom, or conformity, is a value of the highest order. We all live with and on it. Every great culture has developed its system of right conduct. It works more effectively than all talking and educating because it moulds men not only through example and social coercion combined with punishment, but also through pleasing form, art, and participation in ritual. If there were not custom and convention, there would be no orderly society; there would be no protection; and none of us could build up the sense of security and self-respect without which man turns sooner or later to hysteria. The "social contract" of which Rousseau speaks symbolically, well knowing that it never happened as a historical event, signifies the momentous transition from a life of accident and barbarism toward a life in which man's desire for order and collaboration found support among his neighbors. Even the most sublime forms of ethics would have no chance to grow without convention, so often despised by individualists unwilling to

[2] *De Fato* I: "Quia pertinet ad mores, quod ethos illi vocant . . ."

recognize that without it they could not assert their individualism.

Yet suspicion of moral traditionalism and conformism is justified. They are the result of social conditioning, which, while keeping the great majority under discipline, can also harm the outstanding and original individual without whom a society cannot survive. In the morality of conformity speaks the multitude, and, as all that belongs to multitude, it reveals two interdependent characteristics. It is always relative to the habits prevailing in a specific society, and consequently of little universal value. All conformity contains a high degree of regionalism: "In our village one wears that kind of cloth, eats that kind of food, and attends that kind of church." One who does not agree is a "nonconformist," a "foreigner," and in danger of ostracism. Despite, or precisely because of its regionality every multitude tends to consider itself absolute.

Hence the cruelty and rigor of vulgar morality. The man who is a part of the mass does not like exceptions; he feels endangered and offended by the different or extraordinary. Once he has accepted a pattern, he would make it permanent. Incapable of transcendent imagination, he becomes the totalitarian voice of duty and discipline; being essentially insecure in his deeper self, he is arrogant. He does not know the grace of forgiveness. He enjoys slander, the stakes of heretics, and the burning of books, while better men hide their heads in shame for him. Even when awakening from illusion, he does not change his attitude. He merely burns the idols of yesterday. The Italian masses glorified Mussolini when he had the power; they did not protest the mutilation of his body when he was defeated. As long as he was successful and not yet too dangerous he was even admired by influential men in other nations. The same was the case with Hitler.

Conformity expresses itself mainly as legality with its acts of law-giving, judging, and punishing. All these functions have public character and give even the mediocre person a sense of significant participation. In the Middle Ages the burning of a heretic or a witch was a great public festival. Under such conditions, value and virtue become like money which a society coins, evaluates, and devaluates, or more precisely, value and virtue become replaced by the mere sociological category of prestige by participation. Generally, the one who has most power and success has most prestige and is most admired, though he is also most envied and most eagerly watched. But even for him it is dangerous to deviate from the norm; he can but focus it.

Thus, all ordering of human relations through custom and conformity, necessary though it is to a degree, is only a partial answer to the ethical quest. We all know it. In each of us the conflict between majority opinion and our own conscience may have arisen. Organization, adjustment, and all theories which see in them the solution of social problems, touch only the surface. When they claim to express the whole width and depth of human aspiration, they even become dangerously wrong.

What, then, is "moral" or "ethical" in the true sense of the word? In trying to answer this question we pass from the negative to the affirmative.

II. THE AFFIRMATIVE ANSWER

In the field of ethics it is easier to discover fallacies than to give positive answers. As we saw, there is not one good, but many goods, and they all pervade that mysterious totality which is human life. What is good in one instance may not be good in another. And all isolation of variables or attempts at a hierarchical structure lead to artificialities. How can we catch all these evasive phenomena into a comprehensive and persuasive structure?

If we ask the modern social psychologist he tells us that morality means the incorporation of a person into his social environment, achieved by the active understanding of reciprocal relationships and obligations to other persons. A person participates in the collective activity of increasingly wider circles, as we showed in the second chapter. He tries to come to grips with more and more complex and sometimes even contradictory demands encroaching upon his individuality; and he learns to equate his ambitions with his talent. If there is a discrepancy between his aspirations and his environment he acquiesces, or struggles without offending the rights of his neighbors. But does this take us any further than the same realm of convention with its regulating but also its depressive effects?

In addition, we would have then to admit that we will never get out of ethical relativism. For any one group would be right that has succeeded in establishing a dominant pattern of behavior, whether it consists of head hunters or producers, polygamists or monogamists, fascists, communists, or democrats. Such relativism could perhaps even defend itself on the ground that it would breed tolerance and avoid mutual hostility as well as chosen-people complexes with all its horrors. It could also point at the doubtful mythical trimmings by dint of which various cultures and religions have tried to establish the claim of exclusive revelation and righteousness before the Lord.

Here is the crux of the matter. Is it merely prejudice and arrogance for us in the present struggle of ideologies to believe in our right to defend the best in our Western tradition? Is it mere idolatry to wish to preserve its painfully acquired sense of freedom, dignity, and justice against totalitarian systems and especially when our self-defense is accompanied with the necessary degree of self-criticism and an understanding of the values in other cultures?

Here most people wait for affirmation and confirmation. Are they simpletons who should know that one system is just as good as another if it has achieved the necessary degree of power and conformity? Are they egotists looking for rationalization of their selfishness? Or are they morally entitled to believe in, and fight if necessary for their values?

To be sure, there is no philosopher's stone to prevent us from error, no recipe against our foolishness, no unfailing bridle against self-destructive passion, no complete avoidance of tragic conflict. Man's incompleteness and the power of wild forces inside and outside him must always be reckoned with. But amidst all confusing actions there is a criterion and an answer to the quest for certainty; it lies in our concept of man (Chapters III and IV). The good is that which helps a person to widen the narrowness of his ego, to cultivate his emotional and intellectual life, and to develop his rational and intellectual life in its various aspects of contemplation, intuition, and faith. We may also say that that is good which helps him to fulfill his human destiny. Whatever prevents him from doing so is evil.

With this definition of the ethical quest, are we really out of relativism? Is human self-realization, as just described, not as dependent on cultural differences as any other human activity? To a degree, it is. If relativism meant merely the admission that man depends to a high degree on his environment, physically, mentally, and morally, then we would never escape from it. The overcoming of the relativist danger of dissolving everything in indecision and irreverence cannot lie in the denial of the obvious fact that man is dependent, a creature of contingency. This denial would throw us back into the fallacy of absolute freedom, just rejected. But there is something more in human life than just actuality; there is vision, faith, and purpose. There is self-transcendence. Man is within the environment, but he also transcends it. Human destiny is not only here and there, but also beyond. Unless we have the courage to admit this, there is, indeed, no way out of the relativist position. Any one actuality which helps man and his group to survive under some set of rules is then just as good as the other.

In reality, not even the most ardent theoretical relativist believes in such a doctrine. Let us have an example.

In a scholarly discussion one of the speakers, a physician and social psychologist, defended the statement that the only rule to which the scientist has to submit is the specific system of logic and research which his culture recognizes as the most valid. This system, of course, is always relative to changes, hence everything is relative to the decent scientist.

Now we do not raise again the question where "systems" come from (though the answer to this question would also endanger the relativist position, as shown in our chapter on thinking). Nor need we here analyze what is meant by a "decent" scientist, but record further the process of the discussion. One of the discussants asked the speaker whether it was true that medicine and social psychology had progressed far enough to manipulate and arrange the variables in human conditioning so that under a certain number of definable stimuli one could make a criminal out of every child. The next question was whether, from the scientific point of view, it would not be conducive to further research if a number of healthy children were subjected to such a procedure.

"From the scientific point of view," the speaker said, "this would be a most desirable test." Whereupon the disputant asked him why he did not make this test.

Answer: "Because I would not find the children, or respectively, their parents."

The disputant's further question—"But if you found them, would you do it?"—immediately evoked the indignant response: "By God, do you think I am one of the Nazi war crime doctors who tortured human beings for so-called scientific experiments? Who would wilfully turn a child into a criminal?"

What was happening in this discussion was the denial of relativism by its defender. Unconsciously, he had always made his scientific system relative to something he apparently considered absolute, namely the human being. This human being was to him not another piece of flesh or another species of animals (with which he constantly experimented). Rather it was sacred, belonging, if one wants to say so, to a system superior to all other systems.

Making a criminal out of a man by scientific means would have meant to him not only degradation of the value and dignity of humanity, but also of science itself.

No one can define in clear scientific terms what "the nature," or "the mission," or "the destiny" of man is. Nor can any one define the "elements" of morality, as he can define the elements of a chemical compound. Yet, every one with whom we like to work, whom we consider a companion instead of an acquaintance, knows what we mean by loyalty, freedom, dignity, responsibility. These values are not merely social conventions, nor is a society which does not recognize them as good as one that does. For a cultured man such a society is evil. Our values are the speaking, or silent, symbols by which civilized people communicate with each other on a plane more important than the plane of knowledge. They are pointing toward the higher order to which life arrives when, out of its mysterious ground, it has developed the powers of reflection and conscious self-direction.

On this highest evolutionary level of self-consciousness life becomes aware also of its individualization. And it is this combination of consciousness and individualization which makes possible morality as the sense of mutual interdependence of all things living, of grateful participation in the whole of the creation, and, consequently of responsibility and reverence for oneself and all other forms of life. It is as if the individual in the state of ethical consciousness knew that in no other way could he fulfill his destiny but by regarding with love and reverence the divine ground from which he came. Man alone has the concept of God. Irrespective of whether he and others can define this concept in strictly logical and empirical terms—they certainly cannot—it is nevertheless the highest expression of life's self-awareness of its inner order.[3]

[3] In modern philosophical discussion "pragmatism" is often described, or blamed, as representative of the modern relativist attitude. No doubt, two of its chief American advocates, William James and John Dewey, often lend themselves to this interpretation. But it is not relativism in its negative aspect, in spite of all protest against the religious tradition. A profoundly religious expression of faith is in an article on "Evolution and Ethics" (*The Monist,* Vol. VIII, April, 1898, No. 3, pp. 340–341) by John Dewey. See the following words:

"There are no doubt sufficiently profound distinctions between the ethical process and the cosmic process as it existed prior to man and to the formation

We must accept the theory that in our ultimate moral decisions we are related not merely to our accidental social environment, but also to a cosmic and universal order, however dimly envisaged. Otherwise we will never be able to explain why exactly the greatest heroes of mankind—a Socrates, a Christ, a Giordano Bruno—have rebelled against their social order or the intellectual doctrines in their period. We all agree that the criminal is the type of man who is below law and convention. Therefore we consider his punishment to be right and necessary. But we are ashamed when the great prophets also are treated like criminals. We admit their right of protest, as we may reserve for ourselves the right to protest against our social order, and even against our beloved country, when we feel that they become a prison to our most sacred ideals. This right of protest, however precarious, marks the distinction between free men and a free nation, or enslaved men and a totalitarian state.

In decisive hours a person may be confronted with an imperative far stronger than the obligations of custom and legality. If you ask him for an explanation, he may speak about his "conscience," or about his "duty to God." Or he may simply say that "he owes it to himself," unconsciously revealing by these words the wonderful aspect of human life that it finds its highest

---

of human society. So far as I know, however, all of these differences are summed up in the fact that the process and the forces bound up with the cosmic have come to consciousness in man. That which was instinct in the animal is conscious impulse in man. That which was 'tendency to vary' in the animal is conscious foresight in man. That which was unconscious adaptation and survival in the animal, taking place by the 'cut and try' method until it worked itself out, is with man conscious deliberation and experimentation. That this transfer from unconsciousness to consciousness has immense importance, need hardly be argued. It is enough to say that it means the whole distinction of the moral from the unmoral. . . . I question whether the spiritual life does not get its surest and most ample guarantees when it is learned that the laws and conditions of righteousness are implicated in the working processes of the universe; when it is found that man in his conscious struggles, in his doubts, temptations, and defeats, in his aspirations and successes, is moved on and buoyed up by the forces which have developed nature; and that in this moral struggle he acts not as a mere individual but as an organ in maintaining and carrying forward the universal process."

fulfillment in dedication and devotion to the sacredness of the individual.

From an immanent or utilitarian point of view, one would regard the suffering prophets of moral progress as pathological. These men acted against their own interest—how silly! Or, briefly, the Hero as Fool. As a matter of fact, he is often told so by his contemporaries, unless there is around him the halo of war, glory, and mutual protection. For us, all explanations of the ethical are of the foreground unless they add the vertical, or inspirational line to the merely social-immanent explanation.

When a person acts out of a genuine moral impulse, he does not deliberate about social advantages, nor is he interested in moral "theories"—just as little as the artist during the act of creation is interested in esthetic theory. Moral man does not obey external authority or the whims of his ego. He is "bound to do"; yet he is in freedom. His selfness is gone, for his self has grown together with the creative forces of the world. To repeat, nowhere have the terms of self-transcendence and participation, so central in all our deliberations, so much meaning as here. For in the ethical situation the individual feels so beyond his narrow interests and so permeated by the spending power of life that he would detest himself as a traitor if he did not listen. If you wish to define it, say that he listens to life which wishes to preserve itself in its unity and integrity, and which has an inner urge towards excellence. Or say that the "Order" of which we spoke in our metaphysical chapter appears to him in its overwhelming grandeur.[4]

In general usage the terms "guilt" and "sin" are interchangeable, but it seems that "guilt" points more toward law, community, and human institutions, whereas "sin" points more toward the ultimate. It has less a psychological than a religious connotation. We constantly hear of "guilt complexes," but we hear less of sin.

---

[4] See the various works by Albert Schweitzer: For a general introduction, especially: *Albert Schweitzer, An Anthology*. Edited by Charles R. Joy. (New York and Boston, 1947).

If we heard more of sin, perhaps we would have fewer "guilt complexes" and their neurotic consequences. For the person who knows of sin also knows of his belonging to a divine order and derives inner strength from this knowledge. It makes him humble but also takes away the feeling of isolation and uprootedness which so often is the cause of emotional disorder.

In symbolic language the Psalmist says (Psalm 69):

I sink in deep mire, where there is no standing: I am come into deep waters, where the floods overflow me.

I am weary of my crying: my throat is dried. . . .

That they sit in the gate speak against me; and I was the song of the drunkards. . . .

But in the same psalm he also says:

But as for me, my prayer is unto thee, O Lord, in an acceptable time: O God, in the multitude of thy mercy hear me, in the truth of thy salvation.

Deliver me out of the mire, and let me not sin: let me be delivered from them that hate me, and out of the deep waters.

Here are united in one great synthesis the various levels of which we have been speaking: the social level of isolation: "that they sit in the gate speak against me." But this sense of insecurity and persecution is overarched by the much more powerful religious experience of sin: "I sink in the deep mire, where there is no standing." Yet in all grief there still is the sense of partaking in the divine creation. Hence there is not the neurotic situation of despair: "In the multitude of thy mercy hear me, in the truth of thy salvation."

Though the truly ethical decision, as it is intuitional in character, seems to defy the laws of deliberative logic, it is not anti-rational or a-rational. Rather it is reason's culmination if reason, as we believe, includes more than just the exercise of an intellectual apparatus. Kant's theory of knowledge, as stated in his *Critique of Pure Reason*, still exercises a great influence on the minds of thinkers. In contrast, his theory of ethics, or his

Critique of Practical Reason, is generally disregarded. No doubt, he himself has provided some ground for criticism through his interpretation of the concept of duty, or the ethical act. Many of Kant's readers believe that he intended to sever the sense of duty totally from the emotional life of a person. His real meaning was that the "ought" is not merely an emotive problem but carries with it the character of objectivity. But whatever that may be, in his system of ethics just as much as in his analysis of thought Kant reveals his genius. For what is greater than the acknowledgment by one of the most obstinate intellects that the unity with the ultimate appears not to man insofar as he thinks, but to man insofar as he acts.

There is a seeming contradiction between the critical attitude of the *Critique of Pure Reason,* and the moral philosophy of the *Practical Critique.* The first asserts the limitations to man's knowledge of the world, the second affirms the mystical identity of the two. This fact proves how overpowering the insight into the uniqueness of the ethical act must have been to Kant. Rightly he has been characterized as a thinker of the Protestant tradition. For whenever this tradition had not bogged down into the-oretical argument, it emphasized *Unmittelbarkeit,* or the imme-diacy in the relation between man and God. "For I confide"—so Martin Luther says—"neither in the pope nor in a council alone, since it is certain that they have often erred and contradicted themselves—I am held fast by the Scriptures adduced by me, and my conscience is taken captive by God's Word, and I neither can nor will revoke anything, seeing that it is not safe or right to act against conscience. God help me, Amen."[5]

But in order to prove the nature of ethics one need not refer to such an intellectually suspected field as religion.

Poor must be the person who cannot understand the essential truth in William Faulkner's story of the boy who, against the threats of his father, refuses to become his companion in barn-

[5] Luther at the Diet of Worms, 1521.

burning, though, in a childish way, he admires his heroism.[6]
There is not one moralizing word in the story. Only in a short
conversation with his father does the boy admit the inner conflict:
he would have preferred to tell the judges what he had seen.
Only, "later, twenty years later, he was to tell himself, 'If I had
said they wanted only truth, justice, he would have hit me again.' "
However, he could not stand the secret alliance with crime. So
he did the only thing he could as a helpless boy. He ran away
into a dark and unknown future.

III. CRITERIA OF ETHICAL JUDGMENT

There is danger in references to the intuitional. Not only the
great prophet, but also the eccentric and fanatic live in the consciousness of an immediate relationship to higher forces. Not
only in the boy who refuses to go through constant self-profana-
tion, but also in the growing brigand might arise the feeling that
he defends justice against injustice, the good against the evil.

Where are the criteria?

1. The Nature of Conscience

Whereas the false prophet and the destructive person reverse
the true order of things and use the appeal to higher sanction
merely for their self-aggrandizement, the truly moral man is
ready for sacrifice. This is different from throwing himself away
as we find it in the mentally sick or the desperado. In the moral
decision a person may disregard immediate profit and the superficial approval of his fellow men, not because he has lost the
desire to be happy and respected, but because the totality of his
value system rebels against an isolated temptation. If obeyed,
this temptation, rather than adding to his inner peace and self-
respect, would destroy both; for it would make him lose his
better self and sense of dignity.

We call the voice arising within us in such a situation our

---

[6] "Barn Burning," in *Collected Stories of William Faulkner* (New York,
1950).

"conscicnce," and we define "conscience" as man's inner urge to feel himself in harmony with what he considers to be the productive and uniting forces not only in his society, but in the creation as a whole.

2. Spontaneity

The idea of conscience leads naturally to the second criterion of the ethical attitude: spontaneity. Even Luther, when put before the supreme challenge, asked the Imperial Diet and the doctors of the Church for a day of meditation. Yet, in every great ethical decision the discursiveness of thinking dissolves in the power of the final impulse. Despite all tribulation which may precede, doubt suddenly disappears, and there occurs that meeting of subjective willing and objective necessity in which man achieves the highest degree of freedom. Utilitarian philosophies are not entirely incorrect in connecting the moral act with the concept of usefulness—whatever this ambiguous term may mean. But they commit the mistake of identifying the ethical decision itself with the idea and intention of utility. The truly ethical act has its value in the fact that it is not "intended" to be useful in the usual sense. It "comes"; it emerges and stands in and before man, and man obeys the "ought" and at the same time obeys himself.

It is not the ego and its emotionalism that cries for self-realization, though the emotions are deeply involved. Nor is it conceptual thinking and rationalization that finally enforce the ethical decision, though the latter can never be antirational. Rather the I is being called by its conscience, its *cum-scire,* or its "knowing itself in unity with" the Embracing.

3. The Good and the Useful

This insight reverses the current hedonistic interpretations of moral value. In academic lectures on ethics one may hear the professor stating: "Good is what I desire to desire." Such a statement is mere subjectivity, uncorrected by insight into the fact that "desiring" usually occurs within, and is responsible to a social situation. Even if one arranged an endless chain of inter-related desires, there would be no other criterion for the good than desires. But have not the desires of groups, or of whole nations, been as criminal and disastrous as those of individuals—sometimes even more?

Then one hears: "Good is that which is useful to me and at the same time useful for all." But what is meant by "all"? Further-more, is there a necessary identity between the good that is useful for all and the good that is useful for me? Has not the "all," whatever it is, often suppressed the finest aspirations in the in-dividual, and, on the other hand, has not an individual tyrant, in thinking of the useful for him, often suppressed the good and the useful for all?

All utilitarian formulas boil down to the unrealistic statement that an act is good (or right, or true) just because it seems de-sirable and useful to me and, perhaps, also to others. *In contrast, we say that an act is good not because it is useful, but it is useful because it is good.* In the ethical situation, man recognizes himself as a participant in the creative endeavor of life. He makes it richer by his constructive deed. But whether I, or even my fellow men, will immediately feel its usefulness and profit from it, may be doubtful. The ethical decision may require heroism on my part, or on the part of my whole country or generation. But despite all suffering, it releases the productive and joyful against the negative tendencies in the struggle of living. Sometime people will profit from what I have resolved to do, but I may not.[7] If this heroic concept of ethics disappears from the minds of men, then civilization also disappears, because there is no civilization without martyrdom.

4. Communion or Love

Our previous deliberations may be criticized for the fact that the terms "creative," "productive," and "good" have been in-sufficiently defined. How can we validate the good in order to

[7] See Robert Ulich, *Conditions of Civilized Living* (New York, 1946) p. 234.

differentiate it unambiguously from the not-good? Such impatience is understandable. There remains, however, the human calamity that the desire for logical definitions may lead to answers which are narrow in comparison to the width and intricacy of reality. Whoever tries to lift man out of his often tragic exposure, to give him an unfailing prescription for his conduct, and to play the redeemer, is either a simpleton or a deceiver. The essential qualities of good and evil are so much a part of the warp and woof of live that the attempt to extricate them—necessary though it is—may destroy the fibers of the thread as well as the whole texture. How often, in contemplating the life of a great person, do we ask ourselves: was it good what he did, or bad; creative or destructive? That is why at the beginning of this chapter we warned against the "fallacy of generalization."

However, in the process of this discussion we may achieve an increasing degree of certainty.

The nature and content of the ethical act could be comprehended by the term *love* to which we have already referred.

This term is used for such various purposes that it requires explanation.

a. There is love as the expression of *sexual desire,* or the physiological urge which, if unfulfilled, may lead one person into crime, another toward the heights of sublimation. Since in the plan of nature the sexual urge is the instrument of propagation, it creates in the higher forms of evolution not only the desire for self-release, but also affection. In a cultured person mere physical self-satisfaction, isolated from attachment, creates a feeling of disgust. Then the Latin expression applies: *Omne animal triste post coitum est.* Languages of developed civilizations have expressions such as: "This person has thrown himself away"—a term we do not use even if an individual has lost himself in a great, but perhaps self-destructive passion. Then we deplore, we disapprove, but we do not despise. Wherever we distinguish "eros" from merely sensual lust, we are inclined to pardon. For whereas mere lust is degradation, eros is a power. Eros can be tragic, mere lust is shame.

b. With the attachment that springs from mutual sexual desire there develops the kind of *comradeship* that we find in a good marriage. Our institution of family is based on this combination. From the family, so we often hear, the feeling of comradeship extends over into the community and the nation. This is true in the sense that a person who does not know parental love will have difficulty in joining larger social units. But, as we saw (Chapter 2), family love may be without transcending power and degenerate into a mere aggregate of selfish interests. Still more can this be the case with a big community or a modern nation. Such a nation has many ties: language, tradition, common boundaries, and, to varying degrees, also ethnic feelings. But it is far from representing the highest symbol of human community, whatever chauvinists may want us to believe.

c. Such idealization is even dangerous, for it places the nation and its competitive political interests above that for which all social organization should exist and for which it should feel responsible. This is *humanity as a whole*.

As a matter of fact, the finest forms of loving comradeship may not come from erotic or tribal relations, but from that experience which Aristotle sets above all others, friendship. It crosses the boundaries of races and nations, even when they are enemies. Wars can destroy almost everything, but they have not been able to destroy a fine man's consciousness that there is someone across the border whose sense of friendship has remained undisturbed by national and racial hatred. Bonds like these—suspect in the eyes of the many totalitarians in all our modern States—grow out of the sense of the unity of men as a result of their participation in grounds of life which are deeper than the grounds of nations. Though psychologically less intense in many people than the ties arising from sexual attachment, this sense of partnership is nevertheless included in all self-transcending love.

In the concept of humanity we have the third element of love.

Without the sense of reverence that it engenders, even eros and comradeship could not achieve their consummation. Nor is this reverence a mere numerical concept of "all men together" or a sentimental assertion of equality which makes no difference between a hero and a scoundrel. Without love, "all men together" are merely a scrambling and murderous multitude, and "all men equal" the excuse for the tyranny of mediocrity.

The true sense of humanity springs from the certainty of living in a world which is not merely a congeries of creatures and events, but a world of *communion*. Often this feeling of communion is tragic. A person bursting with creative transcendence may find himself in a hateful and uncreative environment; the wings of the mind may beat against a low roof. Another person who also feels the urge to open himself to the streams of sympathy and brotherhood may suffer from insuperable inhibitions.

One may well speculate on the truth of the suggestion that only such persons are capable of this world-embracing love who also possess a strong sexual eros, the sexual eros being near the roots of life, world-embracing communion representing the crown of the tree with its branches opening toward the skies. However we may answer this question, sexual love is our natural destiny, cosmic love our highest achievement.

IV. THE ETHICAL AND THE RATIONAL

Yet there are still uncertainties. How can we know whether our love is in unity with embracing forces or only with overwhelming desires in our own small ego? The love we feel in ourselves and others may be a subtle form of self-assertion rather than true devotion, or, to call it by a paradoxical term, "self-detached attachment."

But despite the intuitive rather than syllogistic nature of the moral act, it cannot be antirational. If our theory of the rational, or of thinking, as well as our ontology contradicted our ethical theory, our whole philosophy would split apart.

Consequently, the criteria valid for right thinking must be

applicable also to right acting. Its uniqueness, which we emphasized, cannot mean isolation from all the other functions of the world. Nothing is "unique" in the sense of being totally isolated; everything is a link in the chain of life.

In fact, for the evaluation of the ethical act there apply not only the aforementioned qualities of conscience, spontaneity, trans-utility, and communion, but at the same time the criteria of good thinking, as developed in our fourth chapter. In the act of thinking, the individual transcends the boundaries of the phenomenal self and unites intellectually with the world outside. So the moral act, though not merely of intellectual nature, is based on the freedom of transcendence. Further in the ethical act, this transcendence relates to a superior order, which renders applicable to it the second and third criteria of good thinking: transpersonal communication and universality. We could well expand Kant's famous "categorical imperative"[8] of acting to include not only the moral, but also the rational sphere and say: "Act [and think] so that the maxims of your moral willing [and your thought] be in perfect harmony with a universal system of laws."

As the fourth criterion of thinking we established the correlation between thinking and the phenomena of the world. Similarly, there always is inherent in the ethical decision the conviction that it is in harmony with the inner demands of reality. Finally, we related thinking to the concept of survival. One of the characteristics of morality is care for life in the most embracing sense of the word. There is also an astounding similarity between the ethical act and intuitional insight. Both have the character of impressive suddenness; yet they need preparation, for the unprepared mind is incapable of both the true theoretical as well as the true ethical intuition.

The old religious and philosophical wisdom becomes once

---

[8] Kant, *The Critique of Practical Reason,* Chapter I, 7. Translated by John Watson, *The Philosophy of Kant* (New Edition, Glasgow, 1927) p. 268.

more confirmed, that the *summum bonum* and the *summum verum*, the highest good and the highest truth, ultimately converge.

V. ETHICS AND THE THEORY OF MAN

If, despite all apparent differences between thinking and ethics we discover a similarity of criteria, to what degree may also our philosophical theory of man (Chapters 2 and 3) help in the understanding of the problem of values?

In a human environment that provides the possibility of sound growth of the various mental functions, there is more chance for a moral life than there is in barbaric surroundings. A person whose affective and rational life has been allowed to develop harmoniously will open himself more easily to sympathetic feelings than an unbalanced and tense individual. In simple words, a whole person may respond more readily than a split one to the wholeness of life and its productive forces.

But this wholeness of a person must not be mistaken for mere sophistication. On the contrary, sophistication may be adverse to the rise of a genuinely ethical attitude. For sophistication in the sense of intellectualism results from overemphasis of the rational compared to the other parts of human nature.

If the wholeness of the person is gone, he has lost not only in width, but also in depth and energy of inner experience. He may be most skilled in a specialized occupation, but when the moral call challenges him, he may fail to answer. This is the tragedy of all cultures in which the reflective side of man has overshadowed his other qualities. It is also the tragedy of our modern Western civilization.

The second part of our theory of man receives new light from our discussion of the ethical problem. We spoke there of the gradual maturing of the human person through ever-widening circles of experience, from the child-mother relation to the sense of humanity and the cosmic character of the world. But the tribesman who feels his unity with the tree under which he lives

and the child who saves his brother, have small orbits of experience, yet many persons who have directed great enterprises
and traveled throughout the world may be blind to the beauty
and worth of life. Again, the question is one of wholeness.
"What shall it profit a man if he shall gain the whole world and
lose his own soul?" (Mark 8: 36). Only when the best of the
child, or the purity of heart, has remained in the most experienced
man, have real excellence and the highest stage of morality been
achieved. In the eyes of the Divine and the eyes of man there
will be no qualitative difference in the virtue of the brave savior
of a single life and a Mahatma Gandhi. But whereas the first
does not change the history of nations, Mahatma Gandhi has,
and therefore there is a difference in greatness.

VI. IS THE ETHICAL ACT RELATIVE?

This carries us to the last, though already indicated, point
in our considerations on ethics. Is the ethical act relative or not?
It is both. It is relative in that it depends on the subjective values
of an individual and on his physical and cultural environment.
A child brought up in hatred and frustration will probably not
save his brother. Without the background of Indian religion and
philosophy Gandhi would not have arrived at the idea of
Satyagraha (literally, insistence on truth; or nonviolent dis-
obedience). But at the same time the ethical act is not relativistic,
for in it human existence realizes its responsibility for the
preservation of productive life. In the light of this fact it makes
no difference whether our historical anthropologists now discover
that there are, after all, certain moral codes common to all mankind. Though interesting, this is not essential. What matters is
that all, an Arabian horseman and an American flyer, a Chinese
child and a French schoolboy, a Communist worker in Russia
and a mechanic at a Ford plant, can have hours in their lives
when they no longer are Arabian or American soldiers, Chinese
or French youth, Communist or democratic workmen, but men
in whom love and responsibility suddenly burst forth with a

power beyond the contingency of cultures, nations, and political systems. Not only through truth, but also through action men can become the vessel of the ground of being, wherever they live.

If men of diverse backgrounds were not given the possibility of uniting in a common ground, there would be no humanity in the deeper sense. For by the term humanity we mean not merely the sum total of all human creatures, but a value: men overcoming the differences of languages and cultures by their sense of unity.

This consciousness of communication with the productivity of life has created one of the perennial factors in the history of cultures, namely that man lives with values, just as he lives with men and things. When people in a specific period are no longer able to feel the urge of the good, however they may interpret it— when the search for the depth of reality is lost to them, then it is the time of their decay. It makes no difference whether the civilization is poor or rich, old or young, a great empire or a little nation. Like a rotting tree, it is no longer able to resist the growth of the parasites within and around it. Only by an inner world can the outer world be mastered.

CHAPTER 7

The Dilemma of Human Organization

> Whereas the truth is that the State in which the rulers
> are most reluctant to govern is always the best and most
> quickly governed, and the State in which they are most
> eager, the worst. PLATO.

> Thou shalt have none other gods before me. Thou
> shalt not make any graven image, or any likeness of
> anything that is in heaven above . . .
> DEUTERONOMY.

1. THE AMBIGUITY OF HUMAN ORGANIZATIONS

THERE is a strange contradiction in human organization. On
the one hand it enslaves man; on the other hand, it liberates him.
On the one hand, it is the requisite of a moral life, on the other
hand, it contributes to immorality.

The family—read the plays of Strindberg—may be the abyss
of unhappiness; but it also is the foundation of healthy living.
The community may be the source of narrow conventionalism,
but it also provides the sense of belonging. His vocation may force
man into routine and rigid specialization; it also gives him
purpose and self-respect.

The ambiguity of human organizations appears clearly in our
modern financial and industrial corporations. On the one hand,
they represent the apogee of concerted efficiency, on the other
hand they have created social problems of such gravity that our
legislators have drawn up anti-trust and other regulative laws.

166

On the following pages we will deal primarily with the two most powerful institutions of Western history, Church and State. In certain periods they have almost assumed the character of deities. In his so-called *Dictatus Papae* of the year 1075 Pope Gregory VII declared the absolute supremacy of the medieval church over not only the religious, but also the social and political affairs of man.

1. The Roman Church has been founded by the Lord alone.
2. The Roman Bishop alone should be called the universal Bishop. . . .
8. He alone may wear the imperial insignia.
9. Only the Pope's feet must be kissed by all princes.
10. Only his name should be mentioned in the Churches.
12. He alone is permitted to depose emperors. . . .
18. His judgment must not be questioned; he alone may reject the judgments of all.
19. He himself must not be judged by anyone.[1]

In modern times the national State has replaced the medieval Church in the minds of many. Hegel says in his *Encyclopädie der Philosophischen Wissenschaften* (par. 535):

> The State is the self-conscious moral substance, the unification of the principles of the family and the civil community. To the sentiment of love which constitutes the unity of the family, the State adds the principle of the self-conscious and self-developing will. Thereby it receives the form of recognized universality. . . .[2]

Gregory VII could make himself believe that he pronounced his demands in the service of God, and Hegel called the State a "moral substance" because he considered it one of the ways toward the realization of the Spirit, or the ideal goods of mankind.[3] In other words, though the confusion is immanent for

---

[1] Jaffe, *Bibl. rer. Germ.*, II, 174-175, translated by author.
[2] English translation with the title: *Hegel's Philosophy of Mind*. Translated from the *Encyclopaedia of the Philosophical Sciences* by William Wallace (Oxford, 1894). The above is a free translation by the author.
[3] *Loc. cit.*, par. 553.

both, the institution was not the end but a means. Neither of the two men was a totalitarian in the modern sense. That radical consequence and at the same time perversion of the dangerous doctrine of the early philosophers of government after the Renaissance that the State be a power "which recognizes no superior above itself (*superiorem non recognoscens*) appears in the doctrines of the modern dictators.

Mussolini says:

We want to unify the nation into the sovereign State which is above all and can even be against all, because it represents the moral continuity of the nation in history.[4]

The State is one, it is an indivisible monad. The State is a citadel in which there cannot be conflicts neither of individuals nor of groups. The State controls all organizations from outside, but cannot be controlled from inside.[5]

In Hitler's insane mind the *Reich* becomes a strange medley of a sovereign State and a body of racially "pure" citizens.

No, there is only one most sacred human right, and this right is at the same time the most sacred obligation, namely: to see to it that the blood is preserved pure, so that by the preservation of the best human material a possibility is given for a more noble development of these human beings.

Thus a folkish State primarily will have to lift marriage out of the level of a permanent race degradation in order to give it the consecration of that institution which is called upon to beget images of the Lord and not deformities half man and half ape. . . .

[The folkish State] has to put the race into the center of life in general. It has to care for its preservation in purity. . . .[6]

It remained for Hitler, probably the greatest perverter of all values, to state that chauvinism was not an evil, but a virtue. And

[4] Sintesi della Lotta Politica, Aug. 7, 1924, in Mussolini, Benito, *Scritti e Discorsi* (Edizione Definitiva, Milano, 1934–1939), Vol. IV, pp. 244-245.
[5] Legge sui Rapporti Colletivi di Lavoro, Dec. 11, 1925, *loc. cit.*, Vol. V, p. 240.
[6] *Mein Kampf.* Complete and unabridged (New York, Reynal and Hitchcock, 1940), pp. 606 and 608.

the terrible question creeps sometimes into our mind whether, though defeated in the field of battle, he has not been partially victorious in the field of the mind. The chauvinists do not seem to disappear, but to increase in numbers all over the world.

II. THE ABSOLUTIST TENDENCY

There are several reasons why certain institutions such as the Church or the State can be raised to the level of absolutes.

1. Man recognizes his lonely helplessness. The community— not only physical (the State), but also spiritual (the Church)— is for him a matter of survival. In and through the community he develops purpose and self-respect; in it he sees embedded the life of his ancestors, his own life, and the future of his children. He identifies himself with its beauty, its artistic and intellectual achievements, its mountains and valleys, its cities and villages. In heightened historical dimensions, the great powers of life that protect or threaten man's individual existence also protect or threaten his institutions. Destiny, God's grace or punishment, honor or shame, victory or defeat, are over them as they are over him. Institutions may save man, but they may also demand his supreme sacrifice; they may be his blessing, they may also be his curse. So man deals with them as with superior persons. For an English-speaking person his country or even his university is "she," as the ship is for the sailor. And the leaders of such communities, especially if they are not seen in body, but through the vivified imagination, may become deities. Such were the Roman emperors, and one may wonder whether for a certain type of courtier the monarch was not even more important than his God.

2. Church and State, as all institutions of historical importance, spread their time span over the lives of many generations. Mortals go, even nations disappear, but, except in extreme historical cataclysms, institutions remain or grow again like trees on parched land. Thus they not only accumulate the labor and experience of centuries, they also acquire the prestige that

goes with tradition. No one "creates" the ethnic, economic, moral, and intellectual culture of his country, he "grows into" it like a child grows into his parents' house. High officials and priests have been not only the executors of special and elevated functions; they have been also the guardians of the heritage; from its sacredness they have received their own prestige. Pomp, cult, decorations, uniforms, academic gowns, martial music, and public games serve the more effectively as a kind of social cement as they can be connected with a nation's great memories.

3. However critical a historian may be, he cannot deny that without the Christian Church Greek-Roman culture, on which ours is based, might have vanished. Before the Church came, our Teutonic forefathers, at least in some Northern regions, engaged in ritual manslaughter as the Aztecs did in Mexico. Charlemagne's *Capitulare of Paderborn* of the year 785 forbids the Saxons on punishment of death to sacrifice human beings to the devil and evil spirits.[7] Christianity spread not only hell fire, but also the gospel of love; it took care of the souls and bodies of men, it directed their sense of beauty into meaningful art and ritual. The growing national States tamed the feudal lords, replaced revenge and force by law and consensus, banditry by diplomacy, and the slaughter of prisoners by international regulations—often broken, but at least a warning. Hegel saw not only little despots, to some of whom, despite all their defects, Europe owes part of its artistic culture. He also saw the growth of nation-states that took over many of the social and educational responsibilities that the Church had discharged in earlier times. They even added considerably more. Governments and their capitals became centers of culture. Think what France owes to its kings with their residence in Paris.

Yet from every rational and empirical point of view, institutions are not absolute. However long their lives and however great their traditions and merits, however overwhelming their impact on our lives and decisions, to a large degree their goodness or badness depends on the virtue or evil of the men who

[7] *Mon. Germ. Hist.*, Legum Sect. II, Vol. I, pp. 68 ff.

work through and within them. We deceive ourselves when we transfer the burden of responsibility from us upon them. There is some justice in the cruel fact that a people cannot suddenly declare itself free from the sins of its institutions. Willingly or unwillingly, it is responsible for their crimes as well as for their virtues. Our language misleads us when it says: "The government (or this business company) has decided." For neither a government, nor a company, nor any other institution decides as such; only human beings decide. Consequently, they, and nothing else, are responsible.

Furthermore, when seen from a historical perspective, how transient and perishable have been those institutions which felt themselves most absolute and thus became severed from the mutuality, judgment, and self-correction on which all healthy life depends. Self-reliance is a necessity; self-deification is suicide.

The end of Gregory's church was utter dependence upon the kings of France, the "Babylonian captivity" at Avignon, the schism, and the Reformation. Still more than it is a cemetery of ecclesiastical absolutes, history is a cemetery of great empires, from the Babylonian to our modern realms. The artificial creations of Mussolini and Hitler sank into dust after a life shorter than that of a human being. In contrast to authoritarian regimes the governments of our democratic States have provided safeguards against the perils of absolutism. Through parliaments and other councils the citizens hope to determine who should be the rulers and how they should rule. But even the greatest democratic and cooperative effort does not guarantee immortality. No one knows whither the avenues of the future may lead. An accident caused by uncontrollable economic, political, or ideological forces may start a reaction to which wise men may respond more wisely than fools, yet still respond impotently.

III. THE IMMORALITY OF ABSOLUTISM

The claim of absoluteness on the part of institutions, as well as on the part of persons, is not only unrealistic from the practical point of view, it is also immoral because it creates false pretensions and insoluble moral conflicts. All single beings exist within the great matrix of Being and are, for this reason, not sovereign. If, misled by their importance, they consider themselves to be their own law, they act against the self-transcendent nature of all life. Only in a limited sense, indicating the right of authority of a government within its own boundaries as against the potential interference of other governments, can the concept of "sovereignty" be properly applied. Even there it carries with it the marks of the sixteenth century when the Frenchman Bodin and his contemporaries provided a juridical scheme for the rising absolutist States, naturally without the prophetic gift to foresee the different conditions of the twentieth century. Not without reason have some modern thinkers called the concept of sovereignty a "myth."

The social life of man will always be full of polarities and tensions. But whereas in a balanced society the individual has a sense of self-realization, any absolute institution suppresses this sense. There is no freedom, and since many human beings like freedom, and even fight for it, entrenched conservative elements with "vested" interests will call to their help even the most obsolete traditions to obviate change. They will profess faiths and opinions in which they themselves do not really believe. And in order to silence the censure of reason and conscience, they will resort to a wealth of subtle stratagems. They will become hypocrites.

"Right or wrong, it is my Church." "Right or wrong, it is my country." "The man is unjustly persecuted, but how does it help him if I expose myself?" "I do not like this business practice, but if I do not use this opportunity, my competitor will defeat me. After all, I have to protect my company's interests." By sly transfer of responsibility one attributes to the institution qualities which lift it above all human morality. But whereas man can delegate and divide labor, administration, and even research, there is one thing he cannot delegate without surrender of self, namely his moral and intellectual integrity.

Thus in every complex society there arises double morality, the most evil of all menaces to the good life. Actions we never would pardon if they were done in an individual's private interest are considered necessary or even heroic if they are done in the interest of the institution. Then theft, espionage, treason, and murder are no longer called what they are; they are even glorified.

There is, from an ethical point of view, hardly anything more disturbing than to read in one of the greatest documents of mankind, Plato's *Republic,* the unembarrassed assertion that the ordinary citizen should be punished when uttering falsehood, whereas the governors should be allowed to lie in the interest of the State.[8] This assertion has at least the merit of candor, for there has been no State, nor any other great institution which would not have allowed—even asked—its representatives to do in its interest what they would never be allowed to do for their own advantage. The higher one's eye turns toward the summits of power, the more it discovers the precipices of crime. The greater the success, however dubious, the higher is the praise. Every Christian capital is proud of monuments in honor of men whom Christ would not have forgiven, though he forgave all other kinds of sinners. The youth of the nation receive instruction in the Christian religion, but are at the same time told to venerate generals who have invaded foreign territories and shot down "rebellious" colonials, churchmen who have started crusades against "infidels" who were better Christians, and men of business who stole foreign property.

But whereas in earlier times ecclesiastical and political imperialisms could parade as sacred authorities before an ignorant populace echoing faithfully the phrases coming from above, or helplessly gnashing their teeth, modern democracy has changed "subjects" into "citizens," and our modern means of information

[8] *The Republic,* Book III. "Then if any one at all is to have the privilege of lying, the rulers of the State should be the persons; and they, in their dealings either with enemies or with their own citizens, may be allowed to lie for the public good" (*The Works of Plato,* translated by B. Jowett, The Dial Press, New York, Vol. II, p. 89).

have made many of these citizens critical and inclined to draw undesirable comparisons. Thus we have the paradoxical fact that with the increase in public enlightenment there also increases the machinery to undo its results by reckless propaganda, indoctrination, and political persecution.

This, however, is an impossible task for three reasons. First, in the long run one cannot work with people who have lost confidence in what they are told and no longer trust their own and other's judgment—who, in other words, are demoralized. Second, from continual conjuring up the evils that may come from hostile forces one continues to produce these evils not only in the enemy, but also in oneself. Third, preventing free discussion of ideas is an invitation to ignorance, and ignorance is self-destruction.

Yet this insight into the workshop of human history seems to be difficult to learn, and still more difficult to apply. Certain— often the most influential—parts of the population appear to be more afraid of controversy than of death. This is partly the result of insecurity. The arguments, and perhaps also the potential physical power, of the enemy may be so frightening that it is advisable to silence him while there is still time. But whereas one can silence people, it is difficult to silence thought. Even our modern revolutions, which to a large degree have grown out of the people's rebellion against the suppression of intellectual freedom, imitate the old rulers immediately after success. The fight for a new truth becomes the fight for a new untruth. Only in spirals does mankind climb out of darkness.

Involvement in politics changes especially the role of education. The more the traditional unity and community of standards disintegrates, the more education loses the authority that comes from being a trustee of mankind's conscience and succumbs to alien influences. Certainly, no human institution is free from the surrounding powers. Thus education, like every other social organism owes its support to the fact that it in turn supports prevailing social and religious doctrines. But it is a matter of degree. When youngsters no longer believe their teachers, while their parents believe nothing (which is as dangerous as believing everything) then there is a cancer in the body of society. Everyone with a clear sense of values knows that, whereas propaganda works for the profit of those who pay for it, education should be for the welfare, freedom, and continuous self-transcendence of man. We say that we do not wish "to fall prey to propaganda," but—at least so far—we do not use the same phrase in relation to education. The advent of this day would be the doom of Western society; the apocalyptic beast of propaganda will then devour both its shepherds and its sheep.

IV. THE WAY OUT

In this time of bewilderment, with terms such as "crisis," "anxiety," and "end of an era" so much more in vogue than the older terms of "growth" and "progress," what can we do?

First, let us be realistic. If, in the dialectical nature of life, we want to have the advantages of organization and of institutions, we will also have to cope with the disadvantages. Whether our organizations, especially our Churches and States, will lead us toward greater freedom and a world-embracing outlook, or become more and more totalitarian, will depend on the degree to which the human person is able to assert his self-transcending quality not only for and above, but even against the biggest institutions. There is a remarkable sentence in the writings of the late Felix Adler, one of the finest American thinkers and founder of the Ethical Culture Society, a man whose works are remembered by far too few.

. . . we should acquire the habit of looking upon the immediate ends as instrumental, and keep in view the supreme end which they in turn are to serve, and we should beware of what I have called the fallacy of provisionalism—that of supposing that we are at liberty to provide for the lower immediate necessities first, leaving the higher and the highest needs to be attended to later on.[9]

Instead of speaking of the "self-transcending," or "spiritual," or "ethical" quality of man, one could say that above all rights

[9] *An Ethical Philosophy of Life* (New York, 1946), p. 229.

of, and compromises with, institutions there stand the "natural" or "inalienable" rights of man, and under their guidance anything should be denied that encroaches upon the reason and conscience of decent human beings.

These concepts, which have guided the best men of the eighteenth century and the founders of this republic, can be criticized from the historical and philosophical points of view. For they are neither "natural"—they are the result of a long and painful development—nor are they "inalienable," for, as the past decades of totalitarian regimes have shown, people may not only be deprived of them, but may help voluntarily in their own self-alienation.

Yet, essentially and existentially, these concepts are true. Those agents, be they single men or whole institutions, who prevent the person from directing his better vision beyond that which exists at a particular place and time, deprive him of his true nature and render him a foreigner to himself. Insight into this truth is of the essence of all great religions. The particular merit of the eighteenth century lies in having extended it beyond religious transcendentalism into political life. The individual cannot attain his ideal end as a *corpus spirituale* unless he lives with and under a government that conceives of the whole human society as an agent that energizes the most sublime human qualities rather than fettering them. There can be no *corpus internationale*, or no United Nations, as long as the self-transcendent or ethical element in man is denied its function as the *vinculum societatis humanae*—the bond that ties men together.[10]

In connection with the group of values just referred to one could also use the term "liberal," as describing man's ambition to liberate himself for ever greater and more embracing purposes. But this term has fallen into disrepute. In intellectual circles it is identified with the "capitalist" freedom of *laissez aller* ("I can do with my business what I want"), whereas for the political investigator it hints of "subversiveness" and "fellow-traveling."

[10] *Ibid.*, pp. 323 ff.

This is dangerous. For unless we remind ourselves of the truly liberal origin of "democracy," it will become depreciated with many other of our cherished values. Among critical Europeans and Asiatics this process has already begun.

But what are these "inalienable" or "liberal" rights in actual social operation?

Briefly, they are those which make man's life worth living. They range from physical conditions to the most sublime aspirations of humanity.[11] Man must be able to feed and shelter himself ("Give us this day our daily bread"). As long as he is capable he must have a chance to work, not only in order to secure his livelihood, but also to secure his self-respect through a feeling of cooperation and contribution. He must have a chance and a stimulus to improve himself through his own efforts. Finally, he must be able to relate himself rationally and reverentially to the order of the universe on and within which he exists. If there is economic exploitation, unemployment, or slave labor, if wars— or treaties—between victorious and defeated nations uproot and transplant whole ethnic groups, forbid parents to teach their children their mother tongue and to revere and worship according to their best ideals, then the basic conditions of healthy human organization are destroyed. When these "intrinsic" values in the life of man are endangered, even under the supposed pressure of "political necessities," the result will always be degradation, unrest, and threat of war.

This is one of the few lessons to be learned from history. Yet there was no important treaty of the twentieth century by which, despite all pious phrases, this lesson was not utterly disregarded. One may ask himself whether we have really outgrown barbarism, or whether we have only organized it.

In addition to—or rather in accordance with—the concept of the "inalienable," or "liberal," or "self-transcendent" rights of man we have to renew the deeper meaning of the concept of

[11] This whole topic has been discussed in more detail in my *Conditions of Civilized Living* (Dutton and Company, 1946).

humanity. It has already been said that as long as humanity is for us nothing but the quantitative total of human beings we will never arrive at a true international order. Only this can be good for individual man that is also good for mankind, and only this can be good for mankind that is also good for individual man.

Here is one reason why we should not always blame institutions, but instead should blame ourselves if things go wrong. In our discussion of the nature of man we have shown that the circles of experience which he has to traverse toward full human maturity are now expanding beyond the older religious and national orders. But like a mountaineer who must jump over the crevasse, yet does not dare, so the risk seems to us too great. No wonder. Every step from smaller to greater units has brought about a crisis of civilization; the task before us is the most gigantic mankind has ever had to face. Our power of transcendence seems to falter here.

Is it a mere dream and abstraction to believe that "the world" might ever become our "fatherland"? Certainly, the world cannot and never should "replace" the nation. That would be sheer iconoclasm. Also, irrespective of the degree of maturity of advanced individuals, we should have no illusion about the hatred of vested interests in nations big and small against the change from nationalism to internationalism. The proof is before us every day.

There is no reason to despair. Yet the concepts of "community" for a migratory tribesman, or "nation" for some Negro groups in present Africa are mere abstractions. They are not yet felt. More immediate goals have to be reached first. But for us, the nation has become too narrow; humanity appears on the horizon. We know and feel the interdependence of peoples; we sense the distortion of humanity in the disaster of war and its presence in mutual friendships, spontaneous relief actions, and our sympathy for suppressed groups. Perhaps this sense of humanity, or these feelings from man to man irrespective of whether he comes from one or the other country, are more natural and spontaneous than the artificially inflamed national chauvinisms of modern, and the religious chauvinisms of older times. Sound patriotism is co-responsibility within the nation, sound internationalism is co-responsibility within mankind. Unless both are grounded in the conviction that everyone is "his brother's keeper," the noble sentiment of patriotism may be turned into the double morality that recommends religion for the children in schools and may even insist on practical democracy at home, but turns pale the moment one tries to materialize Christ's gospel in the colonies or on a worldwide plane. On the other hand, without the patriotic duties of neighborly life gladly fulfilled, internationalism may become a sort of escape. One may speak of "world citizenship" and "global responsibilities," but fail at one's responsibilities within the nation.

V. THE KINGDOMS OF GOD AND MAN

Many who consider the Church a supranatural or "transcendental" institution may object to placing it side by side with mundane organizations, especially the State. For since the early Middle Ages a distinction has been made between the "spiritual arm" on the one hand, and the "worldly arm" on the other hand; the first representing God, the second representing the world in all its sinfulness.

"Men," so says the bull *Unam Sanctam,* issued by Pope Boniface VIII in 1302, "live on two planes, one spiritual, the other temporal. If the temporal power errs, it must be judged by the spiritual power." This sentence could be defended if it were the mystical expression of the postulate that whatever man does should be done with the Eternal in mind. If interpreted institutionally it is, as we have already indicated in relation to another famous ecclesiastical document, unreal and artificial. As must have become clear from all we have said in this book, the whole division of life into a sphere that is specifically "religious," "transcendental," or "supranatural," and another which is "worldly," sinful, and of less importance, deprives the totality of being of its inner ethos and unity. Even through the Christian, supposedly dualistic, tradition goes the unifying insight that "all that is flows from the one divine ground"—*De divina pulchritudine esse omnium derivatur*. There may even be doubtful interests working behind the idea that "salvation" is "beyond," whereas "the world" is the devil's playground.

But if it is wrong for ecclesiastical institutions to believe that they can be more than merely one of the trustees of human conscience, standing under its judgment as much as any other human agency, so it is also wrong if political men take, so to speak, advantage of the supposed division of responsibilities and believe that they can leave the moral problem to someone else while they engage in rough and rude *Realpolitik*. One error creates the other.

There is no human vocation, however simple, which is not related to the whole. Least of all can it be the most comprehensive and responsible vocation of statecraft. With the degree of comprehensiveness and power given to, or usurped by, the modern State, or with the claim of "sovereignty," the ethical responsibility only increases. And this ethical responsibility lies in the obligation to help each single man in the development of his natural rights and moral qualities. In this respect, there can be no difference between Church and State.

That once the time would come when the "Kingdom of God" and the "Kingdom of Man" would no longer be mutually exclusive, but one, has been the dream of some of the greatest prophets of mankind. Something of it was in the idea of the Roman Empire, which the Christians called pagan. But this vision inspired also St. Augustine's interpretation of the divine plan of history. It gave courage and hope to the Pilgrims in the American wilderness, and it never has disappeared from the dream and myths of the common man. In medieval times when the peoples of Europe so often despaired of the Church, the emperors and kings were supposed to be endowed with Christ's power of healing. This was not mere superstition. Rather it expressed the longing of man that in spite of all conflict, division, and suffering in this "valley of misery," there should be a concrete symbol of divine help and justice.

Let us not deceive ourselves about one fact. In that country where longer than anywhere else God was supposed to dwell in the monarch, namely in Russia, a genuinely pious people accepted the new ideology not only because there was force, but also because there was the promise of unity between life and hope which had been lost in the old system.

In reality this was but another of the idolatries with which history is so rich. But the error was not recognized because behind it was a glimmer of truth that could hold sway over the souls of men and can still be a challenge to mankind. The truth is that man will never emerge from the shadows of darkness until both the spiritual orbit (which we may call "Church") and the temporal orbit (which we may call "the State") join in the attempt to unite human existence under the universal laws of life.

CHAPTER 8

Religion as Devotional Self-Transcendence

> A little philosophy inclineth man's mind to atheism, but depth in philosophy bringeth men's minds about to religion.
>
> FRANCIS BACON

I. THE RELIGIOUS CRISIS

IN HIS Address to the Harvard Young Men's Christian Association of 1895, "Is Life Worth Living?" William James quotes from James Thomson's poem, *The City of the Dreadful Night*[1] in order to illustrate modern man's loss of faith in God and meaning.

> The man speaks sooth, alas! the man speaks sooth;
> We have no personal life beyond the grave;
> There is no God; Fate knows nor wrath nor ruth:
> Can I find here the comfort which I crave? . . .
>
> Who is most wretched in this dolorous place?
> I think myself; yet I would rather be
> My miserable self than He, than He
> Who formed such creatures to his own disgrace. . . .

The British poet lived and wrote at about the same time that the German Friedrich Nietzsche, in the *Fröhliche Wissenschaft*,[2]

[1] *Essays on Faith and Morals,* selected by R. B. Perry (New York, 1934), p. 4.

[2] Stück 125. English translation by Thomas Common: *The Joyful Wisdom,* (London, no date).

expressed his atheism in the often quoted sentence: "God is dead." And he would not have become the most widely read and translated philosopher of his time had not his violent protest against Christianity given word to the feelings of many of his contemporaries.

Against the de-deification of the universe William James proposed his "Pragmatism" as a "mediator."

In his just-quoted address on the worth of life, and also in his "The Will to Believe," he admonishes the American student to believe in God and a supernatural world.

When I look at the religious question as it really puts itself to concrete men, and when I think of all the possibilities which both practically and theoretically it involves, then this command that we shall put a stopper on our hearts, instincts, and courage, and *wait*— acting of course meanwhile more or less as if religion were *not* true . . . this command, I say, seems to me the queerest idol ever manufactured in the philosophic cave.[3]

And, in his *Lectures on Pragmatism* William James tells his Boston audience:

So we are tangent to the wider life of things. But, just as many of the dog's and cat's ideals coincide with our ideals, and the dogs and cats have daily living proof of the fact, so we may well believe, on the proofs that religious experience affords, that higher powers exist and are at work to save the world on ideal lines similar to our own.

You see that pragmatism can be called religious, if you allow that religion can be pluralistic or merely melioristic in type. . . .[4]

Or take the statement, also from *Lectures on Pragmatism.*[5]

Our acts, our turning-places where we seem to ourselves to make ourselves and grow, are the parts of the world to which we are closest, the parts of which our knowledge is the most intimate and complete. Why should we not take them at their face value? Why may

---

[3] "The Will to Believe," in *Essays on Faith and Morals,* selected by R. B. Perry (1943), p. 60.

[4] Pragmatism, New Impression (New York, 1922), p. 300.

[5] *Ibid.,* p. 287.

they not be the actual turning-places and growing-places which they seem to be, of the world—why not the workshop of being, where we catch fact in the making, so that nowhere may the world grow in any other kind of way than this?

There is a strange ambiguity in James' attitude toward religion. On the one hand, it smacks of "Pascal's wager," or the calculating attitude we find in medieval writings such as the *Historia Naturalis* of the English scholastic Alexander Neckam. Believe in God, because "if you win in such a case, you gain eternal beatitude; if you lose, you lose nothing at all."[6]

On the other hand, the words "Our acts, our turning-places where we seem to ourselves to make ourselves and grow . . ." may indicate a profound sense of piety unless the verb "seem" is a merely decorative phrase. For they may reveal the conviction that man is not the maker of himself, the autonomous creator; he only "seems" to be. In reality, he is God's creature.

But is not the same ambiguity, only more deeply hidden than in James, also in Nietzsche, the son of a Protestant pastor? For God is not really dead for the German radical. He knows the power of the idea of God, even if it may be an illusion. He knows that man, while becoming his own law and legislator, is engaged in the greatest of all revolutions. After wresting providence from the hands of the Almighty, would he himself be sufficiently strong, disciplined, superhuman, perhaps even brutal, to develop the new morality necessary for his survival in a new world, or would he be caught by his own fearfulness, vulgarity, greed, and sentimentalism?

A new faith, so Nietzsche thought, was necessary, able to fill the yawning void of disbelief, that was not a liberal-conservative compromise, comfortable for a while but in the end fraught with disaster. For what had resulted in the past from all compromising? Disregarding Christ's essentially heroic gospel, the Christian churches had catered to the avarice of the rich, and the "slave

<hr>

[6] "The Will to Believe," *op. cit.*, p. 36.

instinct" of the poor. The end was the degeneration of modern Europe.

The feeling of uncertainty in regard to the value and validity of the Christian tradition, and of religion in general, has grown constantly. And with it has grown a fear concerning the future of human civilization.

But we cannot even try to answer whether or not this fear is justified unless we ask ourselves the question: what is the role of religion in human history?

II. RELIGION'S ROLE IN HISTORY

There will be no disagreement that religion and the institutions growing out of it have influenced the earth's population. India would be different without Buddha, China without Confucius and Lao-tse, the Arabian countries without Mohammed, the West without Jesus. But there is much disagreement as to whether these religions have made the world better. Doubts are not of recent origin. About the church there were rebellious voices in the Renaissance, even in the Middle Ages. During the period of the religious wars there appeared a pamphlet *De tribus impostoribus* (The Three Impostors),[7] which blamed Moses, Christ, and Mohammed for having deceived their followers. French writers of the eighteenth-century Enlightenment, from Voltaire on, considered the priesthood a parasitical growth. Comte de Volney, in his book *Les Ruines,* said exactly what a hundred years later many leaders of continental socialism believed, that religion was a stupefying factor, "opium for the people." The same anti-creed is preached by modern communism all over the world. Two outstanding Anglo-Saxon philosophers of today, John Dewey and Bertrand Russell, are spokesmen for a large number of modern skeptics. And the best known of the Italian

---

[7] *De Tribus Impostoribus, Anno 1598;* 2. Aufl. von Emil Weller Heilbronn, 1876. The date of this work is still a matter of controversy, but the story dates actually back to the thirteenth century. It is alluded to in the correspondence between the emperor Frederic II and Pope Gregory IX of 1239. (See *Historia Diplomatica Frederici Secundi,* V, Pars I, Paris 1857, pp. 327 ff.)

philosophers, Benedetto Croce, writes in his *Aesthetic:* "Philosophy removes from religion all reason for existing, because it substitutes itself for religion. As the science of the spirit, it looks upon religion as a phenomenon, a transitory historical fact, a psychic condition that can be surpassed. Philosophy shares the domain of knowledge with the natural sciences, with history and with art. . . . There is nothing left to allot to religion."[8] Indeed, every open-minded student of the history of religions will sometimes have difficulty in escaping a feeling of despair if—to speak only of our Western civilization—he reads about the activities at some of the most important ecclesiastical councils, the politics of ecclesiastical princes, the Inquisition, the witch trials, the religious wars, and the artificial retardation of human intelligence and welfare caused by vested churchly interests.

But much can also be said in favor of Christianity. The French historian, Ernest Renan, was denied the chair of Semitic Languages at the Sorbonne for his denial of the divinity of Christ. Nevertheless, he wrote in an essay on "The Religious Future of Modern Societies" about the Catholic Church which, in this context, was for him identical with the Christian churches as a whole:

May it please the Lord that I never appear as one who fails to recognize the grandeur of Catholicism and the part that it still will play in the battle of our poor race against darkness and evil. . . . May we guard ourselves against believing that God has forever abandoned this old church. It will again become strong like an eagle and green like a palm tree, but it is necessary that it be purified by fire, that its earthly pillars break, that it repent to have placed too much hope on this world, that it efface from its pompous basilica: *Christus regnat, Christus imperat,* and that it does not feel itself humiliated when it will occupy in the world a position great only in the eyes of the spirit.[9]

---

[8] Benedetto Croce, *Aesthetic as Science of Expression and General Linguistic,* translated by Douglas Ainslie (Second edition. London, 1922), p. 64.

[9] *L'Avenir Religieux des Sociétés Modernes* (Oeuvres Completes, Edition H. Psichari, Paris, no date), p. 271.

When Renan wrote these and similar words, he thought of several great achievements of Christianity: the replacement of crude pagan rituals by more spiritual forms of worship, the deepening of moral conscience, the refinement of art and imagination in certain parts of Europe, the organization of charitable and educational enterprises, and the spiritual unification of Europe which, to a degree at least, had been achieved during the Middle Ages. Second, and perhaps more lovingly, he thought of the piety of his mother, of the faith and kindness of some of his teachers, of the hours of deep contemplation in his own life. But has all this sufficient weight to throw the scales of the balance toward the side of religion? Perhaps most of it would have come about anyhow, out of man's natural creativeness and his desire to survive, both physically and spiritually.

Here the argument begins to reveal its dilettante character. It turns on the old question: what would have happened if something had not happened. If there had not been *this* religion, in our case the Christian, would there not have been another one? Would it have been better? If there had been no organized religion at all, what kind of expression would humanity have given to its deep interest in an embracing meaning? Also, has there been any great movement, say philosophy, statecraft, technology, has there been even any great moral striving, in the pursuit of which mankind has not often turned good into evil? Instead of blaming the religions would it not be more logical to lay the blame upon the human race, or in order to go one step further, on the polarity of life in which contrasts are so strangely mixed with each other?

Such insight into man's sinfulness and life's eternal hazards should, however, never prevent us from criticizing evil where it appears: in the greed and narrowness of the clergy, in the egotistic righteousness of the pious who are convinced that they alone will at last sit at the right hand of the Lord, in the hindering of intellectual and material progress by minds afraid of knowledge and freedom, in the arrogation by particular churches of the exclusive right of divine ministration. Nothing is more against the spirit of Christ than this self-idolatry, however much uncritical minds may be attracted by its show of certainty.

III. RELIGION AS MAN'S COMPANION

To repeat, if the problem is reduced to its fundamentals, there remains humanity with all its greatness and all its vice, desperately trying to explain itself and its relation to the universe, because this humanity is ineradicably religious. Before every religion which some today would glorify or blame for the evils in the world, there was another creed and quest for certainty. And if one religion recedes from the scene without being replaced by another and better, what fills the gap? Perhaps political chauvinism attracting the people by absolutist claims not dissimilar to the worst forms of religious intoxication, perhaps the untruth of misunderstood science, perhaps a superstition.

Somehow man's desire for connection with the transcendental asks for expression, especially when he finds himself confronted by the extraordinary, astonishing, frightening, exciting, or any other great test. The Mexican torero prays before the bullfight to St. Mary; the soldier prays before battle; and the college students before their examinations—some even pray before football! One could just as well prohibit man from breathing because he may inhale bacteria or from thinking because he may make mistakes, as to forbid him to sense reverentially his relation to the unknown powers of the world. Just as through thinking, through art, or through education, so also through religion man tries to lift himself above the chances and dangers of mere existence. But whereas in the processes of thinking he tries to achieve this goal by means of logical concepts, and whereas in art he tries to accomplish it by means of formal imagination, in religion he does it by virtue of faithful devotion.

For all these reasons it is wrong to believe that the motivation of religion lies in the desire of rulers to keep the people in timid obedience. But it is also wrong to believe that religion is primarily or inevitably of a moral nature.

Certainly, in all higher forms of religion the faithful are admonished to live according to the laws of God. This means essentially the same as living according to the laws of what is understood to be Ultimate Reality. This, in turn, means to live ethically. But the feeling of awe, or solemn wonder, can be aroused in immoral as well as in moral situations. The sacred, to which this feeling is extended, may bless or destroy. As anthropologists tell us, its pernicious power may be invoked by jealous men, as its healing power by sympathetic ones. Even today, when as a result of a long cultural development religion implies an ethical demand, it is difficult to say whether it makes man more righteous. Many of us would hesitate to decide which of our friends lead a better life, those who are interested in religion or those who are not.[10]

Was St. Augustine, who united in his thought the three main elements of our civilization, Greek, Jewish, and Roman, a religious man only *after* he had embraced Christianity, or was he perhaps always religious? Or are the repressed sexuality in the religious-mystical poetry of medieval nuns, the cruelty in Wigglesworth's *The Day of Doom*—in no way exceptional in its period —the hidden hedonism in certain concepts of paradise, and the crude materialism in certain resurrection and assumption myths, are all these modes of religious expression genuinely ethical? Nor would men such as the young Francis of Assisi, or Luther, Pascal, and Kierkegaard fit into the typical moral pattern of a modern Christian community. The more one studies them, the more one becomes convinced that it is first of all their passionate search for the meaning of life which made them sensitive to its

[10] We possess now in Aldous Huxley's *The Devils of Loudon* (New York, 1952) an impressive historical-speculative narrative of the heights of sublime heroism toward which religion may lead persons of quality. At the same time the author tells us of the abysses of cruelty, superstition, and mass hysteria into which ill-directed and irrational religious beliefs may plunge whole communities.

heights and depths and to its cosmic character. The moral impulse was secondary. Is there perhaps some sense in the nonsense of some old Russian sects which considered sin and sainthood to be interdependent? Here was the realization that deep insight often comes from sin; the nonsense lay in the idea that this insight could be fabricated artificially.

It is impossible to define precisely the reality of religion. That which remains as the lowest common denominator is the sense of something "sacred," either because it may bless or threaten, or both, or the sense of the *numinosum*, a term profoundly interpreted in Rudolph Otto's famous work on *The Idea of the Holy*.[11] This sense of the sacred or *numinosum* is one of the most insistent companions of the human soul. It serves the purpose of life's consecration which in turn helps man to assert himself amidst the dangers of his environment and thus to survive. Whenever this sense of the sacred disappears in a society, there may still remain a utilitarian or conventional morality and even a high degree of social efficiency, but the deeper appeals of creativeness are lost. Finally there comes the humiliating end.

IV. THE DOMINANT PHASES OF RELIGIOUS DEVELOPMENT

The religious sense of awe expresses itself in several dominant forms according to man's cultural evolution—in magic, in myth, and finally in the great world religions such as Brahmanism, Buddhism, Christianity, and Islam. They have grown out of the desire of the soul for unification with the Divine. The faithful surrenders to the will of God, feels His grace, His love, and perhaps His ire, in all he does; and thus he frees himself from the curse and despair of isolation.

Despite the growth of church membership in many countries the awareness of man's religious heritage seems to be fading all over the world. Ask men and women born in the nineteenth or twentieth century, even those who received religious instruction,

[11] English translation by John W. Harvey (London, fifth impression, 1928).

what is meant by "grace," "redemption," by the symbols of the cross or the "speaking in tongues," and you will receive no answer. Yet anyone who wants to explain our culture in its conscious and unconscious motivations will have to refer to its religious background. Many scholars and writers try to explain modern civilization as if we lived in a world untouched by a salient or latent respect for the religious tradition. But the most doubtful acts of modern governments are often introduced by prayer. Senators with their families go to church and take care that a photographer is in the neighborhood. Big newspapers hesitate to criticize church politics and those clergy who engage in publicity to a degree that they hardly remind one of a disciple of Christ. Even our dictatorial governments take care that the void created by the expulsion of religious associations is filled by semi-religious symbols.

One may argue that all this is a sign of the disappearance of true religion, a show behind which nothing has been left, and that this is much more pernicious than honesty and a new beginning. There remains, however, the fact of the penetration of our daily life by religious memories. And some of them may be more than mere moribund sentiments. They may be filled with a lingering, though often misled, metaphysical yearning.

The most recent form of religion in the progress of man's civilization is connected with *scholarship*. We may also use the term "science," provided it is applied in the universal meaning of search for truth and not merely in a restricted sense. The inclusion of science in the range of religious attitudes is against the prevailing tradition and probably offensive to the religious as much as to the scholarly camps. For since the times of Galileo and even earlier theologians have persecuted scientists and scientists have despised theologians.

But we do not speak here of the arrogant modesty of the so-called "research worker" who boasts of his ignorance in regard to anything of transcendent human interest—a form of renunciation that should be called intellectual self-mutilation.

Nor do we here mean the kind of scientist who believes naively in the omnipotence of his method with respect to any question man may ask. We mean rather the Galileos, the Newtons, the Faradays, the Poincarés, the Plancks, the Einsteins, who, whether formally religious or not, have pursued their efforts in the devout hope that they may help to lighten the darkness, make more transparent the veil that separates man from truth, and yet leave in him "the sensation of the mystical"—according to Einstein "the most beautiful and most profound emotion we can experience."[12] It does not matter in this respect at what result these men arrive. The spirit in which they work is what matters. The description under an old etching of the fifteenth century astronomer, Regiomontanus, describes him as the mind which, in explaining the wonders of nature, leads man closer to the wonders of God.

Indeed, seen from a wide historical perspective the disunity between religion and science is of a more recent date than the unity. For whenever there was an honest belief in God, He always was believed to be incarnated in the Real. He never was the unreal, a mere object of speculation. In terms of intensity of inner experience, He was the most empirical object of research man could imagine. The Scholastic philosophers such as Albertus Magnus and Thomas Aquinas hoped that their thinking might help to answer the quest of man not merely theologically, but in its universality, in its longing for insight into the mysteries of nature as well as the mysteries of the spirit. If there had not been this claim on the part of theology, culturally justifiable up to the end of the Middle Ages, there would have been no battle on the part of the Church against the early scientists. For they took away that which "sacred science" itself claimed to have done, and in good faith. The struggle between religion and scholarship was within the family, and such struggle is always ardent.

[12] See Lincoln Barnett, *The Universe and Dr. Einstein* (New York, 1948), p. 105; also, H. B. Phillips, "Science and Religion," *The Technological Review,* April, 1953.

But let us return to the present. Is the interest which generations of intelligent youth have increasingly shown in the natural sciences nothing but an interest in better laboratories, better machines, and a better "job"? Or are not many motivated by a wondering curiosity? The whole of truth will never be conquered, but the knowable, however dimly, may reflect that whole. And are the students of humanity concerned with nothing but an accumulation of so-called "accurate" facts; or are not the facts for them at the same time guides to the understanding of the course of action of men and nations? What, after all, is the theoretical significance of a "fact," unless it is understood as a link in the chain of cause and effect which leads us from a mysterious beginning to a mysterious end? Here again, as also in the field of philosophical research, the specific answer the scholar gives is less relevant than the desire to perceive the lasting meaning. This is no defense of modern scholars who write bad metaphysics into their biology or their history and claim to have expounded verifiable truth. We rather mean the scholar who wonders and asks new and profound questions. Once the interplay between event, question, and meaning has begun, there emerge inevitably the great problems of freedom and destiny, of right and wrong, of individuality and community, of power and love, of war and peace. And these are also the issues dealt with by religion.

But we must avoid contradicting ourselves. For the truly religious person, man does not ascend to God before God has descended to man. This means that, in the strictest sense of the term, the religious person is "pre-occupied," whereas scholarship should work without pre-fixed conceptions. To be sure, this goal will ever remain an unachievable ideal. Yet it is not less important for this reason. For without this postulate constant self-criticism and intellectual honesty, the pillars of all science, would crumble. On the other hand, are there not hours in every scholar's work when he feels himself much more the "instrument" than the "creator" of truth, when he "cannot help" marvel at the mysteries of the world, and thus be in an attitude where the "ascending" and the "descending" lines meet each other, not greatly different from the mood of those who speak of "seeking" their God?

V. THE CAUSE OF CONFLICT AND THE NECESSITY FOR RADICAL SELF-EXAMINATION

Why then, despite all the possible contributions from and to a rich religious life, is there so much unrest and confusion? In order to explain this we have to go back to certain notions discussed in our chapter on the theory of man. We there said that an individual cannot really mature unless he has grown through increasing mastery from one circle of experience to the next. When, through some disturbances, too much of childhood remains in adolescence, too much of adolescence in manhood, and too much of early manhood in older age, there is continual conflict. And since in and through humanity there speaks the individual, and since religion's history is part of man's maturation, similar conditions to those prevailing in individual psychology will prevail also in the psychological aspects of collective religious experience. Concretely, if magic is not absorbed, but still lives half frustrated and half rebellious in the later stages of psychic development, then there is no sound evolution. The same is true if mythology still pretends to convey literal truth and refuses to be turned into symbolism, and if, in consequence of that error, clergymen fight the scientists and the scientists identify the narrowness of dogmatists with all that religion has to offer. In other words, if one undeveloped mind fights the other in conversations, conferences, books, radios, newspapers, and on the various political arenas, the result can only be bewilderment. Our development towards spiritual maturity is arrested because undigested elements of the past prevent integration and synthesis. Thus, paradoxically, in its most sublime relation to himself and the world, namely in religion, man will live on the lowest level of maturity. Perhaps only politics can be compared with this state of affairs.

Just as in an individual's development, this situation can be overcome only if there is willingness to submit to a radical self-examination of the past, even if it endangers cherished beliefs of our own or of mankind's childhood.

One of the great problems of the Western world is whether Christianity is capable of developing into a religion deep enough to hold the souls of men, and at the same time open enough to support them in their free and incessant search for truth wherever it may be found. The question can also be phrased thus: Will Christianity be one of the spiritual providers and integrators behind the changing aspects of modern world civilization, or will it become a showpiece engineered by clergymen, by economic and political groups that defend their vested interests, and by the people at large because they dislike communism or want to remain within a protective fence of religious conventionality?

There is real danger that present Christianity, like the Roman cults at the end of antiquity, will be perpetuated simply because of the timid opinion that, though too old for true reform, there is nothing to take Christianity's place.

And I, who had my head with horror bound,
Said: "Master, what is this which now I hear?
What fold is this, which seems by pain so vanquished?"
And he to me: "This miserable mode
Maintain the melancholy souls of those
Who lived without an infamy or praise.

"Commingled are they with that caitiff choir
Of Angels, who have not rebellious been,
Nor faithful were to God, but were for self.
The heavens expelled them, not to be less fair;
Nor them the nethermore abyss receives,
For glory none the damned would have from them."[13]

[13] Dante, *The Divine Comedy,* Inferno III, translated by H. W. Longfellow. (Boston and New York, 1913), p. 10.

The new that finally emerges from pale conventionality is largely unexpected. For the Romans it was first a flood of Asiatic and African cults, and finally the victory of despised Christianity —for us, who can know?

Fortunately, there is today in certain groups of Protestant religious thinkers[14] more search for a new spirit than there is in many other fields of culture. In addition a closer entente grows between religious, philosophical, and scientific interests than one would have expected at the opening of the twentieth century. How far and how deep the influence of the new Protestant theology extends, it is difficult to say. Will it be strong enough to remove the intractable elements of the past and make room for new and vital growth?

There is no need to discuss in detail the ballast of intractable elements that institutionalized Christianity, like all other religious cults, has carried for centuries. First, because during the past two hundred years or more there has been so much criticism of our religious heritage that it would be redundant to repeat all the doubts and questions raised against the Christian dogma. Second, because much of that which one person considers superstitious may be sacred for another.

Nevertheless, there are the doubters, the men and women, young and old, who are not skeptics by temperament, but whose education and analysis of religion have led them away from the Christian tradition. There are the many thoughtful college students who know of science and evolution, of causality and the natural nexus of things and events, of philosophical schools, historical anthropology, and comparative religion. The intellectual conscience arising from this education refuses to be "converted." Such students will not sacrifice honesty of mind because others think we all should return to the Christian fold. The center of their attitude and thought is rational, and they have the right to demand respect.

[14] See, among others, the works by Nels F. S. Ferré, Harry Emerson Fosdick, Mordecai M. Kaplan, Reinhold Niebuhr, Paul Tillich, and Henry N. Wieman. See also Peter A. Bertocci's *Introduction to the Philosophy of Religion* (New York, 1951).

From a certain Christian point of view these people may not be the most important, for the Lord looks at the simple and humble with as much or even more favor than at the wise and particularly the half-wise. On the other hand, it is from among the relatively well trained that teachers, writers, commentators, and political readers emerge. In other words these students are the people who eventually make public opinion and are emulated.

Let us not deceive ourselves about the dilemma in which we live in regard to religion and religious education. On the one hand, there exists a deep urge for a view of life comprehensive enough to construct from the multifarious experiences of modern man a system which can give him a feeling of belonging and a hierarchy of values. On the other hand, the system of thought generally offered by our churches does not satisfy that urge, though certain intellectuals in extreme states of insecurity may suddenly embrace dogmas which they had earlier rejected. On the whole, many of our educated and half-educated contemporaries connect with their concept of the Christian tradition ideas and beliefs they consider false in the light of better and fuller knowledge. The doctrine that Christ had to die on the cross in order to assuage the wrath of his Father over the sins of Adam and Eve, is to them utterly foreign. They are unable to associate a deep significance to the idea of Trinity, the Eucharist, the resurrection of the dead, and salvation. Even such central concepts as "grace" and God's "personality" have lost their significance. Indeed, many clergymen themselves, particularly in Protestant circles, speak, when seriously questioned, of the "symbolic" meaning of Church dogma. But with few glorious exceptions, there are no denominations with the courage to give up officially the literal version of the Bible and the articles of faith; through their reticent attitude they still seem to support the fundamentalist attitude that either you believe all or you believe nothing. But our philosophic—our religious—concept of fellow man is too deep to allow a new Dante to picture Gandhi, like Virgil in the *Divina Comedia,* being stopped before the gates of Paradise. Even in enlightened Catholic circles, the older concept of exclusive salvation is disappearing. It contradicts everything we want to achieve on a global level, which is not merely "toleration," but also "respect," not merely some collectivist or imperialist "uniformity," but "unity" which acknowledges and even appreciates diversity. Any group which under the name of religion acts against these wider principles, acts against the ethos of the future. This purified ethos emerges slowly after thousands of years of moral and political struggles and is still far from accomplishment. Yet either this ethos conquers man's mind, or the human world will be conquered by tyrannies.

Even centuries ago man felt uneasy about the dilemma between the religious and the empirical. And why do we today count Dante among the poetic geniuses of mankind? Not because of his eschatology, but because of the beauty, the noble spirit, and the depth of psychological, ethical, and religious insight which radiates from his work.

Dogmatists defend Christian doctrine on the ground that men become more virtuous under the threat of eternal punishment. But the historical facts deny the efficacy of this "educational" device. If anyone did, the crusaders of the Middle Ages believed in their Church's doctrine of life here and beyond. From this belief they derived their right to wage war against the infidels. They wore the sign of the cross on their armor. But the records do not reveal that their faith prevented them from looting cities, murdering innocent people, and wrecking their own cause out of jealousy.[15] Apparently, as long as human beings are vigorous, as long as they have their passions, their ambitions and hatreds, and enjoy their mortality, they bother little about their immortality. Active discipline in kindness to mankind, response to immediate duty, training in forebearing and foreseeing, though perhaps not very powerful either, might be as good or even a

---

[15] See William of Tyrus' *History of the Crusades* (*Historia rerum in partibus transmarinis gestarum*), especially the description of the Conquest of Jerusalem (German translation by E. & R. Kausler), VIII, pp. 19 and 20.

better incentive to decent behavior than all threat of horror hereafter.

Some modern theologians defend certain obscurities in the Christian tradition by appeal to the idea of "paradoxicalness," as developed particularly by one of the profoundest European thinkers, Sören Kierkegaard. But this idea cannot help us across the difficulty. For if belief in a religion can be upheld only in paradoxical fashion—against the pressing voice of reason—then it is an artifact. True piety is the natural outgrowth of emotionally deep experience from wherever it comes: from the thinker's contemplation and the artist's sensitiveness, from man's horror of the cruelty that is in all life, and the soldier's despair about the slaughter on the battlefield, from a man's love for his wife and a mother's care for her child, from a mountaineer's admiration for the grandeur of a glacier and a gardener's delight in the beauty of his flowers. The religious sentiment may have its beginning in an intensive single experience, a shock, as it were, but in the course of time it enters into *all* experience. From a single intellectual event, it becomes a permeating mood. It shines through a person's eyes as much as it shines through his words and his deeds. There is nothing "paradoxical" about it. Therefore even the term "ecstatic," which some theologians use for characterizing the religious experience, is to be applied with caution. True religion is in the usual as well as in the unusual. It is uplifting, but at the same time grounding and mooring. To use a term that might disturb the theologian, it is even "habit-forming." If it were not all these things together, the uplifting process would lead to split and neurotic behavior.

But though the term of paradoxicalness is of no use if applied for the purpose of making an incredible dogma more creditable, there is a paradoxical, or "dialectical" experience at the bottom of all religion, because it is at the bottom of all human relations to the world. Even for the most critical empiricist, there exists the contrastful and polar nature of life, the inexplicable relation between being and non-being, the togetherness of chaos and cosmos, of death and birth, of grief and joy, of the real and the ideal, of sin and salvation. Religious man knows with the Psalmist that we "walk through the valley of the shadow of death." Far better than the shallow optimist, he recognizes the ugliness that is in the world. Yet he can also say, "I will fear no evil: for Thou art with me."

VI. WHAT WILL REMAIN OF CHRISTIANITY?

One further objection is raised from many sides with equal fervor. After all these criticisms and subtractions, what will remain of Christianity?

To this question let us first give one categorical answer. Of all religions which now are in the world, including Christianity, there will remain just as much as is compatible with the general development of reason and civilization. If, however, human civilization is for some time regressive, many beliefs which we now consider obsolete will receive new strength, for regressive civilizations are irrational and opposed to the great venture of thinking. In our day we have Christian churches whose leaders proclaim as divine truth dogmas which their predecessors of the eighteenth century would not have dared to pronounce. But in periods of escape from reason, as ours is to a degree, religion may also be persecuted. These two phenomena, the relapse of spirituality into superstition on the one hand, and hatred against religion on the other, appear as contrasts. But they are not. For whether religion sinks from former heights into magic, or whether it is looked at as an enemy, either situation reveals its defectiveness. The first state is one of senescence which retreats into the unreal—as in the superstitious cults of late Antiquity and our present fear of intellectual freedom. In the second state people idolize the foreground of life and try to run away from the transcending judgment of conscience. Both, degeneration and persecution of religion, indicate mental selfdom, of its supporters and its enemies.

One could give the radical answer that the preservation of Christianity as a distinct creed is less important than the full development of that of which it is a part—religion as such. Indeed, one may ask himself sometimes whether the time will not come when the various creeds will eventually discover what a creed is for, namely to be religious—without any further definition.

However, in mankind's history religion *as such* and a *specific* religion cannot be separated. Only through logical distillation can one have something like religion in purity; in the life of societies the essence of religion is inextricably bound to living forms within living cultures. Therefore a person reared in a Christian atmosphere may—and will, we hope—realize from the fullness of his heart the depth and greatness of, say, India's religious wisdom, but he cannot become a Hindu. The tree of religious unity can grow only if many roots hold it firmly in the soil of its environment.

Let us now point at the congeries of ideas which forms the core of Christianity, but which at the same time is of such a nature that it does not exclude an understanding of the essence of other great religions.

1. There is, first, the concept of the *world as a unity* which subsists by an ever-spending power which we may call God, or the ground, or Being, or whatever name one may choose. All these terms are but symbols of the ineffable, yet near and realizable enough to take away from man the threat of total isolation and direct his self-transcendence toward an ultimate. Religion—this is perhaps its greatest merit—has taught us the value of that which is unachievable by our human endeavor. There emerges the certainty of our participation in a great meaning, often hidden within and behind the polarities of existence, yet being the power without which there would be neither the abiding nor transient, neither the ultimate nor tentative, neither truth nor error. For even the negative in the world is but an acknowledgment of its cosmic character.

2. There is *the figure of Christ* and His sacred example as the profoundest self-expression of the Divine in our Western culture.

Symbolically speaking, every man who through the excellence and purity of his life arrays the powers of light is a savior, and for this he will be persecuted by the powers of darkness.

We must leave the historical explanation and interpretation of Christ the Messiah to the experts. As in the past, they may also in the future express diverging opinions. There are, however, certain events in the record of humanity so full of meaning that changes in our knowledge of the actual are insignificant in comparison to the depth of its message.

For us this depth lies in the polarity of Christ as the "Son of man" and the "Son of God"—a polarity meaningless from a merely positivist-logical point of view, but of immense profundity as the image of man's tension between death and birth, poverty and grandeur, temptation and victory, love and isolation, honor and derision, despair and certainty. In contemplating the life of Jesus from birth to the cross ("My God! My God! Why hast thou forsaken me!") and from the cross to the final re-unification, one reads the biography of Man—so profound and at the same time so simple that it will be one of the greatest sources of inspiration as long as humanity is permitted to exist. But the less the admixture of superstition about Christ's mission and message, and the more willing the Christian to acknowledge the divine in the prophets of other religions, the greater will be the hope for mankind's spiritual unity despite the diversity of prophetic revelations.

3. For our culture Christ has become the apostle of the *brotherhood of men* because he taught the *fatherhood of God*. Let us not forget, however, that the churches of Christ needed an unwelcome competitor, a dangerous critic, and a ruthless actor on the historical arena—the eighteenth century Enlightenment and its revolutionary movements—before they acknowledged the idea of practical and political, in addition to merely spiritual, brotherhood. In many places of the world they are not yet willing to do so. Christianity is not the only possible guide along the road toward human dignity, freedom, and mutual re-

sponsibility. What it needs is transcendent strength of humane convictions, and that can also be found elsewhere.

4. On the other hand, through Christianity—insofar as it has not been fettered by denominational arrogance—the idea of the *human community* has received a persuasive power much greater than that ever provided by the utilitarian reckoning of politicians and the theories of sociologists. It is the greatness of the Christian and of all other higher religions that in them the concept and experience of community is not of horizontal, but of vertical nature. It grows from the notion of man's coexistence in the common soil of the creation. Early Christianity would have become a milestone in the history of men if it had had no other gospel but that contained in Corinthians: "Though I speak with the tongues of men and of angels, and have not charity, I am become as sounding brass, or a tinkling cymbal."

Today, if Chrisians lived accordingly, this would be enough to revolutionize the world. But how could even the most Christian of the missionaries convince the non-European world of the spirit of Christianity when there marched, before or behind them, the armies of the conquering and colonizing nations?

5. The *agape* of the Gospel—charity, or love—is not only law, it is also *suffering*. There are many people in the world— many more than we would believe—who do not have the courage to love, because they are afraid of suffering. Living with and in others means sharing not only their joy, but also their grief. How much less able is a man to avoid disappointment and distress who includes in his self mankind as a whole, and not only one other person to whom he may be attached through immediate bonds? Christ's cross is the symbol of the millions of crosses that are erected along the roads of those who dare suffer, because they also dare love, enjoy, and participate in the light and darkness of human existence. In contrast to the gospels of withdrawal, even in contrast to the teaching of many Christians, Christ's message teaches us the courage to embrace the world with both its beauty and its thorns. But it also teaches us that

those who run away will live and die in the hell of loneliness. There is no salvation except through sacrifice. But again, in order to understand the companionship of suffering and salvation, we do not need to surround the life of Christ with Asiatic mythology taken as literal truth. Rather we need the depth of interpretation which reaches through the myth into its essence.

6. There is finally the Christian idea of the *poverty of the soul*. It has little to do with material wealth or its absence, though both extremes are equally dangerous. Rather it is an attitude of waiting openness which allows the world and its events to enter into man's soul without being distorted by his tendency to interfere and to impose himself. When this tendency prevails, then all that happens to him happens only partially and superficially; not as something that would allow insight and absorption, but as something to be used, changed, or removed as quickly as possible. We have here the alienation of man from his self and from the world that is characteristic of our technological era; the sterile busy-ness that drives man from place to place until he ends in nothing, and the adulation of efficiency, mobility, and accumulation without any knowledge whither all this moves. "New," "Different," "More," "Better," are the catchwords of the modern advertiser, and when he feels that they lose appeal, he prefers such conservative terms as "old-fashioned," "aristocratic," "imperial," or at least "royal." Finally he patches a colorful coat of arms on his democratic automobile. But whether new or old, it makes no difference—it is a sign of restlessness, constant dissatisfaction, and haste.

The Chinese of today blame Lao-tse's recommendation of quiet listening to the universal wave as responsible for the long slumber and backwardness of their country. This criticism sounds like a repetition of Western man's suspicion of the beatitudes in Christ's Sermon on the Mount. But neither He nor Lao-tse recommended passivity or quietism. Rather they advocated the contemplative attitude without which activity degenerates into mere meddling and flurry. The human soul must first be poor

—aware of its ignorance and open to God—before it is ready to receive, able to understand, and free to join productively the creative forces of the universe.

VII. THE PROBLEM OF CULT

There emerges a further problem that has to be faced realistically. What will be the role of *cult?* On the one hand, the Christian cult, like the cults of other religions, contains a large admixture of magic and mythology. On the other hand, can religious ideas be understood and followed without cult? By depriving religion of this element, would we not destroy its vitality?

It is commonly stated that cult and worship are the characteristics of all religions. If this statement is meant to imply that there can be no religion without cult, it is wrong. A considerable number of men with profound spiritual experiences were never servants of a cult; yet they were as much concerned with man's relation to God and the universe as the servants of official churches. Poets of many countries have uttered the deepest thoughts about religion that their language contains but have had no need for cult. In the United States, Ralph Waldo Emerson felt a deep aversion to any formal fixation and cultic expression of belief. Yet he belongs at least as much in the ranks of the religious as the Protestant ministers who made his life difficult.

Thus the problem of cult appears to be not of primary, but of secondary importance. Yet it is a phenomenon of such great historical, social, intellectual, and educational significance that those are right who combine their interest in a religion with an interest in its cult.

1. Cult is of *historical* significance, because in the fight for survival that is going on in the intellectual as much as in the physical arena only those movements can maintain themselves against others which have acquired visible and somewhat stable forms of self-expression. The ideas they stand for must be clearly

discernible and different from others, else they would be lost among their competitors. They must also arouse the sense of community and common action, which is connected with cult and worship. One may doubt whether the teaching of Christ has gained in simple spiritual depth by the disputes of theologians and the diplomacy of councils, by the development of cults and the persecution of other rituals. But without all these binding forms and formulas Christ would probably have been but another Jewish prophet, and his followers would have become lost in the many oriental sects which swept the Roman Empire.

2. The problem of cult is of *social* significance, because every spiritual movement needs strengthening through mutual friendship, support, and encouragement. Cult gives the faithful the feeling not only of social community but also of living in concrete nearness to the divine. Besides these specifically religious qualities ecclesiastical associations share the social characteristics of community-building which we observe in other groups. They have their festival gatherings, their nomenclature, their hierarchies, their oaths, and their examinations and admission procedures for guaranteeing the necessary standards. Only thus can they perpetuate themselves within the competition of interests to which man is exposed.

3. Like all other collective enterprises religion has to reckon with the whole gamut of *human intelligence,* from dullness and need of the palpable to the extremes of subtle abstraction.

How, then, can we expect that in religious life the magic stage, characteristic of lower forms of intellectual development, would have given way completely to higher forms of understanding? And by not allowing the lower stages to express themselves through religion, what would we create? We would create a vacuum into which could creep urges and desires much more dubious than rituals—which, despite the danger of superstition, have also an uplifting and purifying effect on certain groups of mankind. History shows that the taking away of transcendentalism, however primitive, often produces an idolatry of even more doubtful nature. The secular festivals created for the mob of Paris by the leaders of the French revolution, the adulation of Mussolini, Hitler, and Stalin, in our times, the deification of governments and nations we find all over the world—are they desirable substitutes for burning candles to a saint or singing the hymns of Bach? Even if there is no saint to listen, there may be some saintliness in the soul of the worshipper.

4. These factors are of the greatest import for the *educational* future of mankind. A part of good education is transmission of meanings, and this needs adequate and cogent symbols, in religion as everywhere else. High levels of culture are products of long and slow development. The most talented individual has to go through stages of immaturity, and he reveals their traces even in manhood.

Under these circumstances, can and should organized religion be the only social enterprise addressed exclusively to the highest and most abstract levels of culture—though knowing well that large parts of mankind would be deprived from communication? Christian missionaries and teachers, in their zeal for saving souls, have grafted Christianity on primitive and polytheistic cults. Critics assert that thus they have contributed more to the cultural instability than to the spiritual advancement of their flocks. Others contend the contrary. Who knows?

All these considerations compel us to acknowledge diverse levels of cult, rising from low to high forms of symbolism, as culturally conditioned manifestations of religion. Nothing, however, would be more misleading than to interpret this insight as an excuse for churches which, all over the world, still preserve lower levels of cult, culture, and knowledge where there are already signs of progressive awakening. One cannot keep such a central area as religion on a plain below the other areas of intellectual activity without in the long run doing harm to both religion and social progress. Courageous policy in this respect may involve loss of control and the entering into a period of change and new decisions. On the other hand, lack of such courage involves loss of respect and causes rebellion against anything religious, as for almost two hundred years we have seen in various parts of the world.

Spain and Italy, between the fourteenth and the seventeenth centuries, were cultural leaders of the world. Is it due merely to political and economic conditions that Spain today has about half its people illiterate and that, according to the *Encyclopedia Britannica Yearbook of 1950,* in southern Italy "the great majority" of the people are still illiterate? Or may it also have to do with the grip which reactionary forms of religion have had on these peoples? In addition, may perhaps the lack of religious maturity have influenced their political and economic initiative? Even skeptical physicians agree today that the emotional excitement of a pilgrimage to a holy shrine may cure illness. But, say in the domain of the Madonna of Guadeloupe, might it not have improved the health of the population still more if belief in miracles had been gradually replaced by a religion which appealed also to the free use of experimental reason? In this way the revolutionary conflicts between State and Church in Mexico might have been avoided to the advantage of both. No wonder that political groups which explain social retardation with reference to a religious organization pour out the baby with the bath water and fight not only the institution, but religion as such. At the places of pilgrimage and miracle, there appear fewer and fewer people who have enjoyed a good education.

The two errors of irrationalism and of materialist revolution against anything religious have always worked hand in hand. Culture thus goes in circles and finally dies in the morasses of spiritual lethargy, on the battlefields of civil wars, or the concentration camps of dictators.

Certainly, the lack of health in religion is not alone accountable for social unrest. No one can say whether its beginning lies more in the religious, or more in the intellectual, political, and economic fields. However, the companionship exists. If misguided itself, religion misguides everywhere; if mature, it is man's best adviser in his struggle for better life.

VIII. THE RELIGION OF SELF-TRANSCENDENT PARTICIPATION AND THE WONDER OF ASSURANCE

Whatever we said about the differences of cult and the inevitable individuality of religious expressions, they are of value only if there still flows through them the depth and universality of genuine religious experience. If the religious spirit that should unite mankind before the divine is lacking, an individual religion is of no worth.

So let us now, in form of a final integration, ask for the fundamentals. Our outline of the religious evolution has shown that the sacred that lies behind all religious moods is not dependent on a specific image. It may be imagined in the form of a tree ghost, an idol, a host of gods, a personal God, or the final truth and unity of reality.

If so, whence does the feeling of the sacred itself spring? It emerges the moment man realizes reverentially his intimate dependence on a universal power. Whether he seeks to conjure or to understand it, his concern is for his physical and mental survival in a world to which he belongs but which is infinitely greater than his own strength and comprehension. Every new stage in religious sentiment is a step away from lonely dread and aggressiveness toward awe and reverence in a universal sense, or a step towards freedom. The commandment, "fear thy God" in higher religion is different from primitive man's trembling. And the sense of cosmic wonder in the great mystic, the productive scholar, and the sensitive artist is different from the magic concepts about punishment and hell fire in a fundamentalist who believes he follows Christ, but has never understood Him.

Against the irrational remainders of magical times, as well as against the autonomous arrogance or indifference of our technological civilization, true religion creates in man a sense of grateful participation in the ever-spending and ever-radiating power of life. The capacity of reflecting upon the world, which in the analytical situation produces a sense of search and curiosity, turns in the religious situation into a feeling of belonging to, and of reverential responsibility for, the whole of the creation. This is the driving motive in Christ's Sermon on the Mount and in all the other documents which we admire as expressions of the highest religious ethics.

Religion as defined here does not run parallel or contrary to the other expressions of human culture, but interacts with them. Even in the scholar's restless mind there are moments when the sense of transcendence which drives him from object to object toward ever-distant regions, comes to rest in the assurance that there works an embracing truth and unity behind all the little truths and errors of the human mind. There is no final intellectual answer, but there is nevertheless certainty that individual search derives its single meaning from a final Meaning. He hears the wings of truth over his head, and he may bow in a feeling not less deep and religious than the prayer of the pious. There is the ever-changing finite, but there is also the abiding, out of which it appears; there are the conflicts of the foreground, but there is also the depth of the ground; there is all the cruelty and unholiness of nature, but there is also the divine unfolding. There is assurance.

The wonder of assurance expresses itself in many forms.

1. It provides the seemingly contrasting yet organic mixture of *modesty and elation* which we find among the great religious prophets and their true followers. Modesty there is because all the work and thought of man by himself are idle; elation because once the unity with the Divine is found, a superior and protecting power is felt to reign over and within the work of men. This power renders relative all the things the world values: external merit, rank, prestige, luxury, the force of arms, and the power of governments. Hence in all history the prophets have survived the kings and the inquisitors, though the kings and the inquisitors have killed the prophets. The prophets were the final judges.

2. Religious experience of high quality provides a *vision of perfection* and excellence because it sets before the imaginative

mind the picture of creative harmony, or wholeness, and of infinite beauty. The biologist may look at a flower as the result of natural events deserving further research in the laboratory. But for the same biologist the flower may become transparent, as it were, and in the piece of nature which he then sees he may admire the unimaginable grandeur of the self-manifesting cosmos. He may, then, well reflect why there is cosmos (which originally means "order") and not chaos and whether the final answer does not lead to the assumption of a creative spirit, a unifying One, or "God." In the routine of living, only "great" events arouse the sense of wonder, the "little" things are taken for granted. But what is "little" except that which man renders so by his own smallness?

Yet religious man feels, as the Bible calls it, also "the groaning of the creation," the frightening distance between all that is made and the ground that made it. In contrast to the feelings of infinity, purity, and perfection, there arises the consciousness of death, suffering, failure, and finiteness; the awareness of life's polarity which man has to accept as part of his destiny.

3. Though it is false to explain the origin and essence of religion by reference to morality, the religious consciousness creates a profound sense of *ethical responsibility*. The person who feels the grace of partaking in the spending source of life needs no supernatural event or miracle as external proof and sanction of the moral law, just as he needs no miracle for the confirmation of his faith. He feels the *mysterium creationis* and the resulting commitment to all that lives of his self, his language, his love, and even his suffering. All true self-respect engenders also respect for the neighbor, be he a man or an animal, or the earth on which we live. The lower forms of morality need props from outside, be they magic, fear of punishment, or reward. But the higher the ethical as well as the religious standards, the more the two merge into one, religion becoming the strongest urge toward the good life, and the good life the finest expression of the religious fellowship of men.

Its practical effects were to a utilitarian such as John Locke the justification of religion, though his philosophy might lead to a skeptical attitude. But the desire for practical effects should be a secondary motivation. The prime inspiration of religious man comes from his consciousness of universal participation. Hence the feeling that all that we do of good and evil is done for or against *all* humankind, and that all that happens somewhere within the wide orbit of human history, happens also to us. From a narrowly empirical view, this feeling is nonsensical. Yet nothing is more realistic than this profoundest of all insights. After the suffering of nations during the past half-century, we should have learned it by now.

4. Wherever there is a sense of the ground and the whole, there is also a *sense of law*. Therefore, in certain religions, such as the Mosaic, the sacred is almost synonymous with the lawful. Often such traditions have succumbed to the danger of mere legality. Wherever legality reigns, the spirit is in peril. Only prophets who sacrifice themselves for the Law against the laws can re-open the wells of the soul.

On the other hand, the majesty that is in law prevents religion from drifting into sentimentality. The unctuousness of many of our sermons and the mawkishness in many of our pleas are offenses to the Divine. We should not forget that one of the components of Christian philosophy was the school of the Stoics with its idea of justice, not only as a social institution, but as a derivation from "natural law." The wisdom of the Greek and Roman Stoics replaced the antiquated polytheism of the pagan heaven and paved the way for deeper religious insight. But some of us still treat God like a switchman whose main occupation is to direct or re-direct the trains of human desire. The only way to make humans and their nations mature, morally, politically, and religiously, is to tell them that either they discover the law of reality—of the Divine—and live accordingly, or they will have to pay the price for their deeds. Bullets fly according to mechanical laws, not according to prayers and wishes of mothers, however sincere. According to an old proverb, God's mills grind slowly. Therefore, while good men languish, evildoers may gather honors. Nevertheless, these evildoers distort the order of the world and produce hatred and suffering. To always believe in *individual* justice is wishful sentimentality, but not to believe in justice as an element of life is the epitome of unrealism.

5. Only when we understand law, can we understand *love*. Without law, love easily becomes indiscriminate charity, sentimentality, and lack of courage, rightly attacked by Nietzsche as an element of moral degeneration. Law and love are interdependent like authority and freedom, form and growth, conviction and tolerance. Only where law protects can love create, and only where love prevails can law protect.

Was it mere accident or because of their concept of law that the stern Stoics were the first in the pagan world to create the idea of universal human brotherhood? Christ, too, combines the gospel of love with the gospel of law. In modern literature we have the hero in Ibsen's drama, "Brand," who only after wrestling with the "God of Everlasting Right" arrives at the insight: "He is *Deus caritatis.*"

6. Will people living in our religious mood still use *the name of "God"*? They will, but certainly not in the anthropomorphic sense in which it is often used, as an extension of our little egos into the realm of the transcendental. Nor, like the authors of modern ecclesiastical pronouncements, will they insist that science "proves Him," while others insist that science does not prove, or even denies Him. In all likelihood, our children and grandchildren will also be ignorant about the final nature of being, for they too will have nothing available but finite human reason. The Divine as a reverential symbol of the ineffable ground of life is a matter of faith. To true religion the verbal abuse of the Holy becomes particularly dangerous when it is presented in the attire of argumentative logic, with a divisive rather than a unifying effect. The history of Christian apologetics proves that nothing alienates men intellectually and spiritually

from each other more effectively than dialectic quarreling for the claim of divine approval.

7. Will the new religious man for whom we hope use *prayer?* He will, for as long as human beings live in joy and in fear, so long will they pray. But he will not try to push himself into the center of the world's attention and demand that God change for him the course of nature and history. If thinking people criticize such an attitude as "arrogance," then it is not a malicious form of "debunking," but a wholesome invitation to become realistic. In contrast, the prayer we mean will be an attempt to break the fetters of one's finite ego by securing it to the greatness of the infinite, thus helping to guide us toward inner freedom, peace, courage, and fulfillment.

8. People with the new religion will *no longer approve of the claim of superiority* of one over the other forms of profound interpretation of the Divine. During his imprisonment in Yeravda Jail, Mahatma Gandhi wrote the following words about the Ashram vows to one of his friends:

The word we have hitherto used for the "vow" is a translation of the English expression (religious) "toleration." I have never liked the word either in the original or translation. . . . Toleration implies something wanted in the thing tolerated. Respect savours of patronage. But Ahimsa teaches us to cultivate equimindedness toward all religions. In terms of Ahimsa neither toleration nor respect are sufficient words to denote our conduct as it should be towards other religions. . . .

No doubt admission of the equality of the other religions with one's own presupposes imperfection of the latter. Truth and Ahimsa do teach us to admit such imperfection. If we know the whole truth where is the need for search after truth? Possession of perfect knowledge of truth means possession of divinity. For we believe that Truth is God. It is because we do not know the whole Truth, we engage in an incessant search after it, and that is man's greatest privilege and duty.[16]

[16] *Gleanings Gathered by Bapu's Feet* by Mird (Ahmedabad, 1949), pp. 3 ff.

CHAPTER 9

Art as Imaginary Self-Transcendence

> Art is a human activity with the purpose to transmit to others the highest and best feelings to which men have risen.
>
> TOLSTOY

IN THE foregoing chapter, we have brought art close to the loftiest aspiration of mankind, namely religion.

But why has art always been considered one of the great inspirational forces of mankind? Why do we read a poem, stop before a well-proportioned building, and listen to a symphony?

Various factors interplay in this experience so sublimely that analytical severance is barbarian. But it has to be done for better understanding, provided we do not lose sight of the supra-intellectual quality of real art.

1. ART AND PLAY

In his letters on *Aesthetic Education* (*fifteenth letter*) the German philosopher-poet Friedrich Schiller, perhaps influenced by Hogarth's *Analysis of Beauty,* ventures the categorical dictum: "Man is truly man only when he plays." This statement has been rejected by other thinkers, among them Benedetto Croce in his well-known *Aesthetics*. They rightly emphasize the difference between play as mere outlet or sport, and true art.

Apparently, the term "play" needs definition. Puppies certainly play. And so do children engaged in the building of a fortress. This is not what we mean.

Again watch football athletes risking their limbs, or two chess enthusiasts knitting their brows. Here we are on a higher level, for both play within a scheme, the chess enthusiasts even within a highly ingenious one. Both need talent and training for good performance. But though we may speak of the "art" of chess, and though the demand of "fairness" in all good sport reminds us of play, there remains the competitive aspect and the resulting tension, and there also remains the necessity of moving within a set of rules given from outside. All this is alien to the esthetic experience. A famous football match may be described by a historian of sport or a particularly ingenious chess play may be recorded in the annals of this sport. Certainly its inventor deserves the title of creator, for he put something into the world that was not there before. But his creation shades over into the mathematical-instrumental area with its diminishing degree of freedom. Therefore it is not art.

There are, however, deeper differences. They lie in the fact that art lifts us above our actual environment with its tensions and troubles into something we may call the reality of the unreal. We know that a novel is fiction. Yet we take it seriously, for we also know that the fictitiousness of the story contains a symbolism which liberates man for the deeper experiences of life. Behind sport there are not the worlds of Shakespeare and Tolstoy and the face of Beethoven. Man, even when still struggling for sheer survival, enjoys in art not merely the possibility of relaxation, he also welcomes the excitement which comes from the vicarious participation in the depths of human existence. Yet, the competitive sportsman and the chess enthusiast are not different from the art devotee in that they all possess the marvelous capacity of spending energy for that which from the point of view of parsimony and utility might just as well not exist. In other words, they play. The abundance of life expresses itself in free exercise.

It is the deep significance of play that it provides for man the most basic form of self-transcendence, for in it he can give himself to spontaneous occupation which, as in chess, operates on a high level of intelligence, or consists of mere motor activity or in mere release of physical and emotional tension. The great merit of Friedrich Froebel is not so much that he founded the Kindergarten, and that he was a profound thinker (which most educators do not know), but that through his combined gifts of observation and intuition he discovered the human value of play; the play of the child not being a sign of idleness, but the first step toward a harmonious interrelation between the self and the world. In the great artist, much of the child is retained, and often there is great art in the drawings and paintings of children.

II. ART AND IMAGINATION

Art is not without intellect. A poet, a musician, a painter must not be dull. If they are, they may produce rhymes, or melodies, or pictures, but these works will be insignificant. Even technically, a sonnet, a drama, a sculpture, a fugue are beyond mediocre intelligence. Nor can a dull mind really participate in the artist's work. All he may desire from the artist is the satisfaction of curiosity combined with a hedonistic pleasure. In order to produce art man has to be searching, analytical, philosophical, metaphysical; in order to enjoy it he must feel the reflection of these virtues. In art human existence in all its greatness and peril becomes apparent. Art is the companion of philosophy. Yet the intellect in art, in contrast with the intellect in the work of a scholar, is auxiliary.

Good lyric poetry reveals depth of thought and causes us to contemplate, but, when we sense the labor of thinking, the probe of inquiry, the pedantry of explanation, or the persuasion of the teacher, then we know that the muses have fled the artist. On a long intellectual detour the esthetic impetus runs dry. John Donne's "Anniversaries," "An Anatomy of the World," and "Of the Progress of the Soul," though sometimes poetic and profound, are nevertheless too philosophic and didactic to be true works of art. The same is true of Goethe's "The Metamorphosis of Plants."

For the longing of his soul the artist is not satisfied with either mere description or a nice network of logical concepts. The latter, anyhow, apply only to the *belles lettres* and not to music and the plastic arts. The artist builds a world of his own out of his creative imagination.

To a degree that is also the case with the scholar; he also uses his imagination and creates, as it were, a second world. Perhaps the French rationalist aestheticians of the seventeenth and eighteenth centuries were not so wrong as the Romanticists believed. Mere subjectivity, self-expression, fancy, and liberty have never made a great artist. It may well be that the difference between Racine and Newton, or to choose striking extremes, between Dante and Kant, lies not so much in the creative imagination as such, but in the use to which it is put and for which it is trained. However, the fact remains that the scholar's work is in much closer dependence upon the empirical than the artist's. Whereas the scholar's imagination is inquisitive, the artist's is allowed to have wings.

III. ART AND FORM

But flying must be learned. On his way toward fulfillment the artist also needs discipline and a mastership of technique. Like the intellect, they must be the artist's companions without becoming his tyrants, otherwise they take away from him his birthright of creative imagination. We just said that the French philosophers of the seventeenth and eighteenth centuries, who transferred Descartes' philosophy of "method" into the field of art, were not entirely wrong. But when the practicing artists in France and Germany accepted them as mentors, it was a bad time for art and the appreciation of art. The great Gothic masterpieces and Shakespeare's poetry fell into disrepute; only by a violent revolt against the rationalist jailers could the true artist reconquer his freedom. Yet, the great leaders of the rebellion such as Goethe themselves soon realized that there is a fundamental difference between wild emotionalism and artistic production. Those of the period of Storm and Stress who refused to acknowledge this difference are today nothing but curiosities in the history of literature.

But why can Sophocles' *Oedipus,* Dante's *Divina Comedia,* Milton's *Paradise Lost,* and Goethe's *Faust* describe just as much mental chaos, horror, despair, and cruelty as the wildest dreams of fear and still be great art, whereas the dream is just a nightmare? The answer has been given in part by our reference to the delicate kinship between good art and rational understanding. A dream is a thing of the surface, whereas art looks for depth. But we have to introduce still another concept, that of "form." Poured-out dish water neither assumes the qualities of a brook because it flows, nor of an icicle when it is frozen. Artistic form is not only concerned with the accident of outward appearance or with the impressed discipline of form, but also with the activity of the artist in a world where expression heightens the meaning and meaning controls the expression. Is there a better image of the tension between freedom and control in human society than Dostoievsky's dialogue between Christ and the Grand Inquisitor in *The Brothers Karamazoff?* Just as the intellectual self-transcendence of thought needs "order" to be productive and communicable, so art as imaginary self-transcendence needs "form."

Here is the reason for the distinction between photography and painting, or program and "abstract" music. The distinction is not because it may be easier to photograph than to paint, or to imitate a storm on the piano than to produce the truly musical image of unrest, but because photo and program music lack the power of transcendence which great art possesses. There is, however, no need for dogmatism. For there are photographs which are not merely reproductions of nature but show it, as it were, in its self-revealing mood. Something similar may happen with program music. It is idle to argue about the aesthetic legitimacy of styles, materials, and techniques. The criterion lies in the degree of transfiguration from mere stuff to essence, from appearance to meaning, from im-pression to ex-pression. Styles are significant only as revelations of an artist's or a period's conscious or unconscious aspects of reality, or as means by which to understand Mantegna's or Rembrandt's image of a man, Gainsborough's or Monet's relation to a landscape, El Greco's or Feininger's vision of a town, Goya's or Chirico's sense of a street, Raphael's or Toulouse-Lautrec's concept of womanhood. Not the style as such, but the spiritual continuum within which it dwells determines the quality and character of a work of art. Out of this questions emerge which here can only be suggested: why can we say with a high degree of certainty that a newly discovered painting is a "Rembrandt," though Rembrandt's works have such a wide range of expression? Why is there, despite all differences in individual works, unity in Bach and Beethoven, or even in a whole period such as the Renaissance?

Here the phenomenon of personality enters into the artistic image. But what else is personality but a continuum made incarnate by the form in which a specific psychophysical organism reacts to the world? No wonder, therefore, that the artist's personality and his style are inseparably connected with each other.

IV. ART AND PERFECTION

Hardly separable from the concept of form is that of perfection. In thought and science there is always something more to be done. In the moral sphere man achieves unity and harmony only in brief moments; in religion the vision of the infinite is often broken by doubt and despair. In art alone man can achieve something like perfection.

The German word for "art" is *Kunst,* which comes from *Können,* related to the English "can," being able to do. *Kunst* is that which is *gekonnt.*

What is the reason for this uniqueness of achievement in art? It lies in the already mentioned fact that through it man creates a world of his own. He is dependent on the material he uses, but he can choose it to fit his purpose. He becomes dependent on the object he has in mind, but it is not imposed on him from outside; the world he chooses is the world emerging from his soul. Certainly, he does not always succeed. Before and during the work he may be tortured by doubts about his talent, his subject, his material, and his method. But the moment the work is completed and rightly called great art, then all the birth pains are forgotten in the harmony of the accomplishment. Here man can knit each part so completely into the whole that nothing can be changed. Is it not the criterion of a true work of art that any change would be a cause for offense? In contrast, any scholarly work, however good, or perhaps just because it is good, carries within itself the invitation for correction.

V. WHOLENESS

The four elements of art just described—play, imagination, form, and perfection—provide a feeling of totality which other activities, though they may also aim at wholeness, can rarely achieve. Play frees man from himself and the narrowness of immediate interest. The imaginative character of art allows him to take into the orbit of his mind areas much wider than theoretical or practical concentration on a particular object permits. For in imagination the senses, feeling, and intuition work together in order to give man a picture which in content may be sad, tragic, and even grotesque, but which is nevertheless free from the limitations of the empirical world. On the other hand, the element of form prevents this freedom from degenerating into license. The sense of release which art produces, and the discipline it contains, do not disturb, but support each other.

Finally, the element of perfection, which is in art as a consequence of its freedom from extraneous factors, gives man the certainty that his deep and often tortuous desire for excellence may not always be thwarted by the curse of insufficiency. Vision and achievement can meet.

All this fills man with the sense of completion or wholeness. Though there are pain and longing in Richmond Barthe's sculpture of the Negro—muscular, erect, with his hands and mouth open to reach into the work and wonder of the world, his chest breathing the wind of the universe, yet with his feet fettered, an image of man's existence just as much as an image of the individual Negro—though this tension is the very subject of the work, as an art work it is nevertheless a completed whole.

VI. ART AS CATHARSIS AND LIBERATION

We can now understand the truth in Aristotle's concept of catharsis,[1] or of art as the purifier. We find the expression of noble, tragic, and sacred sentiments also in philosophy or history, but a noble work of art gives man the feeling he has when after strenuous climbing he breathes the air of high mountains. Or, to use another analogy, some of us may have been in the presence of one of those rare persons whose very existence has greatness and inner purity. They bless what is in their neighborhood, and one leaves them with a sense of encouragement. "Here is a person," one feels, "who has made a work of art out of himself." In both the great man and the great work of art the strains of life are forgotten because of ease and freedom with which the final form is achieved.

Whenever we have the desire to shed the limitations of earthly existence we are in the state of catharsis.

Is the catharsis which is in art not also the reason for its historical alliance with religion? True, art has often been used by ecclesiastical powers as a decorative element, just as it has been used to further the ambitions of princes and rich parvenus. What has not been exploited by men? But when art was great, it did not merely decorate. Rather it helped the religious, or the heroic, or whatever element it was asked to embellish, to realize

[1] *Poetic* 1449 b 23 ff.

itself on a higher state of self-formation and self-symbolization. Cult, as an integral element of historical religions, has united the pious by the community of deep and cleansing emotional experience. But cult is art, brought to existence by masters whose names have often been forgotten. And who could ever estimate the contribution to religious life made by the builders of beautiful places of worship?

VII. ART AND CULTURE

We have now indicated the functions of art in human culture. We may next approach the same topic from another point of view.

In his drama *Torquato Tasso,* which symbolizes the esthetic genius, Goethe has the suffering Tasso say:

> Und wenn der Mensch in seiner Qual verstummt,
> Gab mir ein Gott, zu sagen, was ich leide.
> (For if man suffocates in silent grief,
> A god gave me to say from what I suffer.)
> Act 5, Scene 5.

Here is a beautiful expression of the liberating power of art. But something else is indicated. Goethe, who in the figure of Tasso represents parts of his own personality, speaks of a god within the poet. Character, self-discipline, passion, depth of experience, all this is necessary for the artist. But for these qualities to mould themselves into form and rhythm requires a divine gift. Even the greatest of all human efforts could not produce it. For us today, with our false notions of "originality," the great artist, or the great thinker, or the genius of any sort, appears as the most "individualist," autonomous, and sovereign type of man. We regard him as the supreme expression of the human self. In a way he is.

But why? Not because he represents the autonomous and self-seeking ego (though in his inevitable loneliness he may give this impression to his fellow men) but because he has broken through the spiritual isolation in which most of us live. In a sense, the truly creative man is less of a separatist and individualist than the average person; his creativeness does not come from the egocentric self, but after immersion in the grounds of the creation. Therefore the true artistic genius reveals the same apparent contradiction of simultaneous pride and humility as the religious prophet: pride because he is the carrier and conveyor of a higher force; humility because the best in him is not his own, but has come to him. Often the genius cannot explain the completed work. He wonders *who* did it. He speaks of a power to which he listened or of a voice which dictated to him.

All this sounds strange to the modern experimentalist: hallucinations and delusions of grandeur, or signs of neurotic hyperexcitement. By its very nature, the extraordinary is not ordinary. That "psychopathic" states occur, no one would deny. But it depends in whom they happen, whether in the ego-centered uncreative, or the ego-forgetting creative type. The first may be subject to hallucination; the second testifies to an act of self-transcendence for which, so far, we have no scientific explanation.

The artist's mystical concept of his intuitions is new witness of a fact that we observed in various other contexts. Only as long as we live in the foreground of reality do we feel ourselves as sovereign or autonomous individuals. But when we arrive at the deeper form of life, we stand before a great wonder. The artist is the sovereign player; his intellect obeys his creative imagination; he re-forms the forms of the world; he purifies the human soul through the image of the great. All this seems to be his own, yet it is not. It is—to use Goethe's symbol—"a god" who forms in the man whom he chooses. Much does the god demand from him; unless he fulfills the divine command through discipline and devotion he will be thrown aside. Many feel themselves chosen, but only a few are. These few throw the spear of imagination far beyond the limits set to others, and thus

CHAPTER 10

Education as Cultural Self-Transcendence

Being also the Book's Summary

> To make the internal external, and the external internal,
> to find the unity for both, this is the general external
> form in which man's destiny is expressed. Therefore,
> every external object comes to man with the invitation
> to determine its nature and relationships.
>
> FRIEDRICH FROEBEL

I. THE AFFINITY BETWEEN PHILOSOPHY AND EDUCATION

WHENEVER philosophy becomes its true self: not merely the
exercise of scholarly skill but an attempt to help men in the
understanding of themselves and in the mastery of their lives, it
meets education. One could even say, it *becomes* education in
its highest form.[1] On the other hand, those rightfully entrusted
with educational responsibility not only search for better methods
of teaching, but also ask fundamental questions such as: What
is life's deeper meaning? How can man's greatest good, his freedom of transcendence, of thought, and of choice, be directed
for the good of mankind? In the great periods of civilization,

[1] Topics similar to those in this chapter are discussed in various books by
the author, especially in *Fundamentals of Democratic Education* (New York,
1940), *Conditions of Civilized Living* (New York, 1946), and *Crisis and Hope
in American Education* (Boston, 1951). See also my essay "The Meaning of
Liberal Education" in *The Teaching of Religion in American Higher Education*,
edited by Christian Gauss (New York, 1951).

constantly expand man's vision and aspiration ov
landscapes of civilization. Without the artist, just as
religious prophet, we would sink into the bog of routi
company can we breathe the air of finality, in order
later with fresh courage into the areas of daily duty.

those we like to call "classical," both philosophy and statecraft were closely related to the task of education.

II. THE MODERN CONFLICTS IN EDUCATION

In these classical periods, so we believe (perhaps with a slight admixture of hope), the important concerns of life were still interrelated. Today, we think, they are separated and often treated as if incompatible.

Most of our modern philosophical movements remain esoteric schools of thought. In our educational systems we are for, or against, not only one, but several traditions at once. Consequently we have none that could unite us. On the whole, there prevails in modern countries the heritage of rationalism, but on its way to the twentieth century it has lost much of its initial faith and energy. It is, therefore, incapable of fighting successfully modern nationalism, modern relativism, and modern irrationalism with all their relapses into superstition and sentimentality. We are longing for a new community of men, but we cannot produce it. For it needs souls animated and drawn together by the sense of inner kinship.

Our unrest is connected with external factors which have been described in so many books that they need only be listed.

Technical civilization—whatever its many advantages may be—isolates man by taking away the more personal bonds and attachments characteristic of earlier forms of production. At the same time it makes the security and employment of large groups of the population dependent on uncontrollable changes in the world market. Thus it becomes increasingly difficult to persuade the modern adolescent that he can use for the struggle of life a liberal education drawing from and leading towards historical continuity and human enrichment. In many countries the industrial population is worse off than the old journeymen who saw something of the world before they settled. If the workers in Europe and Asia move around, they mostly do so not on their own initiative; they are moved around by forces beyond their grasp. The complexity of modern life makes even the well-educated man despair of the usefulness of his political effort. He leaves politics, once the most noble and elevated office of the citizen, to "politicians." Highly developed means of communication make our earth appear to be smaller, but they also make it more inflammable; for mutual interdependence, coupled with differences of habits and outlook, are an advantage only if one likes one's neighbor, not if one is afraid of him. The modern State, though in a few democratic nations still the protector of freedom, has become in many countries the grand inquisitor, the grand jailer, and the grand executor at the same time. Even in democratic nations certain groups and individuals try to use the political machinery for undemocratic purposes. One has to be an expert to know whether agencies and associations which claim to work for loyal citizenship mean, or do not mean, the freedom of the people. There is hardly a country where a person who has worked a life long in thrift and industry can enjoy in old age the full fruit of his work. Consequently, man has developed another sense of time; he no longer wants to wait, he wants to have immediately.

All these factors are so powerful that one may well wonder whether thought and education can still be of assistance in the striving for a good and rational life. Everybody has to go to school. This is true. But at the same time it is for many nothing but a convention. All that results from such an enforced schooling is information, often unwillingly acquired, ungratefully remembered, and quickly forgotten.

For the Protestant reformers of the sixteenth and seventeenth, and for the political reformers of the eighteenth centuries, education was the requisite of man's Christian and political freedom. It still is. But has it developed to the degree it should in face of the gigantic problems which, if unsolved, will destroy our liberal civilization? Will it make the modern citizen, irrespective of wealth, rank, and status, capable of mature and responsible participation in the complex affairs of our cultural and political life? In other words, are we headed toward a truly democratic society, or a mere mass culture, with the terrible alternative of fascist or communist tyranny?

For let us not deceive ourselves about one fact. Despite all useful information which organized education has disseminated over wider and wider areas of the world; despite the assistance it has brought to great numbers of people in their strivings for mental and physical improvement; despite the protection it has granted youth and adults—and these are values to be deeply grateful for—it has been unable to be the independent guide of man in the decisive changes of his historical destiny. Modern education suffers from a frightening loss of inner substance. And this loss may become the greater, the more education turns away from the humanities in order to become a "social science" in the superficial sense in which this term is often understood. Even more than has institutional religion, education has served with equal zest in the preparation of war and the preparation of peace; it has been at the command of tyrants as well as of democracies; it has helped to preach fundamentalism and atheism, relativism and agnosticism; and it has been more the instrument of the competitive than of the cooperative trends in society. Except in rare instances, education has been the handmaid of power rather than the conscience of humanity. There are even academic teachers—not to speak of typical government officials—who no longer know the difference between education and propaganda.

III. EDUCATION AS THE GUARDIAN OF SOCIETY

But criticism of our time is easy. Let us not forget the positive values on which it is built and for which, in many parts of the world, our ancestors fought on battlefields and barricades. Unhampered inquiry and discussion, tolerance of divergent opinions even about sacred taboos of society, the liberation of man from need and disease through science and technology, the unfolding of human energies by tearing down the barrier of castes, the emergence of the modern State out of tribal organizations and the petty domains of absolute princes, the gradual winning of the right of public and nondenominational education for all who are able to learn—should all this lead to the end result of a bewildered generation? Even our international situation, frightening though it is, must not be considered merely a burden and a curse. Should we not more often tell ourselves that we live during the period of a momentous transition as difficult as the one from the lawlessness of the Great Migrations to medieval feudalism, from feudalism to absolutism, and from absolutism to the modern nation state? Before us, of course, is the most difficult stretch, that from the old concept of sovereignty (the hangover from absolutism) to a world of freely cooperative nations. Failure in this attempt will lead us into the abyss; success will open up a new era of human development.

But today less than ever will the circumstances alone determine the future; the deciding factor will be whether man is able to live not merely under, but clearly in front of, and, if necessary, as an enemy of the circumstances that surround him.

It is this kind of man which education must create.

With due regard for the psychological and social nature of man, education must help him not merely to "adjust himself to the changing environment" (one of the most confusing slogans of modern pedagogy), or to regard himself as an advanced species of ape, *un singe arrivé*, but to transcend the existing conditions by a vision of things as they should be. Only when man has an inspiring, rather than a depressive image of himself, can education become a directing force in his social evolution.

But how do it?

IV. FUNDAMENTALS OF EDUCATION

When we ponder this question we discover that the general philosophical considerations of this book apply directly to the educational process.

1. In our chapter on the *theory of man* we showed that only that person can achieve maturity who unfolds his powers within

organically widening circles of experience and realizes that he lives within, and with the help of, the whole of human society. But the more he understands the heights and abysses of experience, the more he sees that all human life, individual as well as social, exists only through its participation in the mysterious process of life. Man, consequently, is responsible not only to himself and his society; he must also try to identify himself with those cosmic forces which, in the light of his best knowledge, are of universally productive rather than of destructive nature.

2. Often the purpose of education has been found in the individual's desire for self-realization. *But what is the individual?* What is the human self? We are here before a mystery which we experience the moment we make ourselves the object of contemplation. The human person, being at the same time within and outside the embrace of the physical creation, being a part of his own reflections, can feel his unity with all that lives and strives, but also his utter loneliness. He can be split within himself. The great philosophies and the great religions have grown out of the endeavor both to understand the depth of this conflict and to find means for its reconciliation. They all arrive at the paradox, that the individual finds himself only by losing himself within a superindividual purpose, or by means of devotion. But is this really a paradox? Yes, if by individuality and self-realization is meant a process of growing egocentricity (which is bound to defeat itself because it leads toward self-isolation and thus toward self-impoverishment). No, if we understand that never does an individual life become fuller and richer than it does through sharing, sympathy, and love.

All education, therefore, is wrong which is based on a false image of the individual. Whether we emphasize onesidedly the ascetic or the hedonistic aspect of education, whether we advocate ruggedness or softness, both polarities are but facets of the same erroneous attitude about the nature of human fulfillment.

It is necessary to be wisely concerned with one's own welfare, to assert one's critical self-interest in the face of flowering words and sparkling ideologies, but it is also necessary to know of the final blessing which is in devotion and sacrifice. A system of education in which immediate personal reward is the main criterion of success helps in ruining the nation for whose future it is responsible. Only that education makes a nation great which teaches youth that the path toward one's true self is the ever-widening sense of communion.

3. The chapter on *thinking* led us to similar considerations. Only when a teacher or learner feels that the laws of his thinking are a cosmic gift and not his own invention which he can use or misuse according to his choice, can he teach or learn the real nature of reality. For just as no man, so also no fact or event, is in and by itself. It always is a window to a deeper reality. The logic by which we connect our prehensions to each other and to the objective world, this logic works in *all* human minds. In some it works more obscurely, in others more clearly, but it is the result of the same great evolutionary process by which man has emerged from lower forms of life into the state of reflection and self-awareness. Through our common participation in the world of mind we not only feel the unity of human intellects, but we also have the right to hope that there is something like truth within and beyond our searching and learning. To be sure, all our human truths are but little verities, paths which stop short before the summit that would allow us to see the whole. Yet the higher we climb, the wider is the vision of reality and the greater the chance that we may arrange our lives according to universal laws. True thinking that refuses to be satisfied with the superficial solution of the problem at hand—in other words, has perspective—provides man also with a touchstone to distinguish that which is important and that which is unimportant. The transcendent tendency in reason comes here close to the transcendent tendency in religion. It saves man from being overwhelmed by the threat of the immediate, particularly by the threat of his own little self, the latter being the greatest of all human menaces.

4. But the more we think about thinking and the individual, the more we are driven to reflect not only *on our relation to reality*, but *on the aspects of reality* itself. While engaged in this ontological, this metaphysical endeavor, we stand in the twilight between scientific philosophy and poetry. All human language is symbolic. In and through it man realizes his greatness, but also his limitations. Yet never does he become so aware of the dilemma of human existence as when he discovers that the unity of life, which is a postulate both of science and philosophy, appears to him only in polarities. Wherever man looks around he meets the contrasts of becoming and being, of dependence and freedom, wholeness and singleness, energy and form, birth and death, good and evil. Man cannot prove whether the logos, or the order of thought within and toward which his thinking progresses, is itself related to the ultimate or whether there are spheres of being and non-being totally beyond even our keenest imagination. No philosophical or scientific system has provided the answer. Probably none ever will. But man's metaphysical quest is not useless play; it represents the finest manifestation of man's endeavor to give himself an account of the universe—or the multiverse—within and on which he lives. Though the answers he receives will turn again into questions, only a shallow generation will stop asking. For this asking opens to man's eyes the horizon of infinity without which he loses the realistic knowledge of his finiteness and runs into the danger of wavering between arrogance and despair. An education, therefore, which believes it thrives better without deeper metaphysical interest may produce a materially informed and busy society, but it will be one without depth. Sooner or later even its efficiency will run dry for lack of inspiration. It may be remembered for its quantity, but not for its quality.

5. Such a society will lack the great *ethical impulse*. For a while it may live prosperously on legality and convention, but neither of them will produce the creative individuals who are the leaven of civilization. Whether or not people are aware of it,

productive morality—as we have already indicated—lives not only on such considerations as one's own and one's neighbor's well-being. Every normal person wishes to be happy within a happy group of people. This is no problem except for men who have lost the natural strength of life. But can a mature life be built only on pleasure and not also on strain and failure? Is not the person who constantly runs away from conflict sure to land in sickness, just like one who would insist on living only in sunshine and never in shade? Only he will receive life's benediction who boldly opens its arms to its fullness, knowing well that he will clasp its coldness as well as its warmth. He alone will be capable of true ethical action. The liberating uplift of our existence into the truth of life that comes during the truly moral act —this sense of unity between fragile individuality and creative wholeness—occurs only to the courageous person who knows that there is no self-realization without self-sacrifice. There are many generous people and many useful acts in the human world for which we should be grateful. But the really great event— though it may happen in the simplest life—is the confrontation of man with the moral demand in the fulfillment of which there is no doubt and hesitation. When education forgets to bear witness to this heroic element in mankind's history, then the end of excellence is near.

6. Destiny wishes to give freedom to man by appealing to his *sense of the beautiful* as well as to his sense of the heroic. By virtue of his imagination he is capable of building above the structure of the actual a world of form and rhythm through which the fuller meaning of the actual becomes surprisingly evident. For superficial minds, just as virtue is supposed to be for nothing but usefulness, so art is supposed to be for nothing but pleasure. If one wishes a broad definition—which, however, would apply as well to other fields of culture—then one might give to art not only the title of liberator from the frictions of existence, but also the title of enricher. For art widens the scale of our sensitiveness in teaching us to understand the depth of

ideas, to sense the delicacy and color of forms, to feel the roughness or smoothness of lines and surfaces, and to hear the rhythm and melody of sounds. But, more important, it also allows us to project ourselves into scenes and feelings which otherwise would be far beyond our power of emotional and intellectual creation. There are few Tolstoys in the world, but many who can read *War and Peace*. And despite the inner excitement a great work of art may cause in us, it gives us at the same time a unique sense of perfection and fulfillment, whereas in all other human activities there are always unfinished fragments.

Our age has provided the most amazing techniques of artistic production and reproduction. But neither in society nor in education is art considered an essential element in the formation of the personality. For many people it does not exist at all, for others it has no more value than that of entertainment or decoration. Only a few are still willing to attune their souls to the rhythm and depth of a great poem. Through the radio, classical music has become more and more popular. But how often does it receive the listener's full attention? Is it not more often a rhythmical noise which helps us to "relax" or fill the void within the background of life?

7. But thinking in its profound intuitions, metaphysics in its universal contemplation, the moral act in its heroic decision, and aesthetic fulfillment in its vision of the perfect form are, despite all their greatness, confined within the narrow boundaries of human power. What, then, is the meaning of human existence in the vastness of the universe?

Philosophical considerations as such are bound to remain limited by the uncertainties of seeking—even with the vital experiences and visions of truth; it is *the religious experience* which gives man the feeling of unity with the All-Embracing. Also here he can speak only in symbols; also here he may sometimes be tortured by doubt. But whereas discursive language often reminds us painfully of our distance from the core of reality, in religious symbolism lives the deep hope of certainty.

This certainty is grounded in experiences beyond the competence of science and can, therefore, live in peace with it, though only under two conditions.

The first demand which education must raise is that science does not arrogate to itself the right to drive out of man's conscience and consciousness whatever cannot be proved in laboratory fashion, but that it understand itself as only *one* of the means by which man participates in the logos and understands, at least in part, the laws of life.

The second demand of education is that religion itself be careful in distinguishing essential religious meaning from the historically and environmentally conditioned forms of religious expression. There are many profound myths in all religions, but in their literal form many of them can no longer be upheld without arousing the opposition of man's intellectual conscience.

Nor, in spite of the necessity of specific cultural roots, should there be hostility and exclusiveness among the various creeds and denominations. No doubt, with the evolution of cultures there have developed not only more and more rituals and theological disputes, but also a seemingly endless splitting of religions into subreligions, the latter often displaying the highest degree of hostility against each other. Yet there is also hope that with increasing international contact and insight into humanity's inspirations and aspirations a sense of unity might pervade the plurality. More and more will men feel that the call of the Divine is one and the same, though it may resound differently in each of the valleys of the earth. Reality, just as it speaks to mankind in different vernaculars and nevertheless remains the same, speaks to mankind also in different religions. No one, after the first formative years, can deny his origin. So it would be idle for the Christian, or Buddhist, or the follower of Confucius to try to forget whence he comes and to create the language of all religious languages, or the symbolism of symbolisms. He would create nothing but a rootless abstraction. In other words, our Western religious life, our culture, and our education, in order to avoid the danger of contributing to modern man's spiritual lack of heritage, must be of the Judaeo-Christian tradition. We all look at the world along the vista of our own vantage point; this is in the nature of human reason.

The point at issue is whether the boundaries of this vista will open up to increasingly wider insights, or whether they will suddenly close in and shut us up in a narrow conspectus. If the first is the case, the religious mood and mode of living can and will embrace and penetrate whatever happens to us, however far our intellectual discoveries take us. And there will be no conflict but mutual delight in the enrichment of life by new knowledge. For the main factor in religion is not this or that knowledge or cult, but reverential living. Some, throughout their lives, may need to assemble in worship at their holy places, while others may prefer solitude. But just as deep in the Divine may live a young woman who prepares herself for her child; a farmer who looks at his fields as a guardian of the nature which provides for mankind; a scientist who takes away his eyes from the microscope to meditate on the mysteries of life; a young man who plans his future in the hope that thus he may help not only himself but mankind; or a child whose soul is for the first time captured by the harmonies of a great religious hymn.

8. The more such experiences occur in the life of a group and of all mankind, the greater is the hope for the future. Every step in the *organization and disorganization of mankind* creates new concepts of man's nature and his goals, new contacts between nations and nations, new interpretations of man's relation to God and the universe. Much more rapidly than our grandfathers anticipated—after a relative quiet of only slightly more than a hundred years—our generation faces probably the most gigantic task ever imposed on humanity. We must bring order on a world-wide basis to the contacts of nations, with most of them in a state of revolution. If in the execution of this task man lacks the energy of transcendence, or the inspiration which helps him to evolve from barbarism toward dignity and freedom,

from what source will he derive his strength and directives? He will be told again and again that this is society. Thus that which he tries to change will at the same time be his God. What a paradoxical situation!

Many of our politicians and even of our so-called statesmen fight for their parties and countries as if these were the absolute ends in the historical process—ends which will lead us only from internal disappointment to international war. In our understandable aversion against the rootless and ruthless individualism of the not too distant past we are now in danger of swerving over toward another rootless and ruthless concept of man, which sees him merely as a part of a collective. Essentially, these two concepts have the same source—man's isolation from the common ground. In this situation he first becomes inflated with the pride of selfhood and thinks of himself as the master of the earth. And when this pride collapses under adverse social conditions, he runs away from himself and seeks shelter in the multitude.

Only self-transcendent man who feels himself as a participant in the unending work of the creation will have the courage to create a new education, and through it one more weapon in the struggle for the liberation of humanity.

There can be schools which no longer educate despite the desperate attempts of devoted educators. There can be refined methods of teaching which nevertheless breed barbarism. There can be the cult of Greek and Latin without a humanist tradition, and much learning of modern tongues, yet the spirit does not speak. There can even be ideals which mislead, rather than lead. This, perhaps, is the greatest of all perils. All our endeavors can become achievements only when they grow out of a society wherein the relations of man to himself, his fellow men, his knowledge, and his institutions are enriched by a sense of common belonging. We may often feel lonely and like foreigners whose language is not understood. This is in the nature of human existence. But living as a foreigner all the time is degeneration.

Even the highest degree of sophistication does not help; on the contrary, it only aggravates the situation.

The base of education is deeper and wider than the overt educational process. If it fails to recognize this fact, it becomes uprooted and can be used for any purpose. But if it understands itself in its transcendent nature, it can become the bulwark of mankind.

CHAPTER 11

Postscript

THOSE of my readers who are used to the old philosophical dichotomies of "realism" and "idealism," "naturalism" and "supernaturalism," "pragmatism" and "perennialism," and so on, may leave this book with a feeling of perplexity. For what I have tried to say does not fit into any of these categories.

Not that I consider these divisions useless. We all like to look at the label of the wine bottle we are ready to empty; it serves for quick identification. However, a collection of labels does not make a good wine, and a collection of "isms" darkens more than it illumines man's insight into the philosophical enterprise.

In fact, no great philosopher was ever interested in mere abstractions. He hoped they would simplify rather than complicate the process of human understanding. He was passionately concerned with explaining the meaning of life to himself and his fellows. Even when he started with an a-priori concept, it was for him not a pale and unreal illusion, but an intuitive conviction; perhaps one which he should have examined more carefully with respect to its empirical background, yet one that was grounded in his personal experience. The "schools of thought" are the assemblies of minor talents, of the commentators who have to draw on their masters' wells because there is none in their own house. And woe to him who criticizes the master and the water they bring home!

But though I believe that the "isms," on the whole, have done more harm than good—even to the neophyte—I do not share the now fashionable rejection of philosophical systems. In the progress of humanity systems are necessary because they unify and crystallize our ideas; therefore they emerge usually at a turning point of history. They are like quiet lakes in which men can recognize their faces and the trees around them, but from which also they can set their sails toward new waters. They clarify and elevate man's aspirations; they also serve as foci for new criticism. Of course, great systems are sometimes careless about details; especially, they have not much regard for those who believe their own precious individuality to be at the world's center.

So, from such an individualistic point of view, they are wrong. But behind *all* challenging philosophy, whether systematic or impressionist, synthetic or analytical, there is man, not as a mere bundle of psychological reflexes, but man in his existential situation, confronted with the great mysteries of life, with birth and death, progress and failure, belonging and loneliness, finiteness and infinity.

If one tries to comprehend all these forces, partly within, but partly also beyond the grasp of human reason and language, if one looks at this vast cosmic enterprise we call "life," and especially this greatest of all wonders, the life of man, can one then still believe in the exclusiveness of "schools of thought," their intellectual absolutism and their second-hand categories? Can one then still contrast "idealism," as right, with "realism" as wrong, and so on in the endless series of philosophical quarrels?

Now, of course, there arises the fear whether with this rejection of clear-cut definitions one does not sink into the bog of confusion—no answer, no decision, no commitment. Had we not better quit the whole business and study something else?

But let us assume, for argument's sake, that there is no answer but the agnostic's or relativist's. There is nevertheless an urge in man to ask, and often it seems to me that the great questions are as productive as the attempted solutions. Ask we will until we die, and not to ask is living death.

Furthermore, though I defended relativism as a decent and even not unrewarding position, I am far from believing that we have to be content with it.

For when, as we have done, you place man in the center of your thought, you arrive at three basic concepts that are not relative, but that give us certainty about our place in the world. Man—as the ever self-transcendent being—not only reaches constantly beyond his immediate environment, but he understands himself—and here is the second concept—as a participant in a greater order. Third, this understanding participation is not a vague abstraction. Rather it gives him direction, for it invokes in him the sense of reverence and responsibility for the powers within and on which he lives and to which he may contribute.

Dwell on these ideas and you will comprehend that they are the essence of all search, religion, and morality. In various cultures they undergo different forms of expression and are clothed with different rituals. But without them man would be a fake; scholarship would be a play; religion would be dead; morality empty; ritual a show, and life a futility.

The universe, as far as we can see, is a gigantic unity in plurality. Unless—against all evidence—we insist on believing that it is chaos (which would make our asking and believing meaningless) we must assume that it is an interacting order; that which we call "mind" and that which we call "matter" being two appearances united in the same hidden ground of creation. Unless we are sodden with dullness, the unscalable yet alluring mystery of being hovers before our minds—we ourselves are part of it. If two climbers start from different directions, hoping they might come closer to the summit and thus have a wider view of the landscape, they will not hate but help each other, as it behooves seekers of the highest. The partition is not between those who, however different the approach, try to climb toward the summit, and, knowing of their own limitations, have humility and charity. Rather the partition is between all these reverential seekers and those who either refuse to look out of their windows, or believe they alone march on the right route. They may even not try the ascent but remain in their valley, chattering and laughing at those who are restless because of their transcending, and ascending, inclination.

One may nevertheless object that this religion of the seeker is without clear content, is nothing but an aspirational mood. Indeed, that is the criticism offered by the orthodox.

But whatever the religious attitude may be, the religion of the seeker is for me just as little a fluctuating sentiment as it is a particular dogma or institution. Rather it is a permeating response to the events of life, a state of mind which sees every point on the surface as an inviting signpost toward a deeper uniting reality. There is nothing too small to be excluded, yet there is a hierarchy to distinguish the important from the unimportant. And this I call important which liberates us from the narrowness in the ego, gives us a sense of belonging, and thus gives purpose to our seeking and doing. It is a relation to the world that accompanies us through diverse moods and experiences, in joy and grief, in the company of our friends and in solitude. In changing and enriching our selves, it also changes and enriches our world.

This belief gives me also the answer with respect to the three main world views I mentioned at the beginning of this book: the theonomous, the logonomous, and the autonomous. In each one of them I saw the strength and greatness of humanity, for each of them may cause the mind to spread its wings toward new horizons of reality. But the moment one view invites or even forces the mind to fold the wings and settle down, it bodes decay. All that is great, is always "in the making." And truth is always greater. A Nietzsche who shudders at the idea that God is dead is closer to the religious spirit than a dogmatic churchman for whom God never was alive.

But I do not hesitate to profess my inclination toward the

logonomous, or reason-centered person, though he is no longer fashionable with many who now lead our intellectual and political life. I still hold Voltaire to be one of the greatest men of our civilization. I still admire some lines in Paine's *Age of Reason* and am still deeply touched by Ernest Renan's story of the French republican I quoted at the beginning of this book, or by Victor Hugo's tale in *Les Misérables* of the pious Bishop going out to convert the lonely and sick old revolutionary, and being so profoundly impressed by the greatness of his dying, that he, the Bishop, kneels and asks for the benediction by the soul he considered lost.

If one understands by faith a rigid belief in the statutes of a specific ecclesiastical institution, then the great men of the Enlightenment, in this country especially Jefferson and his friends, were iconoclasts. But if one means by faith the confidence in man's capacity to develop principles of thinking and an organization of society which make possible a creatively rational and free life, then the eighteenth century was one of the great events of humanity and especially of our Christian culture.

Of course, these men had their limitations and prejudices. But even in the prejudices there was evidence of the use of judgment. Thomas Jefferson, as a symbol of his time, felt little appreciation for Plato. This is due to the American aversion against "mysticism," which in this country is so easily mistaken for obscurantism. Yet the feeling of aversion was also due to a deeper sentiment. Jefferson failed to find that in Plato which for him was indispensable for a good life, namely the appreciation of the natural or inalienable rights of man. Plato's *Republic* with its caste system and the inhuman communism of the leaders of the State was to him repulsive, much though he read and liked Greek poetry.

We know that the idea of the inalienable or the natural rights of man was developed by the late Stoic philosophers. However, for us it is connected with the teaching of Christ and with the rationalist philosophies of the eighteenth century. For the rationalists all men were equal in their natural rights, because in all of them was Reason; for Christ all men were equal because in all of them was the Father. The great rationalists were hostile to the Churches not because the latter taught, but because they failed, to teach Christ. Christ's gospel, in which one finds the understanding of man as a being directed by his power of self-transcendence and cosmic participation, had to be rediscovered by the rationalists. The churches had allied themselves with the reactionary powers which used religion for suppressing the people, as Jefferson had seen in France and partly also in his own country. Paradoxically, and in contrast to what we learn in academic books and courses, it is the rationalist enemies of the established Churches who led Christianity back to itself, as the Reformation led the medieval Church. Unless theonomy has the criticism of empirically responsible reason it begins to like its "supranaturalism" so much that it forgets about natural human beings. And whenever there is narrow insistence on a dogma and the arrogant belief in God's personal revelation to a chosen group, then piety changes easily into self-righteousness, minds become closed, and the value and reality of transcendence is gone.

To be sure, the reason-centered attitude may also slip into the righteousness of a self-glorifying humanism; there is especially the danger of petty or proud intellectualism. But if— fallible humans as we are—there is danger even in our virtues, then I prefer the potential error in reason to any other, for reason is eventually self-corrective; dogma is not. If we wish to have an ever-developing religious civilization it must have a rational basis. For reason, as I have tried to interpret it, embraces faith and does not exclude man's dialogue with the divine ground, whereas theonomy has often excluded man's dialogue with the ground of reason; it still does so at many places.

Every great century was piously rational, or reverentially rational. We often forget that even Thomas Aquinas, now the canonic philosopher of the Roman Catholic Church, was originally suspect in the eyes of the ecclesiastical authorities. He used Aristotelian rationalism for Christian philosophy. In modern language, he was a "liberal." Hence those who study not only his words, but also the spirit of his teaching—as we should do with every great thinker—should also be liberal, and ever open to new ideas.

The whole contrast between reason and faith springs not only from a narrow interpretation of both, as I tried to prove in an earlier chapter, but also from a false interpretation of reason's child, namely knowledge.

Francis Bacon said at the dawn of our technological era that knowledge is "power." All depends on what is meant by this statement: knowledge as might, mastery, and conquest, or *knowledge as kinship,* as the friendly encounter of the human and the cosmic order that creates in man a sense of embracing love for the universe in which he lives. When knowledge ends only in might for might's sake, it will become the more hollow the bigger it grows; finally it will be its own ruin.

Out of the modern loss of the realization that knowledge is kinship there grows one of the characteristics of our time: that we feel ourselves "thrown into the world." How can it be different? How can there be anything else but "anxiety," if man no longer knows himself because he no longer knows where he belongs? No, we are not "thrown" into the world but we live on and within it—from the blood of our ancestors, the food they ate, the women they loved, and the thoughts they pondered and wrote, to the last pulse in our own blood and the last idea in our brain.

It is paradoxical that the great liberators have at the same time been man's captivators; religion has often walled his faith into dogmatism, and science every so often has fostered a strangely mixed mood of masterly arrogance and skeptical pessimism. Both have blocked the way to which they have pointed.

We have now to go the road to its end. No religious prayer, however deeply felt, will help us if our knowledge increasingly alienates us from life, rather than serving as a means of universal kinship. And no knowledge, however extensive, will avail us if we allow our lives to be darkened and misdirected by magical concepts even if they come in the name of religion. What we need is the unity of religion and rationality: "rational piety," if you will, or "devout reasonableness."

This was the attitude of the founders of this republic. This attitude alone, because capable of ever new development, can save us in the future. In it alone lies the hope for progress—slow, arduous, short of final achievement, but nevertheless full of hope, joy, and unending vision.

INDEX

Set in Linotype Times Roman
Format by Marguerite Swanton
Manufactured by The Haddon Craftsmen, Inc.
Published by HARPER & BROTHERS, *New York*